Engaging with Linguistic Diversity

Multilingualisms and Diversities in Education series

Editors: Kathleen Heugh, Christopher Stroud and Piet Van Avermaet

Multilingualism and diversity are fast becoming defining characteristics of global education. This is because human mobility has increased exponentially over the past two decades, bringing about an increase in socio-economic, cultural and faith-based diversity with consequences for citizenship, identity, education and practices of language and literacy (among others).

The Multilingualisms and Diversities in Education series takes a global perspective of the twenty-first-century societal diversities. It looks at the languages through which these diversities are conveyed, and how they are changing the theoretical foundations and practice of formal and non-formal education. Multilingualisms and diversities in this series are understood as dynamic and variable phenomena, processes and realities. They are viewed alongside classroom practices (including curriculum, assessment, methodologies), teacher development (pre- and in-service, and in non-formal education), theory-building, research and evaluation, and policy considerations.

Volumes in the series articulate the opportunities and challenges afforded by contemporary diversities and multilingualisms across global settings at local, national and international levels. A distinctive aim of the series is to provide a platform for reciprocal exchanges of expertise among stakeholders located in different southern and northern contexts.

Forthcoming in the series
Languages and Literacies in Higher Education, edited by Zannie Bock and Christopher Stroud
Functional Multilingual Learning for Inclusive Education, by Seven Sierens, Stef Slembrouk and Piet Van Avermaet

Engaging with Linguistic Diversity

A Study of Educational Inclusion in an Irish Primary School

David Little and Déirdre Kirwan

BLOOMSBURY ACADEMIC
LONDON • NEW YORK • OXFORD • NEW DELHI • SYDNEY

BLOOMSBURY ACADEMIC
Bloomsbury Publishing Plc
50 Bedford Square, London, WC1B 3DP, UK
1385 Broadway, New York, NY 10018, USA

BLOOMSBURY, BLOOMSBURY ACADEMIC and the Diana logo are
trademarks of Bloomsbury Publishing Plc

First published in Great Britain 2019

Cover design: Anna Berzovan
Cover image © Joe Dillon

A catalogue record for this book is available from the British Library.

A catalog record for this book is available from the Library of Congress.

ISBN: HB: 978-1-3500-7203-9
       ePDF: 978-1-3500-7204-6
       eBook: 978-1-3500-7215-2

Series: Multilingualisms and Diversities in Education

Typeset by Integra Software Services Pvt. Ltd.
Printed and bound in Great Britain

To find out more about our authors and books visit www.bloomsbury.com
and sign up for our newsletters.

Contents

Figures

Tables

Series Editors' Foreword

Multilingualisms and Diversities in Education

The purpose of this series is to take a global perspective of the way that twenty-first-century societal diversities and the languages through which these are conveyed are changing theoretical foundations and practices in formal and informal education. Particular attention is given to the assets, opportunities and resources as well as the challenges that contemporary multilingualisms bring to learning, teaching, theory and policy in contemporary local, national and global diversities. The series is intended to engage with theory and research emerging from innovative agents in classrooms, teacher education, higher education, policymaking, evaluation and assessment. A distinctive characteristic of the series is an interest in exchanges of expertise in multilingualism and diversity in education among stakeholders concerned with supporting inclusivity, retention, social cohesion and well-being in different 'southern' and 'northern' contexts. To this end, authors from both less and more mainstream contexts are invited to bring their expertise to enrich and expand debates and theoretical advances on the role, functions and practices of language(s) and literacies, and diversities in education.

We anticipate that authors in this series are likely to view multilingualisms and diversities through different lenses. We accept that multilingualism and by extension diversity are multi-faceted and intersectional, and that there is no singularity or exact replicability that can be transferred *easily and without dialogue* from one setting to another. Because both diversity and multilingualism appear in different contexts and in different guises, we place emphasis on adequately representing the plurality of multilingualisms and diversities, in the belief that such an emphasis will open new territory for twenty-first-century concerns in education.

The interest here is with the opportunities and resources that pluralities of multilingualism offer in the development and support of inclusivity in education, rather than an emphasis on problems or deficit views associated with contemporary diversity. Such a thrust remains under-researched and under-represented in educational literature. Likewise, we encourage authors from post-colonial contexts to bring forward for publication their significant expertise of multilingualisms within formal and informal education. Despite a long history of public debate and research, there is a gap in publication and wider dissemination. Gaps include how the identities and systems of knowledge and belief of local communities expand and alter over time in articulation with generations of human diversity and mobility, and they include the consequences of recent displacement and migration for multilingualisms. Missing from the literature is rich documentary evidence of and theorization of how both local and migrant individuals and communities engage in reciprocal effort to strengthen or alter their affiliations, and how informal practices of literacy and oracy can enrich formal education. On a theoretical level, this series is concerned with how historically diverse and mobile communities are accompanied by and circulate alternative systems of knowledge and belief, and how these can enrich existing theories and pedagogies in education. Owing to the rapidly changing pace of both material and virtual mobility of people in countries and regions and across international contexts, now is a timely opportunity to fill the gaps.

We recognize that at this time there are more than 25 million people who have fled their countries as refugees, and another 45 million people who are displaced within their own or neighbouring countries. Currently two-thirds of the world's internally displaced people (IDPs) are in countries of Africa and the Middle East, and many of these will seek refuge in Europe and a significant number also in North America, Australia and New Zealand. Whereas refugees bring challenges and resources to education in host countries, IDPs bring these to education in their own and neighbouring countries. Yet, education systems are seldom well-prepared to receive and accommodate diverse student cohorts on the scales or in the circumstances that we now see and anticipate. This is particularly the case in situations of forced displacement. Even if the material resources were adequate, the linguistic complexities for mainstream or state-provided education are not yet sufficiently understood.

Many innovative responses to societal multilingualisms have been developed in or emerged among displaced, mobile and minority communities. While not well-known in northern literature, multilingualisms in education have for more than a century consistently featured within local and national systems in sub-Saharan Africa, in more recent enterprises in South and South-East Asia, and now also in promising initiatives in Central Asia. While the attention in this series is on multilingualism in education, it may be worthwhile emphasizing that linguistic diversity is often regarded as a proxy for diversities that emerge through culture, epistemology, faith, identity and socio-economic status; language is the mechanism through which differences are mediated, connections and convivialities are forged, and new knowledge and expertise are advanced. Yet, these complexities are often invisible in mainstream curricula, and may simultaneously pose serious challenges unless proactively harnessed and recognized as assets for curriculum, assessment, pedagogy, theory, teacher education, policy and planning.

Recent displacement and the impact of conflict-induced mobilities of people on a large scale reanimate an interest in and concerns with social justice and earlier generations of migrant communities and the potential now for fresh exchanges of expertise. They also turn our attention once more to the diversities of endogenous, often mobile, minority communities in Europe and Central Asia (e.g. the Saami, Welsh, Frisians, Tatars, Kazaks, Romany), the Amerícas (e.g. Cree, Hopi, Guarani, Quechua), Africa (e.g. ||Ani, Hai||om, Tifinagh), South and East Asia (e.g. Saora, Gondi, Khmer, Hmông, Evenki) and Australia (e.g. A̱nangu, Pitjantjatjara, Yankunytjatjara).

We welcome authors whose work explores synergies and differences of multilingualisms, whether these are in localized northern settings, Indigenous southern communities or northern-focused southern cities. We therefore invite authors from and in different global contexts of school, university and informal education to contribute their research and practice-based theory of multilingualisms in education to this series, including in relation to:

a) pedagogical and theoretical understandings of language/s, bilingualism and multilingualism (including code-switching, functional multilingualism, functional multilingual learning, linguistic citizenship and translanguaging)

b) new or alternative approaches that have not yet been identified, but which are likely to emerge as creative and productive exchanges of knowledge, expertise and response to diversity as educators come to grips with what this means in their different and varied contexts, and how these articulate towards transformation and support inclusion, retention and well-being in education.

We anticipate that placing the lens on the assets and opportunities that diversities and affinities bring to support inclusivity and social cohesion alongside north-south exchanges of knowledge signals a radical shift in the thinking on languages, multilingualism and diversity in schools and universities. It is a shift that moves the debates and research beyond the challenges and problems that at present appear overwhelming for policymakers. Such a shift carries implications for teacher development, education planning and policy. It has implications for rethinking both diversity and language learning theory in tandem, and it has broader implications for research in applied and educational linguistics and education. There is every possibility that this shift will underscore the understanding of languages, multilingualism and multilinguality as integral to diversity, and thus as central to education. These opportunities are no more pertinent than in alternative (new) approaches to teaching and learning languages and literacy/ies, and for understanding how individuals and communities establish multilingual repertoires, and express linguistic agency and citizenship. The opportunities are accompanied by the resources of alternative epistemologies (ways of knowing), ontologies (ways of being) and cosmologies (ways of believing) which enrich global education. It is these opportunities, approaches and resources that are likely to inform ongoing theorization of both languages and diversities in the contemporary world.

Introduction to the first volume

The first volume in this series, *Engaging with Linguistic Diversity: A Study of Educational Inclusion in an Irish Primary School*, authored by David Little and Déirdre Kirwan, is unique for many reasons. As an exemplar of what is possible, the authors address three aims of the series which are to demonstrate how multilingualisms and diversities become assets and resources in education, to reveal opportunities that multilingualisms and diversities bring to support social cohesion and a strengthening of affinities, and to acknowledge and identify, with respect, the agency, citizenship and voice of those who contribute to equity and inclusion.

This book is the story of how Scoil Bhríde (Cailíní), a primary school in Blanchardstown outside Dublin, resists the habitus of homogeneity within a mainstream education system. Although Scoil Bhríde (Cailíní) is in Ireland, it could very well be in a rapidly changing urban context anywhere in the world. It is a story which exemplifies how with astute and deft leadership, and through collaborative agency, participation and voice of teachers, students and parents, the opportunities and resources of diversity are seized, and an uncharted journey of educational success is undertaken. The journey leads the school towards an evolving school policy and classroom practices that not only embrace students' multilingual and knowledge repertoires but also harness these repertoires as assets for learning, with a clear aim to develop an inclusive and equity-based school culture.

Although multilingualism and diversity are fast becoming defining characteristics in the context and new realities of twenty-first-century global education, the logic of monolingualism and assimilation-oriented top-down education policies remain in evidence and have been difficult to dislodge. This school, however, led by its principal and innovative teachers, resists the habitus of homogeneity and a perceived need to acculturate migrant and minority students. This book is a case study that traces how a bottom-up school policy can evolve to address the contemporary challenges of social cohesion, equity and excellence in education. It does so through a process of acknowledging and exploiting the assets of multilingualisms and diversities, and in doing so embodies the principles of social justice.

The case study offers an exemplar of the kind of school leadership that is key to sustainable policy development. It is one that illustrates the importance of a professional learning community of teachers, and a culture of shared responsibility among a school team, pupils and parents. It is also a powerful example of how schools and education systems might move beyond binaries and counterproductive debates that pitch multilingualism against monolingualism in school education. The Scoil Bhríde (Cailíní) community not only recognizes and embraces multilingualism but also turns it into pedagogical capital for learning.

The series *Multilingualisms and Diversities in Education* is intended for (and to make sense to) teachers, teacher educators, theoretical and academic specialists, administrators, policymakers, and development agencies with interests in education and linguistics (particularly sociolinguistics, and applied and educational linguistics). This first book in the series accomplishes just this. We are most appreciative of the exceptional inspiration and contribution that both Déirdre Kirwan and David Little bring to multilingualisms and diversities in education, and we are privileged to have their volume launch this series. Jim Cummins has written a most insightful and thoughtful Foreword to this book, in which he makes explicit how much this work is needed, how significant and timely it is, and the sheer depth and quality of its practice-based relevance for education now and in the future. Thank you.

Kathleen Heugh, Christopher Stroud and Piet van Avermaet
January 2019

Authors' Preface

The seeds of this book were sown early one afternoon in November 2012. Déirdre Kirwan, then principal of Scoil Bhríde (Cailíní), Blanchardstown, had invited David Little to discuss self-assessment with Fifth and Sixth Class teachers at the end of the school day. She knew of his interest in this topic because between 2004 and 2009 he had supervised her PhD research, and she was familiar with his work on learner autonomy and the European Language Portfolio. While we waited for the teachers to join us, Déirdre showed David some of the written work that pupils at different levels of the school were producing in two or three languages, including home languages in the case of pupils from immigrant families. When David gave in-service seminars for primary and post-primary teachers of English as an Additional Language, he repeatedly emphasized the importance of home language maintenance, but the large number of immigrant languages present in the Irish education system meant that none of the available models of bilingual education could easily be adapted to support the development of home language literacy. Yet – without additional resources or special allowances, without external prompting and without attempting to teach pupils' home languages directly – Scoil Bhríde had found a solution, bringing immigrant pupils' home languages into every aspect of school life, inside and outside the classroom, and in this way converting linguistic diversity into educational capital.

David was convinced in theory by the Council of Europe's concept of plurilingual education; what Déirdre told him about Scoil Bhríde's language policy and its implementation suggested one of the ways in which the concept could become a practical reality. Examples of pupils' written work showed that they were achieving high levels of age-appropriate literacy in English (the language of schooling), Irish (the obligatory second language of the curriculum), French (taught in Fifth and Sixth Class), and – in the case of pupils from immigrant families – home languages. In addition, Déirdre explained, pupils tended to develop a high degree of metalinguistic awareness and frequently undertook ambitious language learning activities on their own initiative. In the standardized tests in English and maths that pupils take each year from First Class (6+ years) to Sixth Class (11+ years), the school was performing consistently at or above the national average.

By the time David left the school that afternoon, we had agreed to collaborate in making Scoil Bhríde's approach to language education more widely known. It was likely to be of interest not only to other primary schools in Ireland and elsewhere but also to researchers and decision makers concerned with the educational integration of immigrant populations. Our collaboration began with a joint presentation at the conference on Urban Multilingualism and Education organized by the University of Ghent's Centre for Diversity and Learning in March 2013. Other conference presentations quickly followed, some given by one of us and some by both. For a number of years, with the consent of pupils' parents and the Board of Management, Déirdre had been collecting examples of pupils' written work and teachers' reports on especially memorable classroom incidents or lessons. She had also video-recorded numerous classroom interactions and interviews with teachers and pupils. So in preparing our presentations we were able to draw on a substantial corpus of evidence. Within a couple of years Scoil Bhríde's language education policy and practice had been introduced to language specialists and administrators at all levels of education in Ireland and to decision makers and researchers in many other countries; it had also been presented at academic conferences, webinars and seminars organized by the European Commission in Brussels and the European Centre for Modern Languages in Graz. The structure of the book and the way in which we interpret the evidence available to us gradually took shape as we prepared our presentations, answered questions from our audiences, and wrote and revised two articles arising from the 2013 Ghent conference.

Déirdre is grateful to the teachers of Scoil Bhríde (Cailíní) for the enthusiasm and commitment with which they embraced the school's evolving approach to plurilingual education: Patricia Cummins (Deputy Principal); Anne McKeon and Bernie Dunne (Assistant Principals); Marion O'Hare, Kathleen Burns, Siobhán Kirwan-Keane, Renee Moran, Anne O'Connor (Special Duties Teachers); Denise Kearney, Siobhán O'Connell, Ciara O'Shaughnessy, Clíona Forde, Aoife Dowd, Brenda Lavelle, Suzanne Tiernan, Louise Kerins, Sinéad Toomey, John Maguire, Maeve Kilroy, Aisling Kelly, and subsequently Ann Marie McKay, Seán Devlin, Rachel Dudgeon and Laura Cusack; Roberta Breda and Houleymatou Barry (Special Needs Assistants); Maeve Rispin (School Secretary); Dermot Guilfoyle and Hugh McKay (Caretaking and Maintenance). Déirdre also acknowledges with gratitude the unwavering support of the Board of Management: Dr Don Kelly (Chairperson), Rev. Father Kieran Dunne, Zoya Ralph, Rox Remolacio, Rodica Apopie, Peter Fitzpatrick and Siobhán O'Connell; and of the Parents' Association, especially Carol Mendoza (Chairperson).

Our joint thanks are owed to the teachers who shared their classroom experiences, insights and pupils' work with us, and in particular to the small group of teachers who pioneered the inclusion of home languages in their classrooms: Bernie Dunne (Language Support), Siobhán Kirwan-Keane and Ciara O'Shaughnessy (Sixth Class), Clíona Forde and Louise Kerins (Fifth Class). Our thanks also go to all staff members who subsequently contributed by integrating home languages in the development of plurilingual oral and literacy skills, mathematics, music, the visual and dramatic arts, and sport. We are grateful to the many pupils who provided the examples with which we illustrate our account; their obvious delight in the infinite diversity of language has been an inspiration. We are also grateful to the pupils' parents for allowing us to quote their daughters' contributions to classroom interactions and recorded interviews and to quote and reproduce their written work.

We are grateful to Piet Van Avermaet, Kathleen Heugh and Christopher Stroud for including the book in their series *Multilingualisms and Diversities in Education* and to Jim Cummins for writing the foreword.

Finally, Déirdre expresses her gratitude to all those who supported her during the preparation and writing of the book, with special thanks to her daughters Elizabeth-Ann and Iseult and to her husband Joe. David is grateful to his daughter Joanna for preparing the figures for publication and, as ever, to his wife Jean for her inexhaustible patience and unstinting support.

David Little and Déirdre Kirwan
Dublin, July 2018

Foreword

Jim Cummins

University of Toronto, Canada, and Åbo Akademi University, Finland

Among the many vivid images that emerge from this remarkable book, one that stands out for me is the visit to Scoil Bhríde (Cailíní) by a former pupil of Filipino origin who had been in Sixth Class the previous year. The pupil first visited the principal's office and engaged in an extended conversation in Irish lasting more than twelve minutes, telling her about her new school and the subjects she was studying as well as inquiring about the new buildings that Scoil Bhríde had moved into. This spontaneous and fluent conversation in Irish, probably a third language for the pupil, is not typical of pupils who learn additional languages as school subjects. One might reasonably expect this confident linguistic behaviour from a pupil who had attended an Irish-medium Gaelscoil (Ó Duibhir 2018), but the outcomes of conventional second language teaching programmes in Ireland and elsewhere seldom result in either confidence or fluency. For example, French-as-a-second-language teaching in Canada (generally 30–45 minutes per day from Grade 4) has produced dismal results for a large majority of pupils. Canadian Parents for French, a federally funded advocacy group, summarized the outcomes as follows: 'Only 3% of [Ontario] grade nine core French students continue with the program to Grade 12, most graduating with little ability to converse in, or understand French' (Canadian Parents for French 2008: 17). Compare this reality with the spontaneous writing in French (as well as Irish, English and their home languages) that eleven- and twelve-year-old Scoil Bhríde pupils engaged in after less than two years of learning the language.

The story of Scoil Bhríde, however, goes far beyond simply more effective second or third language teaching and learning. Despite an immigrant-background school population of 80 per cent, speaking fifty-one home languages (2015 figures), the school's standardized test scores in English and mathematics (administered every year between First and Sixth Class) have consistently been at or above the national average. This contrasts with the significant underachievement in most European countries of first- and second-generation immigrant pupils, particularly when they are clustered in schools with large concentrations (more than 25 per cent) of pupils from similar immigrant backgrounds (OECD 2015).

What exactly happened at Scoil Bhríde to produce such exceptional academic outcomes and what can we learn from the experience of teachers and pupils that might be applied elsewhere? David Little and Déirdre Kirwan's documentation of the pedagogical approaches that emerged in Scoil Bhríde over a period of twenty years is gripping and inspirational. Much of the book's impact derives from the fact that pupils and teachers speak for themselves. Pupils' writing in multiple languages, their reflections on their growing language awareness, and their evident exuberance for learning point to the potential of education to transform lives. However, the exceptionality of the Scoil Bhríde experience also highlights the fact that in far too many schools, especially those serving socially disadvantaged immigrant-background pupils, instruction consistently fails to generate cognitive and affective engagement.

Teachers profiled in this volume discuss their own pedagogical journeys in equally insightful and powerful ways. Their reflections illustrate how their identities as *educators* expanded as they learnt from their pupils, how collaboration with each other and with parents reinforced their autonomy as educators, and how two-way dialogue within a classroom community of learners enhanced the transmission of knowledge and skills. As teachers and pupils speak to us from the pages of this volume, we see a process of reciprocal empowerment. Power is generated for both pupils and teachers as instruction connects with pupils' lives, affirms their academic and linguistic identities, and transforms linguistic diversity into educational capital. In contrast to many contemporary educational contexts, pupils' plurilingual repertoires are positioned as cognitive and personal resources rather than as deficits to be remediated.

Although similar directions have been pursued by individual teachers (e.g. Cummins and Early 2011) and sometimes entire schools (e.g. DeFazio 1997), the experience of Scoil Bhríde is unique in its sustained exploration of language awareness, intercultural education and plurilingual learning over many years. And yet the *uniqueness* of this experience should be of concern to educators, policymakers and communities the world over. From one perspective, Scoil Bhríde did little more than apply, albeit in creative ways, research findings and mainstream theoretical insights that are endorsed (in word if not in deed) by a majority of educators and researchers in educational systems around the world.

For example, most researchers and educators endorse a focus on *teaching the whole child* and building on the *funds of knowledge* within particular communities. However, it is difficult to argue that we are teaching the whole child when explicit or implicit policies direct children to leave their languages and cultures at the schoolhouse door (for a recent Flemish example, see Pulinx, Van Avermaet, and

Agirdag 2016). Most educators and researchers also endorse the importance of connecting instruction with pupils' lives and enabling them to integrate new information and skills with their prior knowledge and experience. However, few teachers employ pedagogical strategies that explicitly build on the knowledge and skills infused into the home languages that immigrant-background pupils bring to school. Thus, the educational success experienced by pupils in Scoil Bhríde highlights the evidence-based instruction implemented in the school and thereby throws into relief the evidence-free instructional approaches implemented by the vast majority of schools serving linguistically and culturally diverse school communities.

What lessons can educators and researchers derive from the Scoil Bhríde experience? A first consideration is the fact that *actuality implies possibility* – educational initiatives that have been successfully implemented in one context can, in principle, be implemented elsewhere. For example, until recently it was widely assumed by educators and policymakers that in multilingual classroom contexts teachers had little option but to teach exclusively through the school language since they themselves had no knowledge of most of the languages of their pupils. This assumption has been refuted by the plurilingual instructional initiatives implemented successfully by educators in numerous contexts (obviously including Scoil Bhríde) (e.g. Cummins and Early 2011). Clearly context matters, and initiatives implemented in one context are likely to require modification in other contexts. But it is no longer possible to claim that it is not feasible to integrate immigrant-background students' home languages into classroom instruction.

The four major conclusions (paraphrased below) drawn by the authors on the basis of the Scoil Bhríde experience provide a starting point for the development of language policy and pedagogical practice in both teacher education programmes and schools serving diverse learners:

- Encouraging immigrant learners to use their home languages inside and outside the school promotes educational success. In Scoil Bhríde, no restrictions were placed on pupils' use of their home languages within the school.
- Opening up the pedagogical space to include home languages encourages cross-linguistic comparisons and the development of language awareness.
- The development of overall language and literacy skills will benefit from an integrated approach that encourages pupils to transfer skills from school languages to home languages (and vice versa) and supports parents in developing their children's home language literacy skills.

- A pedagogical focus on language awareness and cross-linguistic exploration
  will stimulate pupils' curiosity about language and encourage them to
  inquire actively and autonomously into connections between languages and
  the role of language in human societies.

The credibility of these claims for pupils across the entire primary school
spectrum is amply documented in the chapters that follow. However, a number
of related themes and claims, which I briefly describe below, also emerge strongly
from the data.

Teachers as knowledge generators

Implicit assumptions about the relationships between research and instructional
practice often position researchers as the generators of knowledge who then
'mobilize' it to improve educational effectiveness. Teachers are positioned
within this discourse as recipients of knowledge, which they are charged with
infusing into their instructional practice. This conception of the relationship
between research and practice certainly describes the traditional process, and
it represents a legitimate strategy for improving education. However, it is by no
means the only legitimate strategy nor the most powerful direction for change.

An alternative strategy, illustrated by the experience of Scoil Bhríde and
other plurilingual projects (e.g. Cummins and Early 2011), is to encourage
teachers to pursue instructional innovation and document its effects on pupils'
academic engagement and learning. Within this conception, instructional
innovations *create knowledge*, and teachers who pursue and document these
innovations become knowledge generators. This conception of teachers' roles
extends notions of teacher agency and autonomy emphasized in this volume
into the realm of empirical investigation and instructional inquiry. The
knowledge-generation process often originates in the context of collaboration
and dialogue between educators and university-based researchers (as illustrated
in the early collaboration between Déirdre Kirwan and David Little), but the
specific innovations come from the educators themselves and evolve over time
through classroom-based documentation and discussion with colleagues within
the school. University-based researchers typically contribute to the knowledge
generation by brainstorming instructional possibilities with teachers, based on
both formal research and experiences elsewhere, observing and documenting
teachers' instructional initiatives, analysing the principles or claims underlying

the observed practice, and synthesizing these principles across diverse contexts in order to assess the extent to which they could account for the observed data.

Schools that position teachers as knowledge generators within a community of educators whose insights and instructional skills are constantly evolving are clearly expanding notions of teacher identity beyond the traditional conception of teachers as transmitters of curriculum. Scoil Bhríde teachers readily articulated the fact that they were also learners, expanding their knowledge of both specific languages and language in general by means of dialogue with their pupils. Within this orientation to research, the knowledge generated by teachers and researchers working collaboratively also flows much more readily into instructional practice in other contexts because it was generated within classrooms by teachers rather than from a much more abstract university-directed investigative process.

Shared leadership

Teacher agency and autonomy in the pursuit of shared instructional goals clearly imply a leadership process within the school that values the input of teachers and community members. The instructional directions pursued by educators at Scoil Bhríde were supported by leadership that was clear, authoritative and collaborative. In contrast to popular conceptions of the 'strong leader' who exercises top-down power, often in an authoritarian way, organizational theory increasingly recognizes that effective leadership creates conditions in which team members take on increasing responsibility and self-management in pursuit of organizational goals.

Shared or distributed leadership also implies accountability for making evidence-based instructional decisions. In Scoil Bhríde, teachers gathered extensive classroom-based documentation of their pupils' learning. Portfolios maintained by teachers included results of weekly spelling and mathematics tests, examples of independent work and projects, a record of progress in reading, the pupil's own reports on books she had read, copies of significant examples of written work, and records of memorable contributions to class discussions that focused on language. Teachers also discussed video recordings of classroom interactions and shared examples of their pupils' work and anecdotes from their classroom instruction. This sharing and collaboration among teachers highlighted the extent to which pupils enjoyed exploring similarities and differences between languages and the creative ways in which they used their home languages in the classroom. Teachers inspired one other, and their collective instructional experience reinforced their belief in the validity of an instructional approach that harnessed pupils' entire plurilingual repertoire in the service of learning.

Thus, the instructional focus on cross-linguistic language awareness was not imposed by the school principal but grew naturally from the collective experience of teachers who trusted themselves and were trusted by the principal to pursue innovative instructional directions within the general framework of the school's language policy. This language policy was far from simply a static document to be displayed on a shelf in the principal's office (as sometimes happens). Rather, it represented a dynamic and evolving invitation for teachers to explore the pedagogical opportunities represented by pupils' linguistic experiences and talents. The freedom for individual teachers to innovate, together with ongoing collaboration among teachers, resulted in a coherent whole-school approach that reflected pedagogical consistency and continuity from one grade level to the next. As one teacher noted: *The open language policy has permeated through the whole school ... in any class the children are open to learning all languages and greet you in several different languages and it has almost become a matter of fact, it's just integrated into daily school life.*

Plurilingual literacy engagement

A final point worth noting is the role of literacy engagement in general and plurilingual literacy engagement in particular in promoting language learning and academic success among pupils in Scoil Bhríde. In multiple research studies, some involving hundreds of thousands of pupils (e.g. OECD 2010), literacy engagement has emerged as one of the most potent determinants of literacy attainment. For example, the Organisation for Economic Cooperation and Development's (OECD) Programme for International Student Achievement (PISA) has consistently reported that the level of pupils' reading engagement is a better predictor of reading performance than their socio-economic status (SES). The OECD (2010) also reported that approximately one-third of the association between reading performance and students' SES was mediated by reading engagement. The implication is that schools can potentially 'push back' about one-third of the negative effects of socio-economic disadvantage by ensuring that students have access to a rich print environment and become actively engaged with literacy.

The interviews with Scoil Bhríde pupils and teachers scattered throughout this book testify powerfully to the fact that, from the earliest grades, pupils were immersed in literacy both in school and at home. As described in Chapter 2, the school emphasized the development of literacy skills across all curricular languages (English, Irish, French (in Fifth and Sixth Class)) as well as in pupils' home languages. Pupils were actively encouraged to make connections among their languages, and their creative written work was prominently displayed throughout the school in corridors and classrooms. The school library included books in multiple languages as well as dual-language books, and pupils were encouraged to collect samples of their writing in their personal books and read their writing in English, Irish and home languages to their classmates.

Parents were viewed as essential partners in this process. The school principal and teachers consistently encouraged parents to maintain their language of origin as the preferred medium of family communication and, over time, to support their children in transferring literacy skills in English and Irish to their home language. Parents were also encouraged to read stories to their children in their home languages and to help them in writing stories and other texts in these languages for sharing with teachers and peers at school.

In short, engagement with literacy permeated the educational experience of pupils in Scoil Bhríde. From the earliest stages of learning how to read, teachers connected literacy with pupils' own experience (through the 'language experience' approach described in Chapter 2) and reinforced reading and writing skills across Irish, English and students' home languages, together with French in the later grades.

The wonderfully imaginative writing that students produced in their multiple languages bear all the hallmarks of what we have called 'identity texts' (Cummins and Early 2011). The term is intended to highlight the powerful connections between literacy and pupils' evolving identities. Pupils invest their identities in the creation of various kinds of 'texts' which can be written, spoken, signed, visual, musical, dramatic or combinations in multimodal form. The identity text then holds a mirror up to pupils in which their identities are reflected back in a positive light. When pupils share identity texts with multiple audiences (peers, teachers, parents, grandparents, sister classes, the media etc.) they are likely to receive positive feedback and affirmation of self in interaction with these audiences. This identity affirmation, in turn, fuels further engagement with literacy. Thus, the creative plurilingual writing produced by Scoil Bhríde pupils represents an expression of identity, a projection of identity into new social spheres and a re-creation of identity as a result of feedback from and dialogue with multiple audiences.

Conclusion

We live at a point in human history when xenophobia and racism, fuelled by population mobility, are once again infecting social discourse in countries around the world. I see the experience of Scoil Bhríde, and its brilliant evocation in this book, as a parable for our times – a microcosm of what _can_ happen when we construct diversity as a resource rather than a barrier or threat. Instruction in Scoil Bhríde went far beyond simply transmission of curriculum; underlying pupils' outstanding academic outcomes and imaginative literary accomplishments was a process of negotiating identities – sustained interactions that collaboratively generated personal and social power for pupils, teachers and parents/caregivers.

References

Canadian Parents for French (2008), _The State of French-Second-Language Education in Canada 2008_. Available online: http://cpf.ca/en/research-advocacy/research/the-state-of-fsl-education-in-canada/

Cummins, J., and M. Early, eds (2011), _Identity Texts: The Collaborative Creation of Power in Multilingual Schools_, Stoke on Trent (UK): Trentham Books.

DeFazio, A. J. (1997), 'Language Awareness at The International High School', in L. Van Lier and D. Corson (eds), _Knowledge about Language. Encyclopedia of Language and Education_, 99–107, Dordrecht, The Netherlands: Kluwer Academic Publishers, Inc.

Ó Duibhir, P. (2018), _Immersion Education: Lessons from a Minority Language Context_, Bristol: Multilingual Matters.

OECD (2010), _PISA 2009 Results: Learning to Learn – Student Engagement, Strategies and Practices (Volume III)_, Paris: OECD. Available online: http://www.oecd.org/dataoecd/11/17/48852630.pdf

OECD (2015), _Helping Immigrant Students Succeed at School – and Beyond_, Paris: OECD. Available online: https://www.oecd.org/education/Helping-immigrant-students-to-succeed-at-school-and-beyond.pdf

Pulinx, R., Van Avermaet, P., and Agirdag, O. (2016), 'Silencing Linguistic Diversity: The Extent, the Determinants and Consequences of the Monolingual Beliefs of Flemish Teachers', _International Journal of Bilingual Education and Bilingualism_, Epub ahead of print 27 October 2015. doi:10.1080/13670050.2015.1102860.

Introduction

The increasing linguistic diversity of school-going populations is among the greatest challenges faced by Western education systems today. How best to manage educational provision for linguistic minorities has been a major preoccupation of policymakers and educational researchers since the mid-twentieth century, and various models of bilingual education have been devised to meet the needs of various kinds of linguistic minority, indigenous as well as immigrant (for a historical overview, see Sierens and Van Avermaet 2014). Yet despite strong empirical evidence in favour of bilingual education (August and Shanahan 2006, Genesee et al. 2006), the past decade has seen a rapidly growing tendency for European countries to adopt policies that imply disregard, perhaps even suppression, of immigrants' languages (evolving policy and practice relative to adult migrants are summarized by Pulinx, Van Avermaet and Extramiana 2014). Against this tendency, the Council of Europe promotes a human rights perspective on linguistic diversity (Little 2010). All residents of a given member state have a right to education, they also have a right to use their first language freely, and this implies an obligation to find ways of including minority languages in the educational process. These considerations are fundamental to the Council of Europe's recent project Languages in Education, Languages for Education; they also help to explain the organization's commitment to the concept of 'plurilingual and intercultural education'.[1] In an age of rising xenophobia and hostility to all forms of otherness, it is impossible to overstate the importance of educational integration as a prerequisite for social cohesion.

Many of the measures governments adopt to promote linguistic integration are in fact assimilationist. That is, they envisage a one-way process in which minorities and immigrants somehow suppress their distinctive identities, including their linguistic identities, in order to be more easily absorbed into their

---

[1] https://www.coe.int/en/web/platform-plurilingual-intercultural-language-education/the-learner-and-the-languages

host society. This understanding of integration is reflected in the widespread requirement that immigrant students leave their home language at the school gate. Sometimes justified on the common-sense ground that such pupils need to spend as much time as possible communicating in the language of schooling, this practice is vulnerable to criticism on educational as well as ethical grounds. Banning the use of home languages at school certainly infringes a basic human right, but it also overlooks the fact that the individual's home language is his or her primary cognitive tool and thus plays a key role in all intentional learning. Whatever regulations are imposed on them, immigrant students cannot expunge their home language from their minds while they are in school; it inevitably persists as their involuntary inner voice and the default medium of their discursive thinking. And if we accept the argument of the Council of Europe's White Paper on Intercultural Dialogue (2008), that integration is a two-way process involving reciprocity and exchange, we must in any case find an active role for learners' home languages in our education systems.

Historically a country of emigration, Ireland has experienced significant immigration only in the last two decades. As in other European countries, immigrants have come from many parts of the world, bringing with them more than 200 languages. Some of these languages are spoken by numerically significant minorities – for example, from Poland, Lithuania, Romania, Latvia and Slovakia (Central Statistics Office 2017: 50); other languages have many fewer speakers. The implementation plan for *Languages Connect*, Ireland's ten-year strategy for foreign languages in education (Department of Education and Skills 2017a), promises new school-leaving exams in Polish, Portuguese and Lithuanian (Department of Education and Skills 2017b: 16). But what about all the other immigrant languages? How are they to be included in mainstream education? This book explains in detail how one primary school – Scoil Bhríde (Cailíní), Blanchardstown, Dublin – has answered this question. An exercise in 'thick description' (Geertz 1973), the book seeks to capture something of the rich complexity of classroom life and pedagogical practice and in doing so to offer tentative explorations of underlying processes. Déirdre Kirwan was responsible for initiating Scoil Bhríde's approach to language education and guiding its development; she gathered the extensive records on which we draw and experienced at first-hand many of the teaching/learning episodes we describe. David Little was not directly involved; his role has been that of an external observer after the event, though at the beginning of our collaboration he briefed himself by holding a meeting with all the teachers before interviewing each of them individually. We believe that two features in particular make our study unusual: its wealth of practical examples and its quasi-longitudinal dimension – we illustrate how the school's policy is implemented with children from four and a half (preschoolers in many other jurisdictions) through to the threshold of the teen years.

Inevitably, the book is centrally concerned with the role played by language and communication in the educational process. English-speaking Irish pupils must acquire basic skills in reading and writing and take their first steps on the road to mastery of relevant varieties of academic language, the terminology and text types characteristic of the different curriculum subjects. Pupils from immigrant families – by 2015, they made up 80 per cent of Scoil Bhríde's cohort – must acquire the same skills in English as language of schooling, which for most of them is a new language when they start school. All pupils learn Irish, Ireland's first official language and the obligatory first second language of primary and post-primary curricula. In the last two primary grades, Fifth and Sixth Class, Scoil Bhríde's pupils also learn French. And with help from parents and older siblings, and in some cases the wider community, pupils from immigrant families transfer the literacy skills they are acquiring in English and Irish to the language they speak at home. An integrated approach to language education such as Scoil Bhríde has devised acknowledges that curriculum and home languages are at all times available in the classroom, whether as media of communication or sources of linguistic intuition and insight. As the one second language that all pupils have in common, Irish plays a pivotal role in binding together the plurilingual repertoires present in each class.

Cummins (2007: 222–3) identifies three interrelated principles that have been widely assumed to shape best practice in second/foreign language teaching and bilingual/immersion education: (i) instruction should be carried out exclusively in the target language without recourse to learners' L1, (ii) translation between L1 and L2 has no place in the teaching of language or literacy, and (iii) within immersion and bilingual programmes, the two languages should be kept separate. Scoil Bhríde's integrated approach to language education flouts all three principles. There are fifty-odd home languages present in the school and most of them are unknown to the teachers. These considerations rule out translanguaging practices of the kind described, for example, by Creese and Blackledge (2010) and García and Sylvan (2011), where English as language of schooling alternates with a home language shared by all members of the class. Instead, immigrant pupils are encouraged to use their home language to support their learning in whatever ways seem appropriate to them. From the earliest stages teachers engage pupils in classroom interaction by asking them to tell the class how they express key concepts in their home language. This has very simple beginnings: four-and-a-half-year-olds teach one another to count from one to five and share the words for primary colours in their various home languages, but pupils are quickly led into complex and sophisticated cross-linguistic comparison. Speakers of the same or closely related languages are also encouraged to use their home languages in pair and group work.

A report prepared for the OECD identifies three approaches to the development of immigrant learners' proficiency in the language of schooling: complete withdrawal from the mainstream, partial withdrawal from the mainstream and immersion in the mainstream with systematic language support (Stanat and Christensen 2006). The first approach seems to imply that the language of schooling must be learnt, at least in its basics, before curriculum content can be successfully engaged with; the second, that focused language support bridges the gap between language learning and curriculum learning; and the third, that mastery of curriculum content and proficiency in the language of schooling are essentially inseparable. In Ireland the second approach is the preferred option, but in Scoil Bhríde small-group language classes include native as well as non-native speakers of English, and the integrated approach to language education explores the connections, similarities and differences between languages as a way of helping pupils to engage with and process curriculum content.

The account we give of classroom practice coincides with theories of language learning that emphasize the importance of giving learners opportunities to interact with one another in meaningful contexts supported by explicit attention to language itself (Schleppegrell 2013). Primary schools in Ireland as in other countries seek to develop pupils' literate proficiency in the language of schooling by modelling and extensive scaffolding (Wood, Bruner and Ross 1976); a focus on linguistic form mostly arises from a concern to encourage orthographic accuracy. In Scoil Bhríde, much the same approach is adopted to the teaching of Irish and, in due course, French. Sfard (1998) has argued that educational success depends on maintaining an appropriate balance between learning as acquisition (accumulation of the elements of knowledge) and learning as participation (the process of becoming a member of a particular community). As Larsen-Freeman (2002: 36–7) has pointed out, Sfard's distinction between acquisition and participation recalls the distinction between language learning as a cognitive process and language learning as socialization via language use. The latter view encourages us to think of classrooms and the schools to which they belong as communities of practice (Lave and Wenger 1991, Wenger 1998). In Scoil Bhríde's classrooms teachers' openness to the home languages of immigrant pupils invites participation on the part of those pupils and necessarily entails that teachers give full rein to pupils' initiatives in classroom discourse. Curriculum content is presented, processed and mastered as learners develop the ability to perform interactively with others (Kasper and Wagner 2011), and pupils come to experience learning as 'a form of life rather than a temporary chore' (Evensen 2008: 345).

Considerations like these came into play retrospectively, as we began to develop our 'thick description' of Scoil Bhríde's approach and speculate on the reasons for its success; they played no role, however, in the development of the approach. The key factor was the strongly learner-centred Primary School Curriculum (Government of Ireland 1999a) and its unacknowledged reflection of educational research that emphasizes the importance of exploratory learning and the need to take account of the knowledge and experience that pupils bring with them to the classroom. A foundational text in this research paradigm, and one on which we draw, is Douglas Barnes's (1976) study *From Communication to Curriculum*, which helped to establish a tradition that is continued in the work of Neil Mercer, Gordon Wells, Robin Alexander and others. Closely related work by Britton et al. (1975) showed the importance for successful learning of the immediate social environment and the teacher's role as a trusted adult (Evensen 2008). The account we give of Scoil Bhríde's approach is strongly influenced by these considerations.

We begin our account by focusing on four dimensions of the national context: the linguistic diversity that recent patterns of immigration to Ireland have brought to Irish society, the language policy that results from the bilingual status of Irish society, the language education policy that has flowed from and been constrained by national language policy, and the official response to the challenges posed by a linguistically diverse school-going cohort. Chapter 2 introduces Scoil Bhríde (Cailíní), sketches its history, describes the increasing linguistic diversity of its pupil cohort, summarizes the development of its integrated approach to language education and provides evidence of its impact on pupils and teachers. Against this multidimensional background, Chapters 3–5 describe the implementation of the approach from three interdependent perspectives. Chapter 3 focuses on the role played by immigrant pupils' home languages in classroom interaction and concludes by considering Scoil Bhríde's policy and practice from the perspective of plurilingual education as defined by the Council of Europe's *Common European Framework of Reference for Languages* (Council of Europe 2001). Chapter 4 explores the development of pupils' plurilingual literacy within the trajectory of literacy development prescribed by the Primary

School Curriculum; it also considers how translanguaging in the sense of producing parallel texts in multiple languages contributes to the development of pupils' language awareness and their sense of identity. And Chapter 5 explores the relation between the inclusion of home languages in classroom interaction and the frequency with which pupils undertake autonomous language-related learning initiatives. Finally, Chapter 6 recapitulates the main features of Scoil Bhríde's approach; discusses its sustainability, generalizability and implications for teacher education; briefly indicates some dimensions of our account that could usefully be amplified and extended by further exploration; and offers some concluding thoughts on the Council of Europe's concept of 'plurilingual and intercultural education'.

1

The National Context

This chapter describes recent patterns of immigration to Ireland, summarizes national language and language education policy, explains the official response to the arrival of linguistic diversity in the education system and the role assigned to Integrate Ireland Language and Training (IILT), and briefly considers developments since the demise of IILT in 2008.

Immigration to Ireland since the 1990s

Ireland has experienced large-scale immigration only in the past quarter century; between the 1840s and the 1990s it was predominantly a country of emigration, though small numbers of Vietnamese refugees were received at the end of the 1970s. In the mid-1990s, similarly small numbers of refugees from the Balkan Wars were admitted under the terms of agreements between the Irish government and the UNHCR; then, towards the end of the decade, there was a rapid increase in the number of asylum seekers, mostly from Sub-Saharan Africa and Eastern Europe; migrant workers from non-EU countries were recruited to fill gaps in the labour force; and large numbers of immigrants came from Eastern European and Baltic states when they joined the European Union in 2004. In the forty years from 1956 to 1996 Ireland's population increased by 25 per cent, from 2.9 to 3.6 million; in the twenty years from 1996 to 2016 it increased by 31 per cent, from 3.6 to 4.8 million (Central Statistics Office 2017: 6). In 2016, 17.3 per cent of Irish residents (0.8 million) had been born outside Ireland (Central Statistics Office 2017: 46).

Between 1996 and 2006 net migration (numbers immigrating less numbers emigrating) exceeded natural population increase (number of births less number of deaths), and despite the financial crash of 2008 and the ensuing economic crisis, immigration continued to exceed emigration between 2006 and 2011.

Over those five years, for example, the number of Polish residents increased from 73,402 to 112,259, the number of Lithuanian residents from 25,796 to 36,683, and the number of Latvian residents from 14,186 to 19,993 (Central Statistics Office 2017: 52). Although there was slightly more emigration than immigration between 2011 and 2016, the number of foreign-born residents continued to increase. In 2016, the distribution of the foreign-born population by nationality was as follows: Polish 2.7 per cent, United Kingdom 2.2 per cent, Lithuanian 0.8 per cent, Romanian 0.6 per cent, Latvian 0.4 per cent, Brazilian 0.3 per cent and others 4.6 per cent (Central Statistics Office 2017: 50). This last category conceals significant diversity: in the year to April 2016, non-Irish immigrants arrived in Ireland from 180 countries (Central Statistics Office 2017: 47).

The 2011 census was the first to ask questions about foreign languages spoken at home and how well those who spoke a foreign language at home could speak English (Central Statistics Office 2017: 54). In the 2016 census, 12.9 per cent of Irish residents reported that they spoke a foreign language at home. The question they were asked was: 'Do you speak a language other than English or Irish at home?', and the absence of a follow-up question to establish whether that other language was the dominant medium of domestic communication makes it difficult to interpret this result with confidence. It comes as a surprise, for example, that French was the second most frequently reported foreign language spoken at home (after Polish), though the fact that 75.1 per cent of those who said they spoke French at home were Irish nationals (Central Statistics Office 2017) suggests that perhaps not all of them lived their family life exclusively or predominantly through French.

Despite this uncertainty, the 2016 census returns show that in two decades Irish society has assumed a degree of linguistic diversity that is historically unprecedented and likely to pose a challenge to the education system. Some indication of the extent of that challenge is provided by the fact that of those who spoke a foreign language at home, 19,743 were preschool children (3–4 years), 54,693 were attending primary school and 31,078 were attending secondary school (Central Statistics Office 2017: 54). Further evidence of the educational challenge is the fact that 1,710 of the preschool children who spoke a foreign language at home could not speak English at all, while 5,989 could not speak English well (Central Statistics Office 2017: 56). In other words, some 30 per cent of children who spoke a foreign language at home would have their first immersive encounter with English when starting primary school. It is worth adding that when children whose early life has been lived predominantly through another language are deemed to speak English 'well' or 'very well', English will nevertheless be a much smaller part of their experience than it is for children born into English-speaking families, and the language may well be a challenge for them when they start school.

Ireland's immigrant population is not spread evenly across the country. It has been policy to disperse refugees and asylum seekers – now a small percentage of the immigrant population – to centres around the country, but all immigrants with the right to work tend to live in areas where they can find a job and housing is affordable. Many immigrants from the Philippines and India, for example, work in the health sector, which means that their children are likely to be enrolled in schools adjacent to hospitals; while schools situated close to meat-packing plants often enrol Portuguese-speaking children whose parents have come from Brazil. Some schools have many pupils from immigrant families, some have only a few and some have none at all. The extent of linguistic diversity that such pupils bring with them is also highly variable: a school with (say) twenty immigrant pupils may find that between them those pupils have the same number of home languages, whereas a school with a much larger number of immigrant pupils may effectively be dealing with two or three linguistic minorities. Six months after the 2004 enlargement of the EU, the Diocesan Advisors for Religious Education in Primary Schools carried out a survey of schools in Dublin's western suburbs. They found that the population of non-native speakers of English had risen to almost 50 per cent in some schools and also that some schools had as many as thirty-two different nationalities on the roll (Diocesan Advisers for Religious Education in Primary Schools 2004). The school at the centre of this study is Scoil Bhríde (Cailíní) (St Brigid's School for Girls), Blanchardstown, Dublin. The classroom data presented and analysed later in the book was mostly collected between 2011 and 2015. By the end of this period about 80 per cent of the pupils came from immigrant families, and they brought some fifty home languages with them. These figures make the school unusual but by no means unique.

Over the past twenty years there has been much debate about what to call pupils from non-indigenous backgrounds. To begin with, 'international' and 'newcomer' were the preferred terms, but they were clearly inappropriate to children born in Ireland to immigrant parents. For several years those receiving English language support were sometimes referred to as learners of English as a Second Language (ESL), though officialdom has adopted the term English as an Additional Language (EAL). In the present work, we refer to the pupils in focus as coming from immigrant homes or families because their parents were born outside Ireland and as English Language Learners (ELLs) because the fact that they speak a language other than English or Irish at home entitles them to a period of specially funded English language support.

Language policy in Ireland

Language policy in Ireland is rooted in the nineteenth-century ideology that associates nationhood with language. Article 8 of the Constitution of Ireland (1937) declares that 'Irish as the national language is the first official language', while it recognizes English as 'a second official language'. According to Scollon (2004: 272), 'it has been essential for the modern state to be perceived as having political boundaries that are isomorphic with language boundaries'. Ireland, however, is an exception to this general rule: Irish has been in steady decline since the 1840s. Small Irish-speaking communities have survived, mostly in rural areas on or close to the western and south-western seaboard, but the great majority of the native population is English-speaking and there are no adult monolingual Irish speakers.

In view of Ireland's colonial past it was perhaps inevitable that the founders of the state would give Irish the legal status of first official language. Although the language plays no role in the daily lives of the great majority of the adult population, all official documents are issued in Irish as well as English, and official and public notices are obligatorily bilingual. Government commitment to the preservation of Irish in public life is confirmed by the Official Languages Act, passed in 2003 to improve the provision of public services through Irish, and the appointment the following year of an Irish Language Commissioner. These and similar measures imply an ambition to restore the language to widespread use in Irish society. The education system is chief among the mechanisms (Shohamy 2006) charged with this task: Irish is an obligatory subject from the beginning of primary to the end of post-primary schooling, and Irish-medium schooling is available at primary and post-primary levels. In 2016/2017 there were 271 Irish-medium primary schools, 145 of them outside and 126 inside Gaeltachtaí (Irish-speaking areas), and 66 Irish-medium post-primary schools, 44 outside and 22 inside Gaeltachtaí. As a language through which citizens live their daily lives, however, Irish continues to decline. According to the 2016 census, only 32 per cent of Irish speakers living in Gaeltachtaí said that they spoke Irish daily outside the school system (Central Statistics Office 2017: 69).

The 2016 census asked two questions about the Irish language: 'Can you speak Irish?' and 'If "Yes," do you speak Irish: 1. Daily, within the education system,

2. Daily, outside the education system, 3. Weekly, 4. Less often, 5. Never?' The total number of people who said they could speak Irish was 1.76 million or 39.8 per cent of respondents, compared with 41.4 per cent in 2011 (Central Statistics Office 2017: 66). It is reasonable to assume that a significant proportion of those respondents were school-going children and adolescents; yet 30 per cent of respondents aged between 10 and 19 said they could not speak Irish (Central Statistics Office 2017). As regards frequency of use, 73,803 respondents said they spoke Irish daily outside the education system (3,382 fewer than in 2011), 111,473 said they spoke it weekly, and 586,535 said they spoke it less often. Twenty-four per cent of those who said they could speak Irish also said they never used the language, while 33 per cent of respondents aged 17 and 18 said they could not speak Irish (Central Statistics Office 2017), though the majority of them would have been taught Irish at school for at least thirteen years. These responses suggest that 'speak Irish' may have been interpreted in at least two ways: 'can conduct a (simple) conversation in Irish' and 'have learnt Irish and can produce bits of the language when prompted'.

The perceived lack of communication between the anglophone and francophone communities in Canada has sometimes caused them to be described as living in 'two solitudes' (see, e.g. Cummins 2008; the phrase comes from the title of a novel by Hugh MacLennan first published in 1945). Although there is no comparable lack of communication between the Irish-speaking minority and the English-speaking majority in Ireland, their languages certainly coexist in two solitudes. This is reflected in the absence of bilingual education. Schools are either English-medium or Irish-medium, and it is a matter of economic necessity rather than educational policy that Irish-medium schools are often obliged to use textbooks written in English to support teaching through Irish. This helps to explain why Ireland has not been significantly involved in the debates surrounding bilingual education in its various forms over the past half century (for a summary, see Sierens and Van Avermaet 2014). Because English and Irish are strictly separated and Irish speakers are a small minority, adult residents who live at a distance from Gaeltachtaí easily forget that they are in an officially bilingual country, and those whose schooling makes them fluent in Irish find it difficult to retain their fluency in later life unless they become teachers of Irish or members of Irish-language associations.

Certainly, English is the language that adult immigrants must learn if they are to establish themselves as independent agents in Irish society. In this respect, it is worth noting that Ireland has not been infected by the testing culture that has attached itself to the linguistic integration of adult immigrants in so many other countries (Pulinx, Van Avermaet and Extramiana 2014). There are two reasons for this. In the 1990s the immigrants for whom official English language programmes were provided were refugees, whose status gave them security of residence that could not be undermined by failure in a language test, and since 2004 the overwhelming majority of immigrants have come from other EU member states and thus have freedom of movement independent of their language proficiency. Because it is the dominant language of schooling, the children of immigrants must acquire near-native proficiency in English if they are to fulfil their educational potential, but before we describe the arrangements the Irish government has put in place to support this process, it is appropriate to explain how Ireland's language policy impinges on its language *education* policy.

Language education policy

As we have already noted, Irish is an obligatory curriculum subject from the beginning to the end of schooling. In some English-medium schools Irish is used as a medium of spontaneous communication on a daily basis, but in most it enjoys the same solitude as it does in Irish society at large. Traditionally, four foreign languages have been taught at post-primary level: French, German, Italian and Spanish. More recently, special projects of the Department of Education have introduced foreign languages to the last two years of primary schooling and supported the introduction of Japanese, Chinese and Russian at post-primary level. The Irish system makes no provision to teach immigrants' languages as curriculum subjects, but it offers school-leaving exams in fifteen EU languages that are not part of the curriculum: Bulgarian, Czech, Danish, Dutch, Estonian, Finnish, Modern Greek, Hungarian, Latvian, Lithuanian, Polish, Portuguese, Romanian, Slovakian, Swedish. Students qualify to take the exam in one of these languages if they come from another EU country, speak the language in question as a first language, are following a general programme of study leading to the Leaving Certificate, and are entered for the Leaving Certificate exam in English. Although aimed at native speakers, these exams are modelled on the first foreign language final written paper of the European Baccalaureate, which invites the suspicion that their chief if unintended purpose is to provide candidates with easy points for university entrance.

From the perspective of curriculum and pedagogy, languages (including English as the majority language of schooling) exist in isolation from one another. Although this replicates the situation of English and Irish in society at large, it has not reflected the views of language education specialists in Ireland for more than thirty years. In 1986, the report of the Board of Studies for Languages set up by the newly established Curriculum and Examinations Board offered this definition of language:

> Language is
> - the chief means by which we think – all language activities, in whatever language, are exercises in thinking;
> - the vehicle through which knowledge is acquired and organized;
> - the chief means of interpersonal communication;
> - a central factor in the growth of the learner's personality;
> - one of the chief means by which societies and cultures define and organise themselves and by which culture is transmitted within and across societies and cultures. (Curriculum and Examinations Board 1986: 2)

Starting from this definition, the report argued in favour of an integrated language curriculum in which the relation between first, second and foreign language learning would be made explicit both in the structure and content of the curriculum and in classroom practice. The same argument was made almost twenty years later, first in a discussion paper on languages in the post-primary curriculum commissioned by the National Council for Curriculum and Assessment (Little 2003) and again in the Language Education Policy Profile that the Council of Europe's Language Policy Division developed in collaboration with the Department of Education in 2006 and 2007 (Council of Europe and Department of Education and Skills 2008). This latter document recommended that policy should 'decompartmentalise' languages and 'aim to develop in each individual citizen *a single plurilingual competence* …, rather than what is evident at present, namely an unrelated set of fragmentary competences in particular languages' (Council of Europe and Department of Education and Skills 2008: 33; emphasis in original). The argument was repeated in *Towards an Integrated Language Curriculum in Early Childhood and Primary Education*, a research report by Pádraig Ó Duibhir and Jim Cummins commissioned by the National Council for Curriculum and Assessment (Ó Duibhir and Cummins 2012). This time it was underpinned by reference to Cummins's linguistic interdependence hypothesis (Cummins 1979), which claims that in favourable conditions skills developed in one language can be transferred relatively straightforwardly to another language. The later chapters of this book provide detailed evidence to support this claim, confirming that significant benefits accrue from what the Council of Europe's *Common European Framework of Reference for*

Languages (2001: 4) calls the 'plurilingual approach'. But until recently the official curriculum remained firmly wedded to the belief that languages should be taught and learned in isolation from one another. Inevitably, this (largely unexamined) belief helped to shape the official policy response to the challenge posed by the need to educate large numbers of children and adolescents whose home language is neither English nor Irish. The beginning of a shift in official attitudes was marked by the introduction of a new Primary Language Curriculum in 2017. Focused on the first four years of primary schooling, the curriculum aims to integrate the teaching of English and Irish in order to exploit the potential for transfer between languages (Department of Education and Skills 2015: 8); it thus responds to the arguments articulated in the report by Ó Duibhir and Cummins (2012).

The official response to linguistic diversity in education

In Ireland as in other countries, the rights and entitlements of adult immigrants depend on their status. All children and adolescents between the ages of 6 and 16, however, are legally required to attend school, so by the later 1990s a significant minority of primary pupils and post-primary students had home languages other than English or Irish. This posed a major challenge to the education system, and the Department of Education responded by funding two years of English language support for each English language learner (ELL). If a primary school had more than two and fewer than fourteen ELLs it received additional funding to pay for extra teaching hours; there were two tariffs, one for between three and seven ELLs and a second for between eight and thirteen. Primary schools could recruit an additional teacher if they had fourteen or more ELLs and two additional teachers if they had twenty-eight or more. Prior to the financial crash of 2008, some primary schools with very large numbers of ELLs had as many as six language support teachers; after the crash public spending cuts put the system under a pressure from which it has never fully recovered.

It's unclear why the Department of Education decided to fund two years of English language support rather than (say) one or three years, but it seems likely that the decision was taken on grounds of common sense and affordability. To begin with, the provision of English language support was seen as a necessary but temporary arrangement: it was widely believed in official circles that when the Irish economy went into recession, immigrants would leave as quickly as they had arrived. This underestimated parents' unwillingness to disrupt their children's education and overestimated the economic attraction of other countries, including immigrants' countries of origin, even after the collapse of the Irish economy in 2008. The official view that immigration was likely to be a short-lived phenomenon meant that it was difficult for schools to develop a coherent and integrated approach to the provision of English language support. In particular, the allocation of funding on an annual basis created uncertainty for schools whose numbers of immigrant pupils/students hovered around the various funding thresholds. Another limitation was that if newly qualified teachers were recruited to teach English, that could not be counted as part of their probationary process. However, many schools preferred to assign experienced class teachers to English language support, replacing them by newly qualified teachers on a temporary basis.

Broadly speaking, education systems have devised three ways of providing for the development of immigrants' proficiency in the language of schooling: by teaching them separately from the mainstream, by assigning them to mainstream classes but organizing separate instruction in the language of schooling and by providing them with language support in the mainstream classroom. In principle, of course, the three modes could be used in sequence, the first in an initial phase of reception, the second in a period of transition and the third when immigrant pupils are deemed capable of participating fully in mainstream education, even though they still need language support. In practice, however, most countries tend to emphasize one or other of the modes in their policy documents, though the boundaries between them may not be firmly fixed. According to a report prepared for the OECD (Stanat and Christensen 2006), most countries favour immersion in the mainstream, though the report acknowledges that this does not guarantee provision of systematic language support. In Ireland, the Department of Education allowed schools to make their own arrangements; there was nevertheless a general expectation that they would provide English language support on a withdrawal basis. In other words, they would assign ELLs to an age-appropriate mainstream class from which they would be withdrawn regularly for special English lessons in small groups.

It quickly became clear that schools needed more than additional funding if they were to provide effective English language support. Those charged with teaching English had the same qualifications as other teachers in their sector. At primary level they were generalists, though they were required to teach Irish and thus had some language teaching experience. At post-primary level they had a degree in the subject(s) they taught and a postgraduate qualification in teaching; unless they taught a foreign language, they had no language teaching experience. At both levels teachers' pre-service education had not considered the challenges posed by linguistic diversity, and even post-primary language teachers were unlikely to have studied the processes of language acquisition in any detail. Coming under pressure from school principals and teachers' unions, the Department of Education decided that it must provide schools with more than funding. In 2000, it gave IILT the task of developing a range of supports and mediating them to English language support teachers in a series of in-service seminars.

The role of Integrate Ireland Language and Training

Integrate Ireland Language and Training (IILT), a not-for-profit campus company of Trinity College Dublin, was fully funded by the Irish government (Department of Education) from its establishment in 2000 until 2008, when funding was withdrawn; David Little was the organization's non-stipendiary director. IILT was already providing intensive English language courses for adult refugees when it was given the task of developing support for the school sector. Its terms of reference were as follows:

1. To analyse the linguistic demands of the primary and post-primary curricula and to describe the proficiency ELLs needed to develop if they were to participate fully in the educational process. This prompted the development of *English Language Proficiency Benchmarks* for both sectors.
2. To create teaching materials and other resources to support the learning of EAL in primary and post-primary schools. IILT responded to this requirement by devising primary and post-primary versions of the European Language Portfolio (ELP), tailored to meet the needs of ELLs. It also developed teaching/learning materials that were closely related to the ELPs.
3. To provide ongoing in-service days for English language support teachers at primary and post-primary levels. From 2000 to 2006 IILT offered two days for each sector in each school year, one in the autumn and the other in the spring. Demand was much higher in the primary sector, partly because there were more ELLs at that level and partly because it was easier for principals to release English language teachers (at post-primary level most English language teachers were also teaching a mainstream curriculum subject). Thus 2005 saw a total attendance of 956 at thirteen in-service

days for primary teachers, compared with 124 at two in-service days for post-primary teachers.

All aspects of IILT's work were informed by the findings of relevant international research, for example in L2 acquisition, bilingual education and language teaching, and supported by a programme of ongoing research and development in Trinity College's Centre for Language and Communication Studies. IILT's in-service days, moreover, promoted a strongly interactive dynamic and involved teachers in the development and piloting of teaching materials and other resources.

English Language Proficiency Benchmarks

The two versions of the *English Language Proficiency Benchmarks* (Integrate Ireland Language and Training 2003a, b) are based on the first three proficiency levels of the Council of Europe's *Common European Framework of Reference for Languages* (CEFR; Council of Europe 2001): A1, A2 and B1. This approach was chosen for three reasons. First, IILT wanted to provide teachers with a 'map' of learners' English language development, from zero to a point at which they should be able to participate freely in mainstream classroom work. The CEFR defines B1 as the level at which language learners are able to act as free agents in interaction with speakers of their target language; it seemed an appropriate target for primary pupils and post-primary students receiving two years of English language support in an immersion situation. Secondly, the CEFR adopts an 'action-oriented' approach to the definition of L2 proficiency, using 'can do' statements to describe the communicative tasks that learners are able to perform at each level. This feature reflects a positive rather than a deficiency view of L2 development, and its lack of emphasis on linguistic form is calculated to encourage a communicative approach to teaching. Thirdly, the use of 'can do' descriptors implies a focus on the individual learner.

The CEFR is a reference document that provides a complex taxonomic description of language proficiency in terms of language use; by contrast, the *Benchmarks* were conceived as a practical tool that teachers could use on a daily basis to plan their work and monitor the progress of individual learners. Accordingly, both versions are built around a series of grids designed on the model of the CEFR's so-called self-assessment grid (Council of Europe 2001: 26–7): proficiency levels on the horizontal axis and five categories of language activity on the vertical – listening, reading, spoken interaction, spoken

Table 1.1 Descriptors for spoken interaction from the CEFR's self-assessment grid and the primary version of the *English Language Proficiency Benchmarks*

	A1	A2	B1
Self-assessment grid, CEFR (Council of Europe 2001: 26)	I can interact in a simple way provided the other person is prepared to repeat or rephrase things at a slower rate of speech and help me formulate what I'm trying to say. I can ask and answer simple questions in areas of immediate need or on very familiar topics.	I can communicate in simple and routine tasks requiring a simple and direct exchange of information on familiar topics and activities. I can handle very short social exchanges, even though I can't usually understand enough to keep the conversation going myself.	I can deal with most situations likely to arise while travelling in an area where the language is spoken. I can enter unprepared into conversation on topics that are familiar, of personal interest or pertinent to everyday life (e.g. family, hobbies, work, travel and current events).
Global Benchmarks (IILT 2003a)	Can greet, say please and thank you, and ask for directions to another place in the school. Can respond non-verbally to basic directions to a place in the school when the other person supplements speech with signs or gestures. Can give simple answers to basic questions when given time to reply and the other person is prepared to help. Can make basic requests in the classroom or playground (e.g. for the loan of a pencil) and respond appropriately to the basic requests of others.	Can ask for attention in class. Can greet, take leave, request and thank appropriately. Can respond with confidence to familiar questions clearly expressed about family, friends, school work, hobbies, holidays etc., but is not always able to keep the conversation going. Can generally sustain a conversational exchange with a peer in the classroom when carrying out a collaborative learning activity (making or drawing something, preparing a role play, presenting a puppet show etc.). Can express personal feelings in a simple way.	Can speak with fluency about familiar topics such as school, family, daily routine, likes and dislikes. Can engage with other pupils in discussing a topic of common interest (songs, football, pop stars etc.) or in preparing a collaborative classroom activity. Can keep a conversation going, though he/she may have some difficulty making him/herself understood from time to time. Can repeat what has been said and convey the information to another person.
Benchmarks 'People who help us'	Can use gestures, keywords and simple phrases/sentences to ask for help (e.g. in Stay Safe role plays). Can reply using keywords and simple phrases/sentences to basic questions about the jobs of people who can help (e.g. Where do we find a ....?, What does he/she do?).	Can ask and answer questions about what people in familiar roles do in their jobs. Can talk with the teacher or another pupil about personal experiences with people in roles of responsibility (e.g. visit to doctor, parent is a nurse/doctor, school traffic warden, postman).	Can ask and answer questions about different jobs and responsibilities. Can ask questions of a speaker who has been invited to the school to talk about his/her job. Can answer typical questions that may be asked by a person in responsibility (e.g. in role plays involving emergencies, danger etc.).

production, writing. Each grid contains descriptors adapted from the CEFR (the self-assessment grid but also the relevant illustrative scales) to make them age-appropriate and domain-specific; the communicative tasks and language competences they describe reflect the communicative processes of primary and post-primary education. The primary *Benchmarks* (Integrate Ireland Language and Training 2003a) consist of fifteen grids: global benchmarks of communicative proficiency, global scales of underlying linguistic competence (vocabulary, grammar, phonology, orthography), and thirteen 'units of work' that focus on recurrent curriculum themes: myself; our school; food and clothes; colours, shapes and opposites; people who help us; weather; transport and travel; seasons, holidays and festivals; the local and wider community; time; people and places in other areas; animals and plants; caring for my locality. The post-primary *Benchmarks* (Integrate Ireland Language and Training 2003b) comprise three global scales, of communicative proficiency, linguistic competence, and general communicative ability; four transversal scales – personal identification, classroom interaction, learning to learn, and cultural awareness; and five scales for different curriculum areas – physical education, mathematics, science subjects, history and geography, and English. By way of illustration, Table 1.1 brings together descriptors for spoken interaction from the self-assessment grid, the global benchmarks for primary level, and the unit of work 'People who help us'. Empirical research subsequently showed that the developmental trajectory described by the primary *Benchmarks* corresponded to the actual language development of ELLs over their two years of English language support (Ćatibušić and Little 2014).

The European Language Portfolio

The Council of Europe's foundational values are human rights, democratic governance and the rule of law. Their effective promotion depends on international exchange, which in turn depends on effective language learning in the education systems of member states. This explains the succession of language education projects implemented by the Council of Europe since the early 1970s. The organization's chief instrument is the European Convention on Human Rights, hence the emphasis its education projects have always placed on the empowerment of the individual learner as a social agent and participant in the democratic process. These considerations underlay the development of the ELP, which was conceived as a companion piece to the CEFR that would allow individuals to manage and document their own language learning, potentially in a lifelong perspective. The ELP has three obligatory components: a language passport that contains a regularly updated summary of the owner's experience of learning and using second and foreign languages; a language biography that provides a reflective accompaniment to learning; and a dossier where the owner collects samples of her/his work. In keeping with the Council of Europe's focus on individual agency, effective use of the ELP depends on regular self-assessment using checklists of 'I can' descriptors organized according to the proficiency levels and language activities of the CEFR.

IILT developed primary and post-primary versions of the ELP, with 'I can' checklists derived from the *Benchmarks* and organized according to their respective structure – thematic for primary, by transversal skills and curriculum areas for post-primary. Because the *Benchmarks* seek to describe the development of ELLs' capacity to participate in curriculum learning, most descriptors refer to the language activities characteristic of Irish primary and post-primary classrooms in relation to curriculum content. They nevertheless assume that cultural issues will be acknowledged and discussed. In the primary *Benchmarks* unit 'Seasons, holidays and festivals', for example, one of the B1 descriptors for spoken interaction reads as follows: 'Can describe and respond to questions about what takes place during a festival or celebration in his/her family or community'. Designed exclusively for pupils and students whose home language is neither English nor Irish, the ELPs make space for *all* the languages that the individual learner knows (this was in any case a Council of Europe requirement) and encourage reflection on differences between life in Ireland and life as he or she has experienced it elsewhere.

The primary ELP was especially widely used: IILT distributed 5,000 copies in each of the last two years of its existence. The ELP was valued pedagogically because it helped teachers to organize English language support and, via guided self-assessment, raised pupils' awareness of their developing proficiency. It also served an important documentary function, informing class teachers, principals, school inspectors and parents of the individual pupil's progress. Together with the *Benchmarks* the two ELPs provided a firm basis on which to develop other supports.

Additional supports

As noted above, the primary sector engaged much more fully with IILT's work than the post-primary sector; accordingly, it was for the primary sector that IILT developed most additional supports. Because in-service days were provided twice a year for a number of years, it was possible to respond to teachers' needs as they emerged over time and to arrange for newly developed materials to be piloted so that they could be revised as necessary prior to publication and dissemination.

The ELP presupposes that the owner has at least basic literacy skills. Some teachers used it successfully with pupils who were in the early stages of learning to read and write English, but that still left pre-literate pupils unprovided for. *My First English Book* was designed to fill the gap: a workbook that contains relatively little text but an abundance of pictures to colour in and focuses on seven of the *Benchmarks* themes – myself and my family; school; clothes; food; colours and shapes; seasons and festivals; animals. *My First English Book* was as widely adopted as the ELP (2,000 copies were distributed in each of the last two years of IILT's existence) and served the same pedagogical and documentary functions.

In 2006 IILT published a book, *Up and Away*, that contained up-to-date versions of all the supports developed for the primary sector so far: general information for schools, guidance on setting up and delivering a language support programme, the *Benchmarks*, resources for pupils to use with the ELP and *My First English Book*, a large collection of classroom activities, materials to support the literacy development of older pupils, and a collection of photocopiable worksheets and activities.

One of the intended functions of the *Benchmarks* and the ELP was to help schools to monitor the progress of their ELLs, but from an early stage language support teachers expressed a need for more finely tuned assessment instruments. They wanted to be able to identify specific weaknesses in individual learners' competence, measure their progress at the end of their first and second years of language support, and in some cases, use the evidence of formal tests to argue for an extension of language support. IILT responded by developing assessment kits based on the primary and post-primary *Benchmarks*. Each kit had four sections – listening, reading, speaking and writing; assessment tasks were derived from *Benchmarks* descriptors; and listening and reading tasks were designed with an inbuilt scoring scheme, while rating grids were provided for speaking and writing tasks. The various sections of the kits were developed, presented at in-service days and piloted prior to publication in 2007. The piloting of the primary kit involved fifty schools and the analysis of a significant body of data; teachers achieved a high level of accuracy and consistency in rating their own pupils.

In all its work with schools IILT emphasized the importance of acknowledging linguistic and cultural diversity and respecting the languages, experience and beliefs that ELLs brought with them. The same policy underlay the work of the Southern Education and Library Board (SELB), which had similar responsibilities to IILT in Co Armagh, Northern Ireland. Between 2004 and 2007, IILT and SELB collaborated to produce common guidelines for the development of school policy and classroom practice and then, on the basis of the guidelines, a toolkit to promote an inclusive ethos in primary schools. The development of the toolkit was informed by regular consultation with primary principals and teachers from both sides of the border. Published in 2007, *Together towards Inclusion* was the first resource book to be distributed to all primary schools in Northern Ireland and the Republic.

After Integrate Ireland Language and Training

The Department of Education withdrew funding from IILT in the summer of 2008 (an account of the complex causes of IILT's demise is provided by Little and Lazenby Simpson 2009: 121–2). For the nine years of IILT's existence the Department showed no interest in the detail of its work. It knew, for example, that *English Language Proficiency Benchmarks* had been developed in fulfilment of IILT's terms of reference, but none of the Department's officials engaged with the detail of the *Benchmarks*, far less considered the implications of their CEFR-informed approach for language education more generally. The consequence of this official indifference was all too predictable. Between 2000 and 2008 the Irish government invested more than half a million euros in IILT's work for the school sector, yet as soon as funding was withdrawn, the organization and its work might not have existed. It's true that all the resources developed by IILT were immediately made available via the website of the National Council for Curriculum and Assessment, but there was no longer an organization devoted to the educational inclusion of children and adolescents from immigrant families, and the prospect of further research-driven development was (and remains) remote. Teachers newly recruited to teach EAL were no longer able to attend an in-service day and receive induction into the *Benchmarks*, the ELP, other learning materials and the assessment kit. Consequently, with two exceptions these resources were quickly forgotten.

The two exceptions were the primary and post-primary assessment kits. A Department of Education Circular of 2009 entitled 'Meeting the needs of pupils learning English as an Additional Language (EAL)' recommended the use of the kits for general proficiency testing, thus failing to acknowledge the context –

Benchmarks, ELPs and related resources – for which they had been developed. Indeed, the Circular cherry-picks *Benchmarks* descriptors in an attempt to align the toolkits with the Department's own attempt to define three levels of EAL proficiency:

Level 1: Very poor comprehension of English and very limited spoken English.
Level 2: Understands some English and can speak English sufficiently well for basic communication.
Level 3: Has competent communication skills in English. (Department of Education and Science 2009: 3)

This distorted if indirect afterlife of the *Benchmarks* is also evident in *Delivery for Students with Special Educational Needs*, a report of the National Council for Special Education published in 2014. The report recommends that the assessment toolkits should be used to identify 'EAL students', defined as 'those whose command of English is so limited as to serve as an impediment to accessing the curriculum and participating meaningfully in mainstream classroom life' (National Council for Special Education 2014: 42). Given the general focus of this report, it is perhaps not surprising that ELLs are here presented in terms of deficit rather than potential, something that IILT had always strenuously opposed.

Conclusion

In this chapter we have used findings from the 2016 census to sketch the linguistic diversity that has recently come to characterize the Irish population and the challenge that such diversity poses to the education system. We have also summarized Ireland's official language policy and shown how the two solitudes that Irish and English occupy in the political and social spheres have been carried over into language education policy and practice. English, Irish and other languages continue to exist in isolation from one another in the great majority of schools, despite the strong arguments that have been made periodically over the past thirty years in favour of adopting an integrated approach to language education policy and practice. Because IILT's work was informed by the considerations and arguments that underpin this approach, there was an inevitable tension between the assumptions that underlay official policy and the classroom practice IILT encouraged. This virtually guaranteed that once funding was withdrawn from IILT the impact of its efforts would be lost to the system. The account we have given of IILT's work is nevertheless relevant to the remainder of this book. From the beginning, the principal and language support teachers of Scoil Bhríde (Cailíní), Blanchardstown, attended IILT's in-service days and made extensive use of the *Benchmarks*, the ELPs and the primary assessment kit. In other words, the school's response to a steady increase in the diversity of its pupil population was based partly on the educational understanding and ethos promoted by IILT. This will become clear in Chapter 2.

In conclusion it is necessary to acknowledge a significant shift in language education policy that has taken place since Déirdre Kirwan collected the data presented and discussed in later chapters. As noted earlier, a new Primary Language Curriculum (Department of Education and Skills 2015) was introduced in 2017 with the aim of integrating the teaching of English and Irish, and *Languages Connect*, Ireland's strategy for foreign languages in education for the period 2017–2026, was launched at the end of the same year. In Chapter 6 we briefly consider the implications of this strategy for the growth of plurilingual education in Ireland.

2

Scoil Bhríde (Cailíní) and the Evolution of an Inclusive Language Education Policy

We begin this chapter by briefly describing the structure of primary education in Ireland and summarizing the ethos, structure and content of the primary curriculum. We then introduce the school at the centre of our study, Scoil Bhríde (Cailíní) – St Brigid's School for Girls, Blanchardstown. We sketch the school's history, documenting the growth in the number of pupils from immigrant families; describe the evolution of the school's response to the challenge of linguistic diversity; recapitulate policy and practice in five principles; and summarize their impact on pupils and teachers.

Primary education in Ireland

Most primary education in Ireland is state-funded and most schools are managed by the churches, the majority (90 per cent) by the Roman Catholic Church and the rest by the (Anglican) Church of Ireland on behalf of itself and other Protestant denominations. Catholic schools are generally larger than Protestant schools and thus have more teachers; some Catholic primary schools are single-sex. Since 1984, Educate Together has been formally recognized as a patron body that is independent of religious affiliation; its patron functions are discharged by a company limited by guarantee. There are currently eighty-two Educate Together primary schools in Ireland. The first state-funded Islamic school was established in 1990 under the trusteeship and patronage of the Islamic Foundation of Ireland; at present there are two Islamic primary schools.

All primary schools have a Board of Management comprising two direct nominees of the patron, two parents of children attending the school (a mother and a father) elected by the parent body, the principal, one other teacher elected by the teaching staff and two additional nominees agreed on by these six members. The Board is responsible for all activities of the school, including the employment of teachers, the great majority of whom qualify by taking a BEd degree at a College of Education associated with one of the universities. As noted in Chapter 1, primary teachers are generalists, required to teach all curriculum subjects, including Irish.

Primary schooling in Ireland comprises two preliminary years (Junior and Senior Infants) and six grades or classes. Equivalent to preschool provision in other countries, the two Infant years are optional, though most children take them. Children are admitted to Junior Infants when they are between four and five years old, which means that they move on to post-primary school when they are between twelve and thirteen.

The Primary School Curriculum (PSC; Government of Ireland 1999a) was developed by the National Council for Curriculum and Assessment through the 1990s and introduced in 1999. Various adjustments have been made since then, but broad curriculum content remains unchanged: language (Irish and English); mathematics; social, environmental and scientific education (history, geography and science); arts education (visual arts, music, drama); physical education; social, personal and health education (SPHE); and religious or ethical education, responsibility for which lies with the relevant patron body.

The PSC is divided into four two-year bands: Junior and Senior Infants, First and Second Class, Third and Fourth Class, Fifth and Sixth Class. This facilitates the organization of teaching in smaller schools, which commonly combine two or more classes. Delivery of the PSC is intended to exploit links between different curriculum areas and topics. There is an expectation that development of listening, speaking, reading and writing skills in Irish will be associated with their development in English and that individual topics will be explored in relation to different content areas. For example, when water is discussed as a topic in the SPHE curriculum, links can be made to most other curriculum areas – science, mathematics, geography, art etc.

The ethos of the PSC is strongly child-centred, emphasizing the individual's cognitive and social development. Its general aims are 'to enable the child to live a full life as a child and to realize his or her potential as a unique individual; to enable the child to develop as a social being through living and co-operating with others and so contribute to the good of society; [and] to prepare the child for further education and lifelong learning' (Government of Ireland 1999a: 7). The principles on which the curriculum is founded include the following:

'the child is an active agent in his or her learning' (Government of Ireland 1999a: 8), 'the child's existing knowledge and experience form the basis for learning' (Government of Ireland 1999a: 8) and 'collaborative learning should feature in the learning process' (Government of Ireland 1999a: 9). The PSC emphasizes the central role of language in learning: 'Much learning takes place through the interaction of language and experience. Language helps the child to clarify and interpret experience, to acquire new concepts, and to add depth to concepts already grasped' (Government of Ireland 1999a: 15). The PSC also stresses the importance of establishing a dynamic and interactive relationship between education and society (Government of Ireland 1999a: 6), acknowledging that 'parents are the child's primary educators, and the life of the home is the most potent factor in his or her development during the primary school years' (Government of Ireland 1999a: 21). One of the specific aims of the curriculum is 'to enable children to develop a respect for cultural difference' (Government of Ireland 1999a: 34).

The current relevance of the last of these aims notwithstanding, the PSC was developed before the Irish education system was faced with the challenge of significant linguistic diversity in the school-going population. For all its emphasis on the role of language in learning, the PSC makes no concession to the fact that pupils' first language may not be (a variety of) the language of schooling. Language in the PSC consists of English and Irish, which in most schools exist in their two solitudes; English is often used as the medium of instruction in Irish lessons.

Scoil Bhríde (Cailíní), Blanchardstown and its linguistically diverse pupil cohort

Scoil Bhríde (Cailíní) belongs to the Roman Catholic parish of Blanchardstown. It was founded in the early 1940s, when Blanchardstown was a village rather than one of Dublin's western suburbs. The school's first accommodation was a superannuated railway carriage parked next to the parish church. Subsequently, it moved first to a building on the site of what is now the community centre and then, in 1956, to a purpose-built single-storey building with eight permanent classrooms. The number of girls enrolled at the school increased significantly with the appointment of the first administrative principal (Déirdre Kirwan) in 1987, and in due course, seven prefabs were erected adjacent to the main building. In 2005, the Department of Education formally requested the Board of Management to expand the school to accommodate two streams of pupils at each class level, making a total of sixteen classes. This expansion required a new school building, which finally opened in September 2013. The teaching staff grew from nine teachers, including the administrative principal, in 1987, to twenty-two teachers, including the administrative principal and various ex-quota support teachers, in 2009. Budgetary cuts subsequently reduced the teaching staff to seventeen.

Until the mid-1990s, the school's immediate catchment area had an ageing population, so the enrolment policy allowed for the inclusion of a significant number of children from Blanchardstown's growing hinterland. Traditionally, there had always been a demand for places from outside the parish. Scoil Bhríde had the reputation of providing a high standard of education, and the fact that it is a single-sex school was an added attraction for some parents in a system that is increasingly co-educational. As the number of girls attending the school grew, so too did the diversity of their origins and backgrounds. Several thousand apartments were built on land that had previously accommodated Blanchardstown Hospital, and their occupation by families led to a new and pressing demand for places in the school. Children of foreign medical professionals from Blanchardstown Hospital had been enrolled in the school from time to time, but they had always been fluent speakers of English. The mid-1990s saw the first admission of children who spoke no English.

This was an experience without precedent for the staff and pupils of Scoil Bhríde. While maintaining a positive and welcoming outlook, teachers had concerns about the skills needed to address this new challenge and doubts about the likely outcomes. In 1994, a ten-year-old refugee from Bosnia came to the school. She proved to be a great ambassador both for her country and for the many non-native speakers of English who would follow her. She adapted very quickly to school life, was highly motivated to learn, and surprised everyone by making rapid progress, particularly in English. In 1996, four more Bosnian girls were enrolled. They gave the impression of being much more traumatized than the first girl (Bosnia was at this time a war zone), and their progress in all areas of school life was not so dramatic.

By 2003, 20 per cent of the school's pupils came from immigrant families. By September 2004 this had risen to 30 per cent because 50 per cent of the Junior Infant enrolment was non-Irish. The following year, 80 per cent of Junior Infants came from immigrant families and were entitled to English language support. This increase was mostly due to the new housing mentioned above, which was occupied almost exclusively by foreign nationals. Socio-economically, they ranged from homeowners to those who had their accommodation paid for by the Department of Social Protection. By 2008, the school had pupils from all five continents and forty countries, and by 2015, 80 per cent of all pupils came from immigrant families. Most of the 80 per cent had little or no English when they were enrolled in Junior Infants, and between them they had fifty-one home languages: Afrikaans, Amharic, Arabic, Bangla, Benin, Bosnian, Cantonese, Cebuano, Dari, Estonian, Farsi, Foula, French, German, Hebrew, Hindi, Hungarian, Igbo, Ilonggo, Indonesian, Isoko, Itsekiri, Italian, Kannada, Kinyarwanda, Konkani, Kurdish, Latvian, Lingala, Lithuanian, Malay, Malayalam, Mandarin, Marathi, Moldovan, Polish, Portuguese, Romanian, Russian, Shona, Slovakian, Spanish, Swahili, Tagalog, Tamil, Ukrainian, Urdu, Vietnamese, Visayan, Xhosa, Yoruba. These languages are as reported by pupils' parents; it seems likely that 'Benin' refers to the variety of French spoken in Benin rather than to one of the country's indigenous languages.

It is important to acknowledge the multiple diversities that underlie this large number of home languages. The parents of some pupils come from communities in Africa and India where multilingualism is widespread and often extremely fluid; other parents come from European countries that tend to identify the nation state with a single language. Some languages – for example, Polish, Latvian and Lithuanian – are spoken by a minority of pupils at all levels of the school, whereas others are represented by just one family or a single child. Some pupils immigrated to Ireland with their parents, having undergone primary socialization in their country of origin, while others were born in Ireland and had much the same preschool experience as their Irish peers, though it was filtered through a language other than English or Irish and may have been framed by a home life shaped by very different cultural practices. The extent to which immigrant families are in contact with other speakers of their home language in Ireland is infinitely variable, as is the strength and frequency of contact with their country of origin. Pupils from Polish families, for example, often spend holidays in Poland, whereas pupils whose parents have severed links with their country of origin may never visit that country, at least during their time at school. Plurilingual families whose repertoire includes a variety of English sometimes choose to speak English at home, which means that the children do not acquire their parents' other language(s) of origin. Some immigrant communities organize weekend schools to support the development of literacy in their language, though there is no guarantee that pupils from those communities will attend. Finally, the socio-economic diversity of pupils' parents, noted above, is reflected in great diversity of educational background, experience and achievement.

The evolution of Scoil Bhríde's inclusive language policy and practice

In response to the challenges posed by increasing linguistic diversity, Scoil Bhríde developed a language policy that seeks to integrate school languages – English as the principal medium of instruction, Irish as the first second language of the curriculum, and French in Fifth and Sixth Class – with whatever other languages pupils bring with them from home. There is no fixed methodology but a general pedagogical approach based on accepting that all languages available to pupils have a role to play in their cognitive, social and educational development. To this end, pupils from immigrant families are encouraged to use their home language for whatever purposes seem appropriate to them, inside as well as outside the classroom, and their parents are encouraged to support the development of their daughters' literacy in the language of the home. There are obvious divergences between this policy and the de facto language and language education policies described in Chapter 1. Scoil Bhríde's policy is, however, fully harmonious with the principles that underpin the PSC. If 'the child's existing knowledge and experience form the basis for learning' (Government of Ireland 1999a: 8) and language 'helps the child to clarify and interpret experience, to acquire new concepts, and to add depth to concepts already grasped' (Government of Ireland 1999a: 15), it follows that whichever language has been the medium of the child's primary socialization must have a role to play in her/his early education. The PSC's insistence that the life of the home is the most potent factor in primary pupils' development (Government of Ireland 1999a: 21) leads to the same conclusion, which coincides with the human rights perspective that informs the Council of Europe's language education policy, especially as it is elaborated in publications that promote the concept of plurilingual education (Beacco and Byram 2007, Beacco et al. 2015). Scoil Bhríde's language policy was also influenced by an historical consideration. English was the sole medium of instruction for Irish-speaking children attending national schools in the nineteenth century; they were forbidden to use Irish in school (Ó Ceallaigh and Ní Dhonnabháin 2015: 182), which contributed to language loss. Scoil Bhríde's principal and teachers were determined that their pupils' home languages should not suffer the same fate as Irish.

Laying the foundations

As noted in Chapter 1, starting in 2001 Scoil Bhríde's principal and English language support teachers attended IILT's twice-yearly in-service seminars and made use of IILT's tools and materials. The *English Language Proficiency Benchmarks* (Integrate Ireland Language and Training 2003a) helped them to see their pupils' English language development in the context of the activities and discourse of the classroom, while the European Language Portfolio introduced them to the concept of learner autonomy and the practice of self-assessment. Scoil Bhríde was also among the fifty primary schools that participated in the extensive piloting of the *Primary Assessment Kit* (Little, Lazenby Simpson and Finnegan Ćatibušić 2007), of which the school made regular use. The in-service seminars also provided information on key issues in second language acquisition and their implications for language teaching, emphasizing in particular the importance of home language maintenance.

Another important influence was Déirdre Kirwan's PhD research, begun under David Little's supervision in 2004 and completed in 2009. Over the course of a school year, Kirwan studied four groups of ELLs ranging from Junior Infants (4–5 years) to Fifth Class (10–11 years), gathering data on their language acquisition (English and Irish), curriculum learning and general development. She regularly video-recorded classroom interactions, collected samples of pupils' written work and plotted their progress against the *English Language Proficiency Benchmarks* (Kirwan 2009). And she used the successive stages of this project – literature review, data analysis and interpretation, findings – to contribute to the professional development of teachers at small-group and staff meetings.

The work of IILT and Déirdre Kirwan's PhD project were both influenced by David Little's writings on the theory and practice of language learner autonomy (see, e.g. Little 1991, Little, Dam and Legenhausen 2017). On the basis of successful classroom practice and empirical research findings, Little argues that the most successful language learning environments are those in which, from the beginning, the target language is the communicative and metacognitive medium through which, individually and collaboratively, learners plan, execute, monitor and evaluate their own learning. This translates into a pedagogical approach that helps learners to become active agents of their learning, recognizes that what they already know is always the basis for new learning, develops their capacity for collaboration, fosters respect for what other learners contribute to the work of the classroom, and makes explicit the essential role that language plays in all learning. In a linguistically diverse primary school, the success of the approach also depends on establishing strong links between school and home and involving parents as fully as possible in the education of their children. Such a theory dovetails neatly with the aims and aspirations of the PSC summarized above.

English language support classes

As we explained in Chapter 1, the Department of Education provides schools with additional resources to support the English language development of pupils and students from non-English/Irish-speaking homes. All pupils and students in this category are entitled to two years of English language support, and there is a general assumption that this will be provided by regularly withdrawing them from their mainstream class and teaching them in small groups. Precisely how schools organize English language support, however, is for them to decide. Scoil Bhríde takes advantage of this flexibility to include native speakers of English in language support groups of four to six. There are two reasons for this. First, all primary pupils benefit from lessons that focus on language because long-term educational success depends on mastering the different varieties of academic language. CALP (cognitive academic language proficiency) as defined by Cummins (e.g. 1981, 1991) is not a phenomenon that suddenly emerges in the later years of schooling; its development is fostered from the very beginning by all classroom activities that focus on elements of language detached from their immediate context of use. In English language support lessons all roads should lead to CALP. Secondly, native speaker pupils can support the efforts of their non-native speaker peers to use and thus learn English, while benefiting from exposure to a multilingual microcosm that has the capacity to generate all manner of insights into language, implicit as well as explicit. Although the great majority of ELLs receive their two years of English language support in Junior and Senior Infants, support must also be provided for older pupils newly arrived in Ireland. It sometimes happens, moreover, that a pupil's two years of support are interrupted by a temporary return to her country of origin. Children who have already had their full allocation are provided with additional support if they need it and can be fitted in.

Scoil Bhríde's English language support teachers aim to start from what their pupils already know, which includes their home language. They recognize that language support is not another variety of learning support (provided for pupils with learning difficulties): if pupils from immigrant families participate in classroom interaction and are fully engaged in what they are doing, they will quickly enough become proficient in oral English. Language support classes thus aim to be relaxed and to allow each pupil plenty of room in which to communicate spontaneously. Perhaps because pupils know that they can always resort to their home language if they need or want to, very few of Scoil Bhríde's pupils have been reluctant communicators; use of the home language may be the most effective cure for the so-called silent period in immigrant pupils' early acquisition of the language of schooling. Language support teachers frequently make use of activities that encourage pupils to interact spontaneously with one another. Knitting and gardening are two examples. The former helps pupils who are learning to read because they have to follow a pattern; the latter teaches the names of plants and garden tools and activities.

Because they teach small groups, language support teachers are well placed to observe individual development, and because they value spontaneity and pupil initiative, they sometimes allow pupils to engage in activities that they would not themselves encourage. For example, half way through First Class a Hungarian pupil who had come to the school towards the end of Senior Infants insisted on reading page after page of flash cards. This was not how the language support teacher would have taught her to read, but she allowed the pupil to take the lead because she was so strongly motivated to do so. By the beginning of Second Class this pupil was writing fluently, composing expressive texts in Hungarian and translating them into English. This might not have happened if the language support teacher had imposed her own preferred method and content on the pupil's efforts to learn to read.

Language support teachers have been the source of a number of ideas that have gradually spread through the school. For example, the now common practice of producing texts with the same content in two or more languages first arose from a language support teacher's concern to involve her pupils in imaginative writing while ensuring that their home languages had a role to play in the development of all their language skills. And it was a language support teacher who first had the idea of bringing pupils from different classes together so that older pupils can provide their younger peers with additional input and stimulation. For example, she took language support pupils from First Class to visit their counterparts in Third Class; each of the latter was invited to say something in her home language and the younger children had to identify the languages used.

Integrating languages in the mainstream classroom

The PSC highlights the role played by language in learning, though in doing so it is evidently referring to English (or Irish) as the language of schooling. Scoil Bhríde's integrated approach, on the other hand, implies a role for Irish and immigrant pupils' home languages beside English, and its implementation assigns a pivotal role to Irish as the obligatory second language of the curriculum. The overwhelming majority of the school's indigenous pupils have their first contact with Irish as Junior Infants, which puts them in the same situation as pupils from immigrant families. The school has a long tradition of teaching Irish as a living language: Irish itself is the preferred medium of communication in Irish lessons, and teachers often address pupils in Irish outside the classroom, expecting them to respond in Irish. At the same time, writing is given the same importance as speaking so that Irish is a fully integrated part of pupils' developing literacy as well as their oral repertoire. The presence of other languages in the classroom helps them to accept Irish as one more medium of communication and facilitates its integration into the delivery of curriculum content. Regardless of their language background, pupils learn to contribute answers in Irish alongside the home languages of children from immigrant families. In this regard, it is worth quoting the report of the Department of Education inspectors who carried out a whole-school evaluation of Scoil Bhríde in March 2014:

> A very good standard is achieved in the teaching and learning of Irish. A positive disposition with interest and regard for the language is cultivated throughout the school and it is clear that the pupils are proud of their abilities in Irish. Effective use is made of language games, pictures and posters to develop the oral abilities of the pupils. A very good range of poems and songs are recited and sung in every class. The pupils read with understanding and fluency. Good attention is paid to writing. (Department of Education and Skills 2014: 3)

According to the Chief Inspector's report for the period from January 2013 to July 2016, only 12 per cent of schools fell into the category 'very good' for the teaching of Irish (Department of Education and Skills 2018: 9).

Home languages are drawn into classroom discourse and the processing of curriculum content in many different ways, some of which will be discussed and illustrated in later chapters. Again it is important to stress that the school's integrated approach to language education is precisely that: an approach and not a fixed set of pedagogical procedures. It is an approach that recognizes the relation between language and cognition, understands the complexity of plurilingual repertoires, and acknowledges the central role that the language of primary socialization plays in each child's identity and sense of self. It is an approach that is open and spontaneous, ready to take advantage of every opportunity that presents itself to enrich classroom discourse with insights that come from immigrant pupils' home languages. For present purposes, one example of emergent classroom practice will suffice. Several years ago, a Junior Infants teacher completed the year's maths programme in May. She decided to revise it in Irish rather than English, and in due course the principal visited her classroom and observed how well the pupils could perform the prescribed maths functions in Irish. The principal suggested that the teacher might include home languages in further revision, and a week later, pupils from immigrant families were able to demonstrate the same facility in their home languages.

The importance of regular staff meetings

Regular staff meetings have played a crucial role in the development of classroom practice and the evolution of Scoil Bhríde's integrated language policy. Some meetings bring all the staff together, while others are limited to the teachers working within a single curriculum band. In January 2014, for example, the principal met with the four teachers responsible for Fifth and Sixth Class (two classes at each level). The purpose of the meeting was to discuss how the school's language policy should be amended to include a clear explanation of the reasons for adopting an inclusive approach to language education.

The meeting agreed on four points. First, the use of home languages in the classroom releases pupils' energy for learning because it acknowledges the centrality of those languages to their sense of who they are. Secondly, the use of home languages supports pupils' cognitive development, fosters the growth of implicit and explicit skills of reflection and analysis, and thus encourages lifelong learning. Thirdly, because it encourages the development of plurilingual competences and language awareness, home language use fulfils the language education policy adumbrated in the Council of Europe's *Common European Framework of Reference for Languages* (Council of Europe 2001) and elaborated in subsequent documents (e.g. Beacco and Byram 2007, Coste et al. 2009). Fourthly, Scoil Bhríde's integrated approach to language education supports indigenous Irish pupils' learning of Irish by helping them to recognize that *all* languages can be used to communicate information. They come to understand that Irish is not just another school subject to which they devote an hour each morning, and in due course many Irish pupils think of Irish as their 'home language'.

As regards implementation of the policy, the teachers felt that time is always an issue: it is necessary to balance pupils' enthusiasm for linguistic exploration with the need to cover the curriculum. In response to this the principal quoted Howard Gardner's view that 'the greatest enemy of understanding is coverage' (Gardner 1993: 24); pupils learn most effectively when they are engaged in interaction and enjoying themselves, so perhaps teachers need to trust themselves and their pupils when their interest and enthusiasm take them beyond what they have planned or the workbook requires. The principal reinforced this point by recalling an observation made by Ralph Tyler seventy years ago: 'Learning takes place through the active behavior of the student: it is what he does that he learns, not what the teacher does' (Tyler 1949/2013: 63). And she followed this by quoting Shuell's more recent version of the same argument: 'If students are to learn desired outcomes in a reasonably effective manner, then the teacher's fundamental task is to get students to engage in learning activities that are likely to result in their achieving those outcomes …. [I]t is helpful to remember that what the student does is actually more important in determining what is learned than what the teacher does' (Shuell 1986: 429). The meeting agreed that an updated language policy document should help to ease teachers' anxieties regarding coverage.

Finally, in the previous school year, Fifth and Sixth Class teachers had introduced their pupils to self-assessment (see also Chapter 5, pp. 137–9 below). In retrospect they thought what they had done had been too specific and led to the parroting of learned phrases; self-assessment needed to have a more general focus if it was to encourage more meaningful learning. It was agreed that the Fifth and Sixth Class of the past two years had been quite exceptional. But while other classes might respond less positively to the school's inclusive approach to language education, it was also agreed that *all* pupils stand to benefit from the approach to a greater or lesser degree.

The role of parents

As we have seen, the PSC acknowledges that 'parents are the child's primary educators, and the life of the home is the most potent factor in his or her development during the primary school years' (Government of Ireland 1999a: 21). The success of Scoil Bhríde's integrated language policy depends on the contribution that immigrant parents make to their daughters' language education by maintaining their language of origin as the preferred medium of family communication and in due course supporting the transfer of literacy skills in English and Irish to the home language. When enrolling new pupils, the principal always describes to parents the school's distinctive approach to language education, explaining that there are two reasons behind it. First, the language in which the child lives her early years necessarily becomes the default medium of her inner voice and thus plays an essential role in her early learning; also, allowing children to use their home language helps to reduce the stress of adjusting to a new linguistic environment (Coelho 1994: 323). Secondly, as the child grows up, her home language may have an essential role to play in maintaining family cohesion. Wong Fillmore has described the serious consequences of 'subtractive bilingualism', the process by which a new language supplants the individual's family language:

> When parents are unable to talk to their children, they cannot easily convey to them their values, beliefs, understandings, or wisdom about how to cope with their experiences. They cannot teach them about the meaning of work, or about personal responsibility, or what it means to be a moral or ethical person in a world with too many choices and too few guideposts to follow. ... When parents lose the means for socializing and influencing their children, rifts develop and families lose the intimacy that comes from shared beliefs and understandings. (Wong Fillmore 1991: 343)

Some parents' initial response to Scoil Bhríde's language policy is sceptical; they are inclined to adopt the common-sense view that if English is to be their daughters' language of schooling it should also become the language of the home. This view is relatively common in families whose plurilingual repertoire includes a variety of English but less common in families who have little experience of using English as a medium of everyday communication. In these latter cases parents tend to be relieved to know that their daughter's home language will be given a role in her education and grateful for the welcoming and inclusive ethos that makes this possible.

Scoil Bhríde's English language support teachers play an especially important role in encouraging immigrant parents to provide their daughters with appropriate support: discussing the events and issues of the school day in the language of the home; teaching them the vocabulary they need to express what they have been learning at school (numbers and the concepts of addition, subtraction and division; days of the week and months of the year; weights and measures; and so on); reading stories to them in their home language; encouraging them to read aloud what they themselves have written in their home language. In school–home liaison, Scoil Bhríde also follows some of the suggestions made in IILT's resource book *Up and Away* (Integrate Ireland Language and Training 2006). For example, parents are made aware that especially in the early stages, their daughters may respond to them in English or Irish, reassured that this is not a cause for concern and encouraged to persist with the language of the home.

Communication between the school and parents can be difficult when parents have little English. Sometimes other parents help by translating basic information and school circulars into their language, and the school makes every effort to ensure that invitations to attend events at the school always include some kind of visual support. The school involves parents directly in some of its language-related activities. For example, it uses them as a source of linguistic expertise when multilingual posters and charts are needed for display in classrooms, and parents are sometimes invited into the classroom to support language learning activities. These occasions serve two purposes. Parents provide a linguistic model for pupils who share their home language, and they show the other pupils that different languages can be used to communicate the same information. A similar effect is achieved by having senior pupils visit junior classes to model home languages, whether in interactive talk or by teaching poems and songs they have learnt at home. Parents also contribute indirectly to their children's education in many different ways, for example, by attending events organized by the school, participating in the activities of the Parents' Association and perhaps serving as a parent or community representative on the school's Board of Management.

Managing linguistic diversity: Five principles

Looking back over more than two decades of evolving policy and practice, it is possible to identify five interacting principles that have underpinned the development of Scoil Bhríde's integrated approach to language education.

Principle 1: Starting from pupils' existing knowledge

As we have seen, the PSC endorses the constructivist principle that what we already know always helps to determine what we learn and how we learn it. According to this principle schools must find ways of accommodating and building on the experience and knowledge pupils bring with them, what

Douglas Barnes (1976: 81) calls their 'action knowledge', González, Moll and Amanti (2005) call 'funds of knowledge', and Heugh (2015: 280) calls 'knowledge repertoires'. The pedagogical *challenge* is to present and process 'school knowledge' (curriculum content) in ways that are accessible to pupils from the perspective of their action knowledge, and the pedagogical *goal* is to help them to convert school knowledge into action knowledge. When children from English-speaking homes attend primary school in Ireland, they bring with them knowledge, experience and skills that they have developed while acquiring English as their home language. The conversion of school knowledge into action knowledge requires them gradually to extend their repertoire in their first language, adding literacy skills, acquiring the words and phrases that embody key curriculum concepts, and in due course mastering the registers and genres of academic language characteristic of the different curriculum subjects. Because they have acquired their action knowledge in a language other than the language of schooling, the task facing children from families with a home language other than English is altogether more complex; it can also be very intimidating. This is how one sixteen-year-old former pupil of Scoil Bhríde recalled her first day at school in Ireland:

> I felt all eyes on me as I walked through the school. My dad talked to the principal and she called a teacher over who then took my sweaty hand and led me to my new class. She asked me something in a language I didn't understand – English. I looked at her helplessly. She introduced me to my new classmates, some were smiling and some were observing me from top to bottom. I was asked something again and again. I had no idea what the class teacher said. I never felt so stupid in my life. I couldn't help but think about how I was one of the smartest in my class in my country and now it seemed I would be the thickest. The recognition of this whole situation made me want to run back home, crawl under my bed and never come out again.

In Ireland educational success depends crucially on the development of proficiency in English as the language of schooling; but this is a process in which each ELL's home language necessarily plays a central role as the core of her identity and the default medium of her action knowledge and discursive thinking. And by acknowledging that role, it is possible to make the process less intimidating and more effective. It is important that the linguistic and cultural diversity of a school's pupil population is made visible in classrooms and corridors. But if the acceptance of diversity is to achieve full educational value, it must go further than this, emphasizing the value of pupils' home languages and finding ways of including them in the educational process.

Principle 2: Use of home languages

These considerations lead directly to the second principle that no restrictions should be placed on pupils' use of their home languages inside or outside the classroom. Irish primary teachers are required to teach Irish, and some of them may have learnt other languages at school, to degree level, or by taking evening courses, but they are unlikely to know even a few words of most of the home languages present in Scoil Bhríde. Because they recognize the role that home languages inevitably play in their pupils' acquisition of English and in their learning generally, however, Scoil Bhríde's teachers seek to give that role an explicit presence in their classrooms from the beginning. This produces a phenomenon that fits the broad definition of 'translanguaging' elaborated by García and Li Wei (2014): communication in which participants make use of their individually different linguistic resources to arrive at common understandings and achieve common goals. Much of the empirical research on translanguaging focuses on classroom discourse that switches back and forth between two languages, in both of which the teacher has at least some proficiency (see e.g. the English/Gujarati and English/Chinese examples discussed by Creese and Blackledge (2010), the English/Spanish examples discussed by García and Sylvan (2011) and Flores and García (2014)). In Scoil Bhríde, however, the teachers must trust the pupils to know how to make use of their linguistic resources. This offers an interesting new perspective on the concept of learner autonomy which we explore further in Chapter 5.

Principle 3: Emphasis on literacy skills

The third principle is that pupils need to develop an age-appropriate literacy in all the languages they know and/or are learning. On the face of it, there is nothing unusual about the strong emphasis Scoil Bhríde places on the development of pupils' literacy skills: literacy is, after all, a precondition for educational success and it has been at the centre of much recent educational debate in Ireland. What is unusual, however, is the place that is given to home languages alongside English, Irish and French. Not only are their written forms visible throughout the school, from Junior Infants to Sixth Class, in classroom and corridor displays; pupils are encouraged to transfer the literacy skills they develop in English and Irish to their home languages. When pupils from immigrant homes are in the very early stages of learning English, Scoil Bhríde's language support teachers use an approach to literacy development that allows pupils to contribute material in English that comes directly from their own experience (action knowledge again, accessed in their home language). The teacher writes whatever the pupil says in her copybook; nothing is changed or added, even though sentences may be incomplete or ill-formed. Then the teacher helps the pupil to read her text aloud. Because it expresses a meaning that is important to her and valued by the teacher, the pupil is fully involved, which means that she is motivated to learn. The agency she derives from her home language contributes directly to her learning.

Principle 4: Pedagogical explicitness

Teachers of monolingual classes have always known that they cannot expect all pupils to understand new curriculum content the first time it is presented and explained. This is not only because some children learn more quickly than others; it is also due to differences of motivation, concentration and action knowledge – each child's out-of-school experience, and therefore action knowledge, being unique. When classes are linguistically diverse, teachers face a much greater communicative challenge, and the teachers at Scoil Bhríde respond by explaining things several times, seeking to vary their language as much as possible with each new explanation. This pedagogical explicitness works to the benefit of all pupils, whatever their language background. It also combines with the sustained focus on language and pupils' plurilingual resources to encourage a generally reflective approach to learning: What are we doing? Why? How? And with what results? (cf. Dam 1995, Little, Dam and Legenhausen 2017). In other words, the general approach to teaching encourages an approach to learning in which self-awareness and in due course self-assessment figure prominently.

Principle 5: Teacher autonomy

Finally, the fifth principle is respect for teachers' professional autonomy. Scoil Bhríde's teachers are expected to observe the school's inclusive ethos and support its language policy, and they cannot avoid placing a strong emphasis on the development of pupils' literacy skills and using teaching methods that seek to be as explicit as possible. But how precisely they implement school policy in their classrooms is a matter for them to decide, and it is assumed that each teacher will adopt an approach that is shaped by her personality, her preferred teaching style and her professional experience. It is also assumed that each teacher's classroom practice will evolve in much the same way as the school's language policy evolved. To begin with, the principal recognized the need to inform herself about language development in general and the linguistic needs of immigrant pupils in particular. In due course this led her to undertake qualitative research that yielded insights she could share with her colleagues. Video recordings of classroom interactions were analysed and discussed, and it became usual for teachers to share anecdotes from their classrooms and show one another samples of their pupils' work. And the enthusiasm with which pupils of all ages explored similarities and differences between languages and made use of their home language in the classroom reinforced the teachers' belief in the validity of their approach. Several of Scoil Bhríde's teachers have followed postgraduate programmes that required them to engage in action research focused on the linguistic diversity of their classes.

The impact of Scoil Bhríde's inclusive approach to language education

Standardized tests

One measure of the success of Scoil Bhríde's integrated approach to language education is provided by the standardized tests in English and maths that pupils take annually from First Class onwards. The tests in question are formulated in English and normed on native speakers of English in the Irish primary school population. This prompts questions about their appropriateness for pupils from immigrant families, and teachers attending the in-service days organized by IILT between 2000 and 2006 sometimes reported that test scores achieved by immigrant pupils did not do justice to the ability they displayed in the classroom. This has not been the experience of Scoil Bhríde, however. The school's test scores have always been at or above the national average, and the individual scores of immigrant pupils do not cluster together at the bottom of the scale. The 2016 PIRLS (Progress in International Reading Literacy Study) results provide an international context for these results: no country in Europe was ranked higher than Ireland for reading skills at primary level (Fourth Class).[1]

---

[1]   http://www.erc.ie/2017/12/05/results-of-pirls-2016-released/

What some of the pupils said

In June 2012, Déirdre Kirwan asked a group of Fourth Class pupils (10–11 years old) what they felt about using their home languages in school. A German-speaking pupil said:

> Well, I feel like you're not only allowing English and Irish into the school but you're allowing other languages, because since this is an Irish school you'd expect only English and Irish would be spoken, but when for example different languages that you wouldn't really find in a school like Ireland, but when you can bring that into the school and do a project it's really nice.

A Romanian-speaking pupil said that when she is allowed to use her home language in class, she has *a smile on my face, I feel excited, I feel like I really want to do it.* When asked if this was because she understood Romanian better than English she replied that she understood both languages equally well. The German speaker added that she liked the way she was being taught because using German involved her parents in her education; she could consult them on matters of German grammar. This prompted the Romanian speaker to say: *You should try to learn more from your parents. I can't write in Romanian but I practise at home.*

Déirdre Kirwan also asked the pupils whether they thought having so many languages used in school was an asset or a source of extra difficulty. Their replies were generally positive. The German-speaking pupil said that having more than one language gives you

> lots of options, you don't just have to learn one language or the usual language like your parents have which is English. You've got lots of options so if you're doing it in the class constantly you'll constantly be learning different languages. So you'll have lots of options when you're older. If you want to move to a different country you've already got the language.

An Igbo speaker said: *Languages are not really hard. You don't give up on a language that you want to know. Keep on learning it every day and like* [the German-speaking pupil] *said, there's lots of options.* A Kurdish speaker added: *It's kind of a good thing as well because if you have the books* [in other languages] *you can learn more stuff.*

The German speaker thought it was a good idea to use all the languages present in the class as a resource for learning:

> Whenever in the class we pick a word and then we get all the people that have different languages to translate it, you find a lot of similarities, and sometimes

when we're learning like in Irish lessons and everything pupils will put up their hands and say this means this in their language and it's quite interesting because there are a lot of similarities and that makes it easier for you to learn different languages.

A Polish pupil agreed, adding:

We did some translation and put it in a book and some of the languages were very similar, but when we put in Polish it was very … like in all its words because it was different 'cause it had those little different kind of alphabet and it looked different.

A Malayalam speaker said:

It improves your ability of learning languages and as [the German-speaking pupil] *said, when you go to different countries you'll know more and if you want to talk to a person you've got a lot of languages in your head and it improves your stamina and your abilities.*

The same pupil said that when she first came to Ireland she did not realize that English was not the only language. She thought it was good to learn Irish as well as English and a home language; when she started school, she found Irish interesting and added: *It still is.* An Irish pupil whose home language was English said that she was teaching her parents Irish as they had forgotten much of what they learned at school. The Polish pupil said that sometimes she feels as if Irish is her *first language because we speak it all the time in our school and it's very good, it's nice and it's interesting.*

In June 2014 Déirdre Kirwan interviewed another group of Fourth Class pupils. When she asked them to try to remember how they felt when they first enrolled in Scoil Bhríde, a pupil whose home language was Hebrew said:

I came to school two years ago in Third Class and I felt really scared and I had no English. I remember first time I was sitting inside teacher's table and I didn't really understand her … first I was little bit nervous and then I started feeling more fine but in a couple first days I went … like my parents took me early from school.

She said she began to feel comfortable about staying in school on her fourth day. A pupil whose home language was Hungarian said that she came to Scoil Bhríde at the end of Senior Infants, so she had now been in the school for four years. At first, she couldn't understand anything, so she *did nothing*; it was *very scary but fine.* She said she began to understand English at the end of First Class (one year later) and that made her feel *fine.* She began to read in Second Class. When asked if she had enjoyed being able to read she said: *I didn't understand every word like properly, so I understand words but not the story.* She said she enjoyed maths: *It was the only thing I could understand.* She still enjoyed maths but also liked writing, though after three pages *it sometimes gets tiring.* She said that when she was in Second Class her mother began to teach her Hungarian and she learned *how to read and write in about one or two months.*

A pupil who had recently arrived from Ukraine said:

> *Very first came, I've been now only little bit of English because I was learning it in my Ukraine, so I don't know how to write and how to read but … I not really good at understanded it … em I first told* [another pupil] *and she sometimes said what does she mean and I started to understand English and to em around eh one fourth of Third Class and I prefer to feel scared and eh and nervous and right now I feel good and happy.*

A speaker of Malayalam said she knew only a little English when she started school in Junior Infants. She found it difficult to read and write Malayalam, but a friend in her early teens was now teaching her. A Vietnamese speaker already knew a little English when she started school in Junior Infants; she said she made a friend of the first girl in her class who spoke to her, but by the end of the year she had several friends.

In June 2012 Déirdre Kirwan put the same questions to a group of Sixth Class pupils and elicited closely similar responses. A pupil whose home language was Yoruba was strongly in favour of learning languages at school:

> *I think learning French and other languages in school is very good because it helps us in life, and if we go to a foreign country like Germany or France we may be able to speak German or French and it's great fun because of the games we play and I enjoy learning French and Irish.*

A speaker of Tagalog, however, expressed reservations regarding the number of languages being used in class:

> *Sometimes I kind of disagree with working with three languages at the same time because when you learn three languages at the same time you have to learn so many words and sometimes you might get mixed up with them.*

An Albanian speaker was quick to agree:

> *Sometimes I disagree as well because when you're learning one and then you go on to the next it can be confusing.*

These negative contributions may not be as straightforward as they seem, however. The Tagalog speaker was a highly intelligent and motivated pupil who had always seemed to cope easily with the four languages in her developing repertoire. Indeed, examples of her written work showed that in learning French she went some way beyond what was explicitly taught. Until she made her negative comment, all the responses to Déirdre Kirwan's questions were positive, and this raises the suspicion that her response may have been prompted by the desire for discussion and perhaps disagreement. The Albanian speaker had not reached the same level in any school subject, and although she expressed disagreement here, later in the discussion she said she was very happy that she was able to use her home language to support her learning because *it's easier than French and Irish and English.*

The way in which another Tagalog speaker expressed approval of Scoil Bhríde's integrated approach to language education shows that pupils sometimes taught one another their home languages: *I like learning languages ... English, Irish and French ... it's very interesting because sometimes I ask some of my foreign friends to teach me some of their languages ... like Romanian.* Using home languages at school also has the advantage that it facilitates private communication, as a Ukrainian pupil pointed out: *It's kind of fun and nobody understands you and you get to talk about whatever you want.*

Two years later, another group of Sixth Class pupils agreed unanimously that learning languages in an integrated way was a really good idea and that using home languages generated interest among pupils and made parents happy too. They also felt that knowing a lot of languages in primary school provided a basis for later improvement and that plurilingual learning should be available at secondary school because it would be good for job prospects and travelling in other countries. One pupil expressed the general view like this:

> *I think it's very exciting and really good to have all the languages that we have, all the different ones. And also in class when we're learning French it's good that our teacher also listens to us when we say that there's a lot of similarity, again, in the words. And I think it's also very interesting for people from other countries because I like really wanted to learn another like language and I can go on the yard and I can talk with my friend and she can teach me the language, like, basics of it. I think it's very interesting that we get to know each other, like, countries and stuff.*

This pupil spoke Polish at home and was learning Spanish from a friend and teaching the friend Polish. She agreed that there are fewer similarities between Polish and Spanish than between Polish and Ukrainian. A Romanian speaker said that Scoil Bhríde was the only school she knew of that taught French in Fifth and Sixth Class: *I think that is really like excellent and amazing* because it makes it *easier to learn French now 'cause if you continue it in first year* [of secondary school] *you'll be, like, the best in your class.* A pupil whose home language was Foula said: *I think it's a great thing to bring your language into school because ...*

I am very interested in learning different languages … it's a great help because you learn more things.

A Lithuanian speaker said that when new pupils use their home language in school it gives them confidence and helps them to make progress in English, especially when they see other pupils using home languages as well as English. A Polish-speaking pupil agreed. She added that the introduction in Fifth Class of Language Boxes to store information on pupils' countries of origin made her very interested in learning more about Poland.

A German-speaking pupil pointed out another advantage of using home languages in the classroom:

It's great because at a very young age you can, like, there might be some other people in your class that can speak the same and you can learn together, like, you can learn from each other … and just to be able to say that I went to a school that supports all different languages and cultures is a great thing to have.

She added that new pupils receive a lot of help from their peers:

Quite a lot of people have come to this school and they don't know any English and in a couple of months they already know so much because everyone around them has helped them and just like by hearing the language and that they're eager to learn more languages to help others.

Pupils were strongly aware of the importance of home languages for their sense of identity and heritage. The German-speaking pupil said:

*Sometimes in school we talk about Irish traditions and some people, like, they originally come from Ireland and they already know it and we don't, so when we're talking about our own countries, it's like when they're talking about Ireland, we'd have nothing to relate to or be proud of and to put our name on and so we'd be, like, we'd be empty. If you know a language that one of your parents knows don't forget it, don't try, like, not to speak it, don't hide away from it, because it's what makes you **you** and it's special and it's … you can't … it's like having an arm or a leg, you can't take it away from you.*

In the same vein, a speaker of Foula said:

For me it would be like pretending that your language never existed. It would be like rejecting your own language. It would be terrible and if it was me I would feel devastated and I would immediately forget about my language and whenever I go visit my uncle I wouldn't be able to speak or understand anything and I would know that my language is not in my heart anymore … it wouldn't be fair … people can be embarrassed if they have a language that no one else has, but don't be afraid, it's interesting to have another language.

A speaker of Amharic expressed the same thought like this:

> *I just want to say to other kids out there that if someone is trying to hide your language or doesn't want you to speak out loud you should be courageous and just say that you want to speak it.*

A Kurdish-speaking pupil made the point that twenty years ago in Kurdistan people were not allowed to speak their own language but were obliged to speak Arabic. This prompted the German-speaking pupil to point out that at one time, Irish was a forbidden language but now people are free to speak it.

What some of the teachers said

Déirdre Kirwan also recorded interviews with some of the teachers. Their enthusiasm for the integrated approach to language education matched that of their pupils. A Fifth Class teacher summed up her experience like this:

> *I think the experience is very beneficial and valuable. The children absolutely love it, they're so engaged with the programme, with the content, with the activities. It has been challenging to implement initially because there's a lot of resources to be made and a lot of work goes into the planning when you're trying to bring in all the different languages, but it's definitely worthwhile and you can see that by the enthusiasm of the children and by their dedication to their work. They absolutely love to have the opportunity to talk about their own cultures and to bring their own language into the classroom.*

A common theme in interviews with teachers was the educational benefit of making explicit the interconnectedness of languages: language awareness informs every aspect of classroom life regardless of the subject being taught. The same Fifth Class teacher explained how this works: *The children absolutely love the opportunity to talk about their own country, where they come from, their cultures, to compare the different cultures, and then if we're learning different new things in French and Irish that they can find out those phrases and words in their own language.* The discourse generated by the coming together of multiple plurilingual repertoires also has a positive impact on ELLs' learning of English: *For the children who are learning English as a Second Language they're learning so much English in an age-appropriate environment that they're not going back to basic words, they're doing the phrases while we're all learning something at the same time.*

An experienced mainstream teacher with responsibility for Fourth Class said that the inclusion of home languages in the classroom had made her revise her whole attitude to language teaching and learning. She had spent the previous eight years teaching junior classes, where pupils were positive about learning Irish, and she wondered what happened to change their attitude by the time they reached the middle grades. The Irish they had learned *must be in there somewhere and it's a matter of getting it out.* She found that when ELLs were encouraged to use their home language *the lights come on* and they became more engaged. Irish lessons provided especially good opportunities to make use of pupils' home languages, and this had a *very positive knock-on effect on the Irish children*; they began to see the possibility of using Irish as their second language. They also took note of the fact that ELLs were autonomously writing in their L1 and Irish and some of them began to do the same. It was particularly gratifying that the spontaneous production of written text in several languages was not confined to high-ability, high-achieving learners. Pupils were always very happy to show their texts to the principal, read them aloud and have their efforts video-recorded.

A Sixth Class teacher noted that the integrated approach to language learning meant that a greater variety of languages was being used not only inside the classroom but also outside, in corridors and the school yard. Pupils were also ready to engage with new languages that were not part of the curriculum; in her own class, a pupil from an Itsekiri-speaking family had chosen to use Swedish in a project on Sweden. When working on the same project an Irish pupil wanted to know what second language Swedish children learned in school. This question would never have arisen in the days when the school had few ELLs among its pupils; now it seemed self-evident.

Having implemented the school's integrated approach to language education for two years, a mainstream teacher considered that the work the children had produced was evidence of its success. The *open language policy has permeated through the whole school ... in any class the children are open to learning all languages and greet you in several different languages and it has almost become a matter of fact, it's just integrated into daily school life.* She cited the example of a German-speaking pupil in Sixth Class who taught a German song to First Class for the European Day of Languages. At the end of the lesson, the pupil repeated one of the phrases she had taught and asked: *Now can anybody tell me how to say that in their own language? Does this sound like anything in your own language?* The pupil did this without prompting: for the moment *she was the teacher, and this is what she has assimilated as the role of the teacher.*

Overall, teachers agreed that the integrated approach to language education had a powerfully motivating effect on pupils, transformed their attitudes to learning and using Irish, brought language awareness to the centre of the educational process, and encouraged pupils of all ability levels to engage with the home languages of their peers. Teachers themselves learned words and phrases in many different languages as well as new pedagogical techniques; they also learned a great deal about how children learn:

> *Children are responding very positively to the open language policy – even their body language, demeanour within class, the speed and accuracy with which they answer questions when their own language is involved. Regardless of subject, their interest increases if it is something to do with home or their own language or their own experience; therefore when they respond it is with much more developed thought ... equally in writing.*

Conclusion

In this chapter we have introduced Scoil Bhríde (Cailíní) and its pupil population within the broader context of primary education in Ireland, described the evolution of the school's integrated approach to language education, recapitulated policy and practice in five underlying principles, and presented some preliminary evidence of their impact on pupils and teachers. The next three chapters explore classroom practice from three complementary perspectives: how multiple languages are used in classroom discourse at different levels in the school, how pupils gradually develop plurilingual literacy, and how the school's approach facilitates the development of a high degree of learner autonomy. In doing so we draw on data that was mostly collected between 2011 and 2015: video recordings of classroom interaction, interviews with teachers and pupils similar to those we have quoted in this chapter, samples of pupils' written work, and teachers' reports from the classroom.

3

Languages in Classroom Discourse: Using Plurilingual Skills to Construct Knowledge

This chapter is concerned with classroom communication, the talk between teachers and learners that frames and shapes the activities of each lesson and presents and processes the content of the curriculum. We begin with some introductory reflections on the nature of classroom discourse and the impact of the acknowledged presence of multiple home languages on its structure and potential; we then present a succession of examples, starting with Junior Infants and ending with Sixth Class; and we conclude the chapter with a discussion of pupils' developing repertoires from the perspective of the Council of Europe's concept of 'plurilingualism' as defined in the *Common European Framework of Reference for Languages* (CEFR; Council of Europe 2001).

Varieties of classroom talk

For more than half a century, educational researchers have expressed concern that dominant patterns of classroom discourse fail to promote optimal learning. What typically goes on in classrooms is believed to conform too closely to the popular image of schooling: the teacher tells and the learners listen; the teacher asks a series of questions to check that they have been listening and have understood; and then she tells them the next thing on her agenda. From time to time the learners' retention of what the teacher has told them is measured by giving them a test. This is the structure of classroom discourse – IRF (initiation, response, follow-up) – uncovered by Sinclair and Coulthard's (1975) pioneering study and labelled 'recitation' in the United States (Tharp and Gallimore 1988). What the teacher tells may also be presented to learners in a textbook whose procedures parallel those of the classroom: the learners read, and their reading is supported by a succession of questions and tasks that allow the teacher to gauge the extent of their comprehension. According to this pedagogical tradition, teaching is a matter of transmitting knowledge to learners, and learning is a matter of receiving and retaining what is transmitted.

Against this tradition, educational reformers have stressed the importance of making use of the knowledge and experience that learners bring with them to the classroom and using participatory modes of discourse. In Chapter 2 we noted three broadly constructivist principles that are fundamental to the Irish primary curriculum: 'the child is an active agent in his or her learning' (Government of Ireland 1999a: 8); 'the child's existing knowledge and experience form the basis for learning' (Government of Ireland 1999a: 8); and 'collaborative learning should feature in the learning process' (Government of Ireland 1999a: 9). We associated these principles with Douglas Barnes's argument that schools should present and process 'school knowledge' (curriculum content) in ways that are accessible to pupils from the perspective of their 'action knowledge' (the complex of knowledge and beliefs, experience and skills they have accumulated outside the classroom). These principles and this argument imply that dialogue – reciprocal communication in which the teacher shares discourse initiatives with her learners – has a fundamental role to play in the educational process. And there is a wealth of theoretical and empirical research to support this implication; one thinks, for example, of the work of Robin Alexander (2006a, b), Neil Mercer (1995, 2000), Gordon Wells (2009), and Mercer and Hodgkinson's collection of essays on classroom talk inspired by the work of Douglas Barnes (Mercer and Hodgkinson 2008).

It is easy to give the impression that 'dialogic teaching', with its emphasis on 'interpretation' and 'exploratory talk' (Barnes 1976), has no room for teacher talk that presents learners with new information. But presenting new information is an essential part of the teacher's task, and Barnes himself sought to strike a balance between 'exploratory' and 'presentational' talk, arguing that each has a role to play, but at different points in the unfolding of a lesson (see also Barnes 2008). In the same way, criticism of the tendency for teachers to dominate classroom talk may be understood to imply that they should somehow withdraw into silence; but if that were to happen, interactional chaos would reign and curriculum learning would be impossible. In their management of classroom communication, teachers at all educational levels must strike an appropriate balance between presentational and exploratory talk; for it is only thus that they will create a dynamic of teaching and learning that brings school knowledge into the kind of interaction with learners' action knowledge that

Barnes envisaged – an interaction that entails the examination of alternatives and encourages learners to be reflective and critical:

> Reflection includes taking responsibility for finding connections and examples, asking questions, reinterpreting experience, and searching for new techniques and new ways of understanding relevant to the matter in hand. 'Critical' learning goes further and implies that teachers should encourage pupils to find alternative ways of looking at topics, and should help them to grasp what evidence may be used to support one or another viewpoint. (Barnes 2008: 15)

Classroom practice in most Irish primary schools reflects this understanding of teaching and learning, although practitioners may not be closely familiar with the research that provides it with a theoretical foundation. It is usual, moreover, for this understanding to be reflected in the physical organization of classroom space. In Scoil Bhríde classrooms are furnished with easily movable tables and chairs; each pupil has her own chair and shares a table with another pupil. When the teacher wants to communicate with the class using the interactive whiteboard, the pupils sit in pairs and rows facing her; this makes it easy to switch between teacher talk addressed to the whole class and pair work. When the teacher wants pupils to work in small groups, their tables and chairs can be arranged accordingly. And when she wants to communicate interactively with the whole class, the tables can be moved to one side and the chairs arranged in a large circle or semicircle. The balance and relation between these different configurations of classroom furniture and space, and the modes of discourse that they support, will depend partly on the topic under consideration and partly on the preferences of the individual teacher.

The question then arises: What impact does the acknowledged presence of multiple home languages have on the structure and potential of classroom discourse in a school like Scoil Bhríde? As we explained in Chapter 2, the school has a long tradition of treating Irish as an alternative medium of communication, inside and outside the classroom, so that pupils' attempts to use Irish play an indispensable role in their learning of the language. A fixed part of each school day is devoted explicitly to Irish, but the language also has a potential presence in every other lesson; in other words, the possibility of bilingual communication is always present. That said, there are two important differences between Scoil Bhríde and multilingual settings like those found in a country like South Africa (for an overview of policy and practice, see Kerfoot and Simon-Vandenbergen 2015): none of the pupils' home languages are indigenous community languages, and most of them are completely unknown to the teachers. From the beginning ELLs are encouraged to use their home languages whenever they like in the classroom and the school yard. In the oral communication of the classroom, however, home languages can fulfil only three overt functions. First, they can be used by pupils in reciprocal communication with speakers of the same or a closely related language when they are engaged in pair or group work; second, they can be used for non-reciprocal purposes of display (e.g. pupils can show the rest of the class how to count in their home language); and third, they can be used as a source of intuitive linguistic knowledge that individual pupils can make available to the teacher and the rest of the class.

In circumstances of extreme linguistic diversity like those that obtain in Scoil Bhríde, the teacher and most researchers have no access to communication between pupils in their home languages, and such communication plays only an incidental role in the account we give of classroom discourse in this chapter. The examples we present illustrate the second and third functions of home language use. Asking Junior and Senior Infants to count aloud in their home languages is intended to serve a motivational and a cognitive purpose: to increase pupils' involvement in classroom interaction and to support their learning by engaging the language that is their primary cognitive tool and the default medium of their discursive thinking. Asking them about their home languages contributes to a growing awareness of the similarities and differences between languages, and as some of our examples show, exploring the literal meaning of a key term in several different languages can offer an intriguing point of entry to new curriculum content. Like the display function, moreover, using home languages as a source of linguistic data and thus a basis for drawing comparisons and contrasts between languages ensures that they remain activated in their speakers' minds. From the beginning of Junior Infants, home languages are the means by which Scoil Bhríde's teachers encourage their pupils to 'tak[e] responsibility for finding connections and examples, asking questions, reinterpreting experience, and searching for new techniques and new ways of understanding relevant to the matter in hand' (Barnes 2008: 15). This in turn helps pupils to 'find alternative ways of looking at topics, and … to grasp what evidence may be used to support one or another viewpoint' (Government of Ireland 1999a). This is the sense in which the discourse characteristic of Scoil Bhríde's classrooms may be said to involve 'translanguaging'. If, as Swain has argued, 'languaging' is the 'process of making meaning and shaping knowledge and experience through language' (Swain 2006: 98), '*trans*languaging' is the process of making meaning and shaping knowledge and experience through multiple languages. It is a dialogic process, yet each pupil's experience of it is unique because her linguistic repertoire is different from all others in the class. That repertoire comprises English, Irish, French (in Fifth and Sixth Class), in the case of ELLs the language of the home, and fragments of all other languages the pupil encounters in the course of the school day: a rich and unpredictable mix.

Including home languages in classroom communication

In this section of the chapter we present a series of vignettes that illustrate the inclusion of home languages in classroom communication. As we explained in Chapter 2, Scoil Bhríde's integrated approach to language education is not a rigid method; there is a great deal of variation among teachers and from one class of pupils to another. English and Irish are taught, English as the primary medium of pupils' literacy development and educational growth, Irish as an alternative medium of communication that has a role to play both in curriculum learning and in the social life of the school. ELLs' home languages are not taught, but their explicit presence in the classroom is encouraged, partly because they can provide ELLs themselves with a cognitive scaffold to support curriculum learning, and partly because they greatly enrich the learning experience of all pupils by enabling them to develop unusually high levels of language awareness. The examples that we give in this chapter are typical but by no means exhaustive; and it's important to stress that the diversity of the pupil population is such that it is impossible to identify a single dominant pattern of individual development, although strong tendencies certainly emerge.

Junior Infants (4+ years old)

In Junior Infants the school day begins with twenty minutes of play during which pupils are free to communicate with one another as they wish; after this the teacher uses discussion to introduce and explore curriculum content that is relevant to the pupils' here-and-now (the weather, bedtime routines, getting up in the morning and so on). Although teachers are free to organize delivery of curriculum content in whatever way they choose, they usually focus first on English – songs, poems, stories and games – and then on Irish. Then, after the mid-morning break, pupils learn maths through play, followed by other curriculum areas, and after the lunch break the school day ends with a story. Although at this early stage the emphasis is on the development of oral skills, the written language is present in labels, signs and charts and frequently referred to; in this way, recognition of written words in English and Irish is strongly promoted.

When they start school, Junior Infants respond to their new surroundings in a variety of ways. Some observe without speaking, while others engage in play activities that may or may not require linguistic interaction. When they need to speak, children can sometimes be observed interacting with each other in different languages. Although they have no apparent linguistic comprehension of what is being said by their partner, they understand that they are engaged in a collaborative, goal-directed activity that can proceed via unspoken negotiation. Routines of this kind are, of course, central to first language acquisition, and they play the same key role in ELLs' acquisition of English and all pupils' acquisition of Irish.

Greetings

One way of introducing a class of Junior Infants to the variety of home languages in their midst is to focus on greetings. The pupils arrange their chairs in a semicircle and the teacher begins by saying 'hello' to the English speakers in the class, who respond in English. Then 'Dia dhuit', the Irish equivalent, is introduced. When the teacher asks whether anyone knows another way of saying 'hello' or 'Dia dhuit', ELLs contribute appropriate expressions from their home languages. The teacher may prompt by asking ELLs what they say to their mother when she collects them from school each afternoon. Children from bilingual homes are likely to be explicitly aware of differences between languages, like the girl from an English- and Italian-speaking family, who told the teacher: *My Daddy says, Ciao! Como esta? Va bene.* Greeting and leave-taking activities can be supported and practised in various ways, for example by using puppets or role plays. In this way pupils begin to understand that there are many ways of saying the same thing and each of those ways is as valid as the next.

Counting and addition

The early stages of learning to count and add show how the use of ELLs' home languages supports their acquisition of foundational concepts. The Primary School Curriculum requires that Junior Infants learn to count from one to ten and understand the concepts underlying the numbers one to five. One Junior Infants teacher introduced a lesson on addition by inviting pupils to volunteer to count from one to five. Individual children chose to undertake this task in a variety of home languages, English and Irish; none of them was a native speaker of either English or Irish. A Lithuanian child explained in English that she would count in Irish as did a Filipino child whose home language was Tagalog. The teacher then invited the whole class to count from one to five in English, Irish and Spanish, another of the home languages present in the class. A Lithuanian child undertaking the same exercise a few months later also did so in Spanish. When asked what language she was speaking she replied: *It's from 'Dora the Explorer'* (an animated television programme for children in which Spanish is used as well as English).

On another occasion, pupils were asked to set up an addition problem using two hoops, some coloured blocks and large foam numbers from one to five. The first child placed blocks in each of the hoops and the second child matched them with the appropriate numbers. The teacher then invited pupils to call out the equation in the language of their choice. The first to volunteer was a speaker of Tagalog. She was followed by an Irish child who used a mixture of Irish and English: *Two agus two sin four*. The teacher asked her if she knew another way of saying 'two'. After some thought the child replied: *a dó* and gave the answer in Irish as well – *a ceathair* ('four'). She then repeated the equation more confidently. The next child stated the equation in Polish. In Irish, the teacher invited her to say it again. Standing in the same place as the previous speaker, the pupil began to answer in Irish but the teacher encouraged her to use Polish instead. The pupil went back to the place where she had first spoken before speaking in Polish again, as though identifying this particular spot as the place where Polish was spoken.

Mixing languages within utterances is quite common in the Junior Infant classroom. Children move from English to Irish and/or their home language, and even though their usage of both English and Irish (and presumably their L1) is correct, they may not be able to identify which languages they have used. For example, a pupil from an Indian family used *agus* as the link between the two numbers she was adding, which she gave in Malayalam, but she strongly disagreed that she was mixing Irish and her home language, insisting that it was all 'Indian'. Asked to add two and two, a Venezuelan pupil mixed Spanish and English: *dos y dos together make quatro*. Similarly, when pupils were asked to add two and three, a Romanian child mixed Romanian and Irish: *două agus trei sin cinci*; a speaker of Bangla used Irish, English and Bangla; and a Filipino child used English and Irish but added an Irish prefix to the English word 'two': *a two agus a two sin a ceathair*.

Colours

Children usually know the names of primary colours before they start school, so work on colours in Junior Infants provides another opportunity to include ELLs' home languages. The teacher may seat the class in a semicircle and place coloured sheets of paper on the floor in a second, smaller semicircle so that all the children have a clear view of them. The teacher chooses a native speaker of English to call out the names of the colours in English in the order in which they are laid out. A second native speaker of English repeats the task, but from a different starting point. Two children are then given the task of jumping over the colours the rest of the class calls out, this time in Irish, although none of the children has Irish as her first language. Next the Special Needs Assistant calls out the names of the colours in French (the language of schooling in her country of origin) as she jumps over the coloured sheets. All the children repeat the words she calls out. Individual children perform the colour-naming exercise in Kurdish, Romanian, Irish and Albanian. It's important to note that Irish is here being used as an authentic medium of communication alongside the various home languages present in the class.

Days of the week

Learning the days of the week provides another pretext for including ELLs' home languages. To begin with, days of the week are taught in English and Irish with the help of a wall chart. The teacher regularly calls on individual pupils to point to the different days in turn and the rest of the class responds by saying the name of the day, first in English, then in Irish. Pupils from a senior class may be brought in to replicate the exercise using their home languages, while the Special Needs Assistant uses French. On one occasion two Junior Infants undertook to say the days of the week in Kurdish but at the last minute did it in Irish. As they explained afterwards, they suddenly realized that they didn't know the days of the week in Kurdish because *our mam forgot to tell us* ('day of the week' is, after all, a concept that many children first encounter at school). They said they would check the vocabulary at home and practise so that they could say the days of the week in Kurdish the next day.

Shopping for food

Learning about the different kinds of food is an important part of the Junior Infants curriculum and thus a recurrent focus of classroom activity. One teacher began a lesson by asking the pupils what a supermarket is. A native English speaker responded: *It's somewhere you buy stuff.* The teacher then asked what kind of things she could buy in a supermarket and individual pupils made suggestions in English. Next the teacher asked if anyone knew 'another way to say supermarket', which she immediately rephrased: *Is there any other language that we could say supermarket in?* One pupil responded with *an siopa* (Irish) and another with *sklep* (Polish), each correctly identifying the language she used. The teacher then asked the same question of a Latvian-speaking pupil, who answered with *veikals*, and a Chinese child, who could not remember the word in her language. 'Supermarket' was not a new topic in this class, and a Congolese child whose home language was Swahili recalled the Chinese word and answered: *diàn*/店. The teacher then drew her pupils' attention to some items of food she had assembled on a table. She asked the class to identify the first item and an Indian child did so correctly. The child was then invited to the table where she held up a carton and facing the class she said *milk*. She was asked to say which language she had used and did so correctly. The teacher's next question concerned the word for 'milk' in different languages. Answers were forthcoming in five languages: Malayalam (*pāl*/പാൽ), Irish (*bainne*), Polish (*mleko*), Chinese (*nǎi niú*/牛奶) and Kurdish (*şîr*). The same procedure was followed for the remaining items on the table – eggs, butter and bread – and answers were supplied in two more languages, Konkani and French.

Music

It is very important for learners to have frequent opportunities to use their various languages as often and in as many different ways and situations as possible. Reciting rhymes and singing songs are a way of giving them practice in vocabulary and grammatical structures without making them explicitly aware of the fact. And teaching Junior Infants the Christmas song 'Jingle Bells' in English, Irish and French is another way of showing them that the same content can be expressed in different languages. The fact that Santa Claus, Daidí na Nollag and Père Noël are all the same person teaches the same lesson. A developing sense of the connections between languages gives pupils confidence and encourages them to pursue more ambitious learning where the use of a language other than the L1 is not a significant barrier to further exploration of knowledge.

Visit by Third Class pupils

In order to support plurilingual learning, teachers in junior classes sometimes invite senior pupils to take part in lessons so that their class can observe a variety of languages in use and begin to see this as a normal part of life both inside and outside school. On one occasion, for example, Third Class pupils came to a Junior Infants class and spoke about themselves in their home languages. A pupil from Latvia did so in Latvian and Russian, then repeated what she had said in English. The teacher then encouraged a short interaction between the Latvian pupil and a Junior Infant who spoke Russian and Hebrew. After that, another Third Class pupil from an Irish family told the class about herself in Irish and English, after which pupils from Polish and Indian families spoke in Polish and Malayalam respectively, each providing an English translation of what she had said. Home languages and lesson content were further supported when a Third Class pupil called out the names of colours in English and Tagalog. As well as giving affirmation to speakers of languages other than English, the teacher was using the lesson to give her pupils an opportunity to use their auditory skills to identify similarities between languages. This is an important first step in the development of explicit language awareness.

Senior Infants (5+ years old)

The curriculum for Senior Infants builds on what has been taught in Junior Infants, with a greater emphasis on the development of pupils' reading and writing skills. In Scoil Bhríde, home languages continue to be drawn into the life of the classroom in many different ways. As we noted in Chapter 2, small-group language support classes are a frequent source of new activities. One language support teacher encouraged pupils to talk about things of interest to them – their country of origin, favourite toys, playing with friends, especially memorable events – in English and their home language. In one group, a discussion of Sunday School prompted an Arabic speaker to read the action song 'Head, shoulders, knees and toes' from a book written in Arabic. The class teacher and language support teacher responded by showing the class how to play a similar action game, 'Hand to hand', in English and Irish. Individual pupils then took turns to lead the game, calling out instructions in Irish, Arabic and Polish (the two home languages present in the group). Action games of this kind became a regular feature of language support classes and provided yet another activity in which plurilingual pupils could engage in enjoyable multilingual activities.

Mathematics/sequencing

As we have seen, days of the week are introduced in Junior Infants and they remain in focus in Senior Infants, both for their own sake and for the role they play in developing pupils' skill in sequencing information correctly. Beginning with English, one teacher printed the name of each day on a postcard to support her pupils' learning. She then used the same technique to revise the days of the week in Irish, pinning the postcards to the classroom wall so that they could act as a visual support. After this, she began to work through the home languages present in the class so that all pupils were able to learn the days of the week in a variety of languages and use whatever language they chose to answer questions like: What day is it today? What day was it yesterday? What day will it be tomorrow? Next, she called out individual days of the week in English and asked the children to tell her the equivalent in another language. Pupils referred to the postcard versions in English, Irish, French, Spanish and Polish to help them with this task, and some offered days of the week in their home language even though this had not yet been added to the set of postcards. In discussion about what it means to know the days of the week in several languages, one pupil pointed out that sometimes a pupil may know them in a language *when the teacher doesn't even know them.*

Healthy eating

One Senior Infant teacher joined forces with a language support teacher for a lesson about healthy eating. The pupils sat at tables in groups of four or five as though they were in a café, and the language support teacher distributed samples of various foods. The class teacher began by addressing a child whose parents used English as their home language because the first language of each was a different African language. She asked, in Irish, whether the child liked cheese. The pupil responded in English but used the Irish word for cheese: *I don't like cáis.* The teacher told the children that they could now taste the different items of food in front of them. The previous week they had been taught about the senses, so she asked the class which senses they were now using. A child who spoke Malayalam at home said: *Eating our toast we touch and we smell and we taste.* The teacher praised the child, recapitulated the three senses that the child had identified and asked her to repeat what she had said in her home language. As she spoke, the child pointed to the parts of her body associated with touch, taste and smell, as though she were instinctively using kinaesthesia to support her utterance in Malayalam. A Rwandan child whose parents had different first languages and so used English, their second language, as the language of the home, put up her hand and added hearing to the list of senses. The teacher praised her and then asked: *What do we hear when we're making toast?* The child answered: *When it pops up.* The teacher listed the four senses identified so far and asked if anyone could name the fifth sense. A child from a Spanish/Irish background offered *see,* a Lithuanian speaker suggested *look* and the Spanish/Irish pupil added *sight.*

In the same lesson, an Estonian child whose home language was Russian put up her hand and said that mayonnaise comes from Estonia. The teacher asked whether the word *mayonnaise* or a different word is used in Estonian. The child confirmed that *mayonnaise* is the Estonian word, adding: *It's nearly like mayonnaise but it doesn't have m at the end.* The teacher asked the same pupil if she could say what was in her sandwich in English. The pupil identified cheese, ham and lettuce, which she translated into Russian when the teacher asked her to do so.

At the end of the lesson the two teachers asked each other in Irish whether they liked particular foods. Individual children immediately translated what they had heard into English to show that they had understood what the teachers had said.

Music

Another Senior Infant teacher incorporated home languages into a song that she adapted (to the tune of 'The Farmer in the Dell') to consolidate learning about transport. Entitled 'Is maith liom bheith ar scoil' ('I like being at school'), the song began in Irish and worked through the seven home languages present in the class – Arabic, Chinese, French, Malayalam, Romanian, Slovakian, Yoruba – the final verse being sung in English. The teacher encouraged children to stand up and sing the verse in their home language (if there was more than one speaker of the same language, they sang the verse together). The rest of the class joined in the chorus which was sung each time in Irish.

Having found not only that the children enjoyed singing in their home languages but that pupils were learning the verses in multiple languages without being formally taught, the teacher decided to take the process further. She asked parents of all the language groups in the class to teach their child a nursery rhyme or simple song typical of their culture. Many parents responded with enthusiasm, providing songs in Tagalog, Malayalam, Spanish, Romanian and Lithuanian. The teacher combined them in a medley that began with a song in Irish accompanied by actions that helped to explain the song's meaning; a chorus in Irish was also sung after each song. Percussion instruments were used to mark the medley's 4/4 rhythm, and the pupils counted 1, 2, 3, 4 in Irish before beginning each song. This was quite a complex undertaking, especially as the songs had entirely different meanings. The pupils thoroughly enjoyed singing together and listening to the contributions of their classmates; some of them learned the words of languages that particularly appealed to them. The medley was sung at the St Patrick's Day Céilí, a special event in the school calendar, but the Spanish speakers were absent. The teacher planned to omit the Spanish song, but when she came to the point in the medley where it should be sung, a Romanian child jumped up and began singing in plausible-sounding Spanish. She was obviously delighted to seize the opportunity to do so.

Language awareness

Already in Junior Infants pupils begin to develop an explicit awareness of similarities and differences between the various languages present in their class. This process continues in Senior Infants, and evidence abounds to suggest that pupils are constantly thinking about language. This is stimulated, of course, by the fact that their teachers are always encouraging them to explore similarities and differences. One Senior Infants teacher reported that during a phonics lesson about the /d/ sound a pupil remarked that both *dearg* (Irish) and *red* (English) contain /d/. This prompted other pupils to tell the class the word for 'red' in their home language. On another occasion, a pupil said of the weather: *It's windy*. When the teacher queried this, she qualified her original utterance: *It's a little bit windy*. The teacher asked the class if this could be said in another way. A Filipino child responded in Irish: *Tá sé …* The teacher tried to help her by saying: *gao …* (the first part of the word *gaofar*, 'windy'). The pupil replied: *No, no! You know, that longer word first*. The teacher offered *saghas* ('somewhat', 'a bit'), which enabled the pupil to say: *Tá sé saghas gaofar* ('It's a bit windy'). Another pupil described the weather as cold. The teacher asked the class to suggest other ways of saying 'cold'. A Romanian child offered *frig*. The teacher praised the child and asked whether *frig* reminded the pupils of any other word to do with cold. A speaker of Malayalam offered *fuar* (Irish for 'cold'), saying that the sound at the beginning of the word, /f/, is the same. Speakers of Tagalog and Polish offered *frio* and *zimno* respectively. Again, the teacher praised these contributions, then checked the word *frig* with the Romanian speaker, asking if this word reminded the class of an English word. A Lithuanian child said *fridge* and the teacher encouraged the class to make the link between *fridge* and *cold*.

The pupils' developing language awareness is often surprisingly sophisticated, as our next example shows. In Ireland, student primary teachers are required to undertake teaching practice in schools. On one occasion, a trainee teacher used the Irish formula 'Dia dhuit' to greet a Senior Infants class. Although the children were very familiar with this greeting, they looked puzzled and failed to respond. The student repeated the greeting several times to no avail. Suddenly, a Chinese pupil recognized the problem. *No, no*, she said, *Is not Jeea. Is d-, d-, d-, Dia. Say d-, d-, d-*. The student had pronounced the word 'Dia' using a different dialect from the one used by the teacher. To understand what was wrong and then propose a solution, the Chinese pupil had to draw on a complex combination of perceptual and cognitive skills.

First Class (6+ years old)

Language awareness

Noticing an introductory Chinese reader on the principal's desk, a six-year-old pupil from a Chinese family demonstrated that she could read Chinese by translating into English a number of words used to label pictures. The word beside a picture of a gate, however, she translated as 'door'. When the principal pointed this out, she acknowledged her mistake, explaining that in her language the same word is used for a means of entry both indoors and outdoors, while in English two different words are needed to take account of the different locations.

Language support

In First Class, language support lessons continue to play a key role in drawing out ELLs' home languages. When the teacher invited one group to greet one another in their home languages, some children chose to greet, and also to give their name and age, in English, Irish and their home language. A Polish child explained that there are two ways to say hello in her language, *cześć* and *dzień dobry*. As the interaction progressed the teacher mentioned a *cupán tae* ('cup of tea'), whereupon two pupils offered similar-sounding equivalents from their respective home languages, *kubek* (Polish) and *kupa* (Bosnian). Another pupil told the teacher that the word for chair in Bosnian is *stolica*. Repeating this word, the teacher drew a link with the Irish word *stól* ('stool'), which was displayed on the classroom wall, then asked all the pupils to tell her the word for stool in their home language. Two Polish children agreed that the word *art* is the same in Polish and English. The teacher said that she had heard that *start* and *extra* are also the same in both languages. While one pupil agreed, the other was unsure; but both agreed that *park* is the same in both languages. One of them explained that there are two ways of saying 'park' in Polish, *park* and *plac zabaw* (which means 'playground').

In language support classes ELLs continue to play games that involve following instructions to touch hands to hands, knee to knee etc. in a variety of formats. A pupil may call out the instruction in her home language with or without the accompanying actions. If she omits the actions, her classmates must use all the skills at their disposal to decide which action is the appropriate response. In another approach, two teachers initiate the game in Irish and pupils copy their actions while calling out the sequence in their home language. This has proved a highly effective way of getting ELLs to translate spontaneously into their home language utterances they hear in Irish or English; it also helps to foster an awareness of the connectedness and equivalence of languages.

Second Class (7+ years old)

English language support rooted in home languages

Language support continues to be provided in Second Class for recent arrivals and pupils who may have spent a year at the school, returned to their country of origin for a year or two and then come back. Home languages continue to play a central role and again pupils are encouraged to recognize similarities and differences between the languages they hear in the classroom. In one lesson a pupil noted that some words in Tagalog are similar to their equivalents in her home language, Spanish. The teacher encouraged her to compare the days of the week, displayed on a poster in Irish and Spanish. Explaining that she herself did not speak Spanish, the teacher then suggested a game in which she 'phoned' the pupil in English and the pupil replied in Spanish. When a Hungarian speaker complained that she couldn't understand what the Spanish pupil was saying, the teacher explained that she couldn't understand everything either but was using the interaction to try to learn. She asked the group the meaning of one word the Spanish pupil had used: *mucho*. A Filipino child answered that it means *a lot*. The teacher then asked if there is a similar word in English. The Spanish pupil suggested *much* and went on to explain that there is another word in Spanish that means *a lot and a lot*.

Teachers often begin language support lessons by naming the topic that will be discussed and inviting the pupils to respond to an introductory question in English and then translate their answer into their home language; alternatively, they can answer first in their home language and then translate into English. For example, the teacher may ask the pupils what they are wearing, and if there are five pupils in the class, there will be five descriptions of clothes in five different home languages and English.

One language support group used the European passport, an EU-produced information booklet, to learn more about their various countries of origin, the languages spoken there and so on. When it emerged that some children knew more than two languages, the language support teacher engaged them in spontaneous translation in their mainstream class; the children were very happy to show off their skills. This exercise had the added effect of encouraging children who were native speakers of English to become involved, citing Irish as their second language.

On another occasion a language support group was exploring the rights and responsibilities of being a global citizen, with particular reference to children under eighteen years of age (the United Nations Convention on the Rights of the Child is used as a resource to address these issues). In a summary of their discussion, children volunteered to identify rights and their corresponding responsibilities in English and their home language. A Polish speaker named the right to play and the responsibility to include others in her play, while a Bosnian speaker named the right of all children to be safe and the responsibility to take care not to damage the safety of others. Both her class teacher and the language support teacher had observed that this latter pupil's grasp of oral and written English had improved dramatically since she started to read in Bosnian; she was also much more involved in classroom activities and discussion. During the lesson on rights, she mentioned *talking in my language* as *my favourite thing in the world*. A Latvian speaker said that all children have the right to learn and others must not be disturbed when trying to learn.

In another lesson a Lithuanian child asked a Bosnian classmate the following questions in Lithuanian: *What is your name? What age are you? What class are you in? What are your favourite hobbies?* The Bosnian pupil answered the first three questions in Bosnian and the fourth in English – perhaps because she didn't talk about hobbies at home and lacked the relevant vocabulary in Bosnian. The language support teacher asked the Bosnian speaker how it was that she could understand questions in Lithuanian. The child attempted to answer, saying *because ...* a few times, but was unable to do so, perhaps due to a lack of English. The teacher thought that she may have guessed the meaning of the questions correctly because of the order in which they were asked.

Third Class (8+ years old)

Language support

In consultation with the class teacher, the language support teacher decided to work with groups in Third Class to explore the United Nations' Millennium Development Goals, a global action plan to achieve eight anti-poverty goals by 2015. During a series of small-group language sessions, the pupils and their teacher discussed individual goals, asking in relation to each of them: *What can we do?* While these discussions took place in English, the pupils were encouraged to use all languages available to them – English, Irish and their home languages (in this case, 'Benin', Igala, French, Igbo, Irish, Italian, Mandarin, Moldovan, Tagalog, Urdu, Yoruba) – and each goal was recorded in the home languages present in the group. Some pupils were able to write unaided in their home languages, while others were helped at home by their parents. When the group had reached agreement on the type of help that could be given, that was recorded in English. Their work was presented in the form of a booklet, which they read to various classes in the school. Some of the younger children heard their home language read aloud in school for the first time; their surprise and pleasure were clearly visible. Table 3.1 lists the eight Millennium Goals and the actions the pupils agreed on.

Table 3.1 The eight Millennium Goals and the actions proposed by Third Class ELLs

Goal	What can we do?
Stamp out poverty and hunger	We can share our food and tools
Educate every child	We can give books
Make sure there are equal chances for women and girls	We can show respect for women and girls
Reduce the numbers of children and babies who die	We can give medicine
Improve the health of mothers	Send doctors and nurses to give help
Fight infectious diseases	We can give equipment and antibiotics
Clean up the environment	We take care of our world
Work together to make the world a better place	We can share ideas, things and money

Use of video recording

Another way of supporting pupils' home languages is to use a video camera to film them telling their classmates about themselves in English, Irish and their respective home languages. Each pupil is given a sheet of paper on which she writes in large letters the name of her country, her home language, English and Irish. This acts as a prompt when pupils translate their contributions, which include details of their age, physical appearance, favourite subjects etc. They speak first in their home language, then in English, then in Irish, for example: *Ja mówie po polsku. I speak Polish. Labharaím Polainne.*

The school garden

When the new school building was opened in 2013 a small patch of ground was developed as the school garden. The school caretaker prepares the ground and provides advice on planting procedures, but the pupils are responsible for tending the garden. We mentioned in Chapter 2 that one of the language support teachers exploited this in her lessons. The tools and plants that the children were working with provided practical reference points for the oral discussion and writing that preceded and followed gardening sessions. Capitalizing on the fact that their Latin derivation means that the names of plants and herbs are often closely similar across languages, the teacher compiled a table that pupils themselves could add to, giving names in Latin, English, Irish and home languages (Table 3.2). This was given to pupils of all ages and at all stages of language support, in the belief that if the practical activity of gardening was accompanied by written information it would contribute to pupils' literacy development.

Table 3.2 The names of plants, herbs etc. in Latin, English, Irish and home languages

Latin	English	Irish	Home language
flores	flowers	bláthanna	
latuca	lettuce	leitís	
helianthus	sunflower	lus na gréine	
sectivi	chive	síobhas	
dolor sit amet	carrot	cairéad	
apio	parsley	peirsil	
herba	herbs	luibheanna	

Language awareness

Pupils continue to exhibit their developing language awareness in a variety of ways. For example, after one Third Class had learned two poems by W. B. Yeats, 'Down by the Salley Gardens' and 'He wishes for the Cloths of Heaven', a Romanian child remarked on the use of the present participle structure in both texts: 'I being young and foolish … ' ('Down by the Salley Gardens') and 'I being poor … ' ('He wishes for the Cloths of Heaven'). Another example concerns the introduction of fractions. The teacher began by calling two pupils to the front of the class, one pretending to have a fractured arm, the other a fractured leg.

When the class had suggested synonyms for 'fracture' – 'break' and 'split', for example – the teacher asked what words they knew for 'break' in other languages. Among the suggestions was *rupt* (Romanian), which the pupils quickly linked to the 'e*rupt*ion' of a volcano; further suggestions included 'inter*rupt*ion' and 'dis*rupt*ion'. This was followed by a roleplay in which a pupil 'inter*rupt*ed' the teacher as she spoke. When asked what had happened, her classmates suggested that the pupil had *made teacher lose her place, she broke your concentration, she broke the class rules by her inter*ruption. This led into a discussion about fractions as broken-up numbers and the pupils drew their 'fraction walls'.

As children's metalinguistic skills develop, they become more adept at making linguistic comparisons. Having listened to a Filipino child read her work in three languages, Tagalog, English and Irish, a child of Russian/Nigerian heritage explained that she now knew the word for hedgehog in Tagalog: *parkupino*. When asked how she had worked this out she said: *because it was almost at the end of the story and the ... the spikes* [of the hedgehog] *reminds me of porcupine's*.

Fourth Class (9+ years old)

Language awareness

By the time pupils reach Fourth Class, the development of language awareness is a fully integrated part of classroom interaction. As one teacher observed: *Much depends on the openness of the teacher and her willingness to exploit unplanned and spontaneously arising opportunities*. For example, one morning during roll call, a Polish child answered *here* instead of *anseo* (Irish is normally used for this activity in all schools). A Ukrainian pupil then used *ici* and her neighbour, also Ukrainian, answered in Polish. The class thought this was hilarious. In the following days, all languages present in the class were used to answer roll call, and some pupils took the opportunity to answer in the languages of their peers. When an Irish child asked the teacher to talk in *our* language, the teacher obliged by using Irish to correct that morning's mental maths test. She reported that switching to Irish presented very few problems for any of the children.

Later, in a discussion concerning the word *chauffeur*, the teacher pointed out that it comes from French. A Polish child said she knew what it meant because *it's nearly the same as the word for driver, 'szofer', in Polish*. A Ukrainian child said that the word for chauffeur *sounds the same in Ukrainian but I'm not sure of the spelling*; she suggested *chofear* or *shofer*. A Romanian child then offered șofer. The teacher drew attention to the shape and position of the cedilla beneath the *s*, explaining that this serves the function of changing the sound from 's' to 'sh'.

Shortly before Christmas, the teacher used a picture of the stable in Bethlehem to stimulate discussion. Pointing to the manger she asked the class to explain its function. Pupils gave the following answers: *a thing for pigs' food; my Granny has one of those for the pigs; it's a thing for animals' food.* The teacher then explained that the French word *manger* means 'to eat'. This was received with a collective *Aah!* Later in the discussion, the teacher gave the English and Irish words for the gifts brought by the Three Wise Men and the pupils gave the equivalents in their respective home languages (Table 3.3).

Table 3.3 The gifts brought by the Three Wise Men, in English, Irish and home languages

English	Irish	Polish	Urdu	Arabic	Romanian	Ukrainian	Russian
Myrrh	miorr	mira	myra	miria			
Gold	ór	złoto			aur	zolat	zolata
Frankincense				francosaura [?]			

When pupils were exploring the use of calculators in a maths lesson, the teacher hinted that an answer proposed by one of the pupils (037) was also the name for a lion: when they turned their calculator upside down they saw that it read 'LEO'. A Romanian child remarked that the *word for lion in Romanian is nearly the same, it's 'leu', you spell it with 'u' but it sounds nearly the same, lay-oo.*

In another maths lesson the teacher asked: *What is an oblique line?* A Romanian pupil suggested that it was like *oblig* in her language, which meant *something you must do*. The teacher realized that the pupil was confusing 'oblique' with 'oblige', and she used the whiteboard to explain the difference in meaning between the two words. This prompted an Irish pupil to observe that *obligatory* was similar to the Romanian *oblig*, whereupon a Filipino pupil offered *obligate*. A Lithuanian pupil then answered the teacher's original question when she said: *There's an oblique line on the end of the letter q.* At the end of these exchanges an Irish pupil remarked that *it's like as if every word you say in one language, you can say it's like … in French or something else.*

The following sentence occurred in the English textbook: 'They did not venture near the cave for fear they would wake the dragon and provoke his anger.' The teacher asked the class to explain the word 'provoke'. A Romanian child commented that *it's like a word in my language, 'provoch', that means to challenge or to dare.* A Polish child added: *It's also like 'provokacia' in Polish and that means to keep annoying someone.*

Figure 3.1 Poster in Igbo explaining how to make a sandwich (Fourth Class).

Examples of this kind arise whatever topic is in focus. One teacher found that a lesson on how to make a sandwich offered opportunities to develop language awareness. First, the class identified the six steps involved in making a sandwich and wrote them out in Irish; then the six steps were written out in English; and after that pupils wrote them in their home languages and other languages they happened to be interested in, and made posters (Figure 3.1). When the posters were read aloud pupils tried to identify the word for bread in the language used – a matter of using their knowledge of the six-step sequence and looking for cross-linguistic similarities.

Fifth Class (10+ years old)

Understanding Italian

An Irish pupil whose parents had been on holiday in Italy brought an Italian newspaper to school; it contained a report on a rugby match between Ireland and Italy. The Special Needs Assistant (SNA) was Italian, so the class teacher asked her to read part of the article aloud to the class. As she began to read, the children realized that they could understand the meaning of much of the article even though none of them had learned Italian. This experience increased their interest in finding connections between languages and enhanced their self-confidence with regard to language learning. The Six Nations rugby tournament also provided an opportunity to discuss sport using several languages. The Italian Special Needs Assistant engaged the class in discussion of the Irish and Italian teams prior to their match. Speaking in Italian, she explained to the children why she had come to their classroom and read an extract from an Italian newspaper report on preparations for the game between Ireland and Italy. The pupils attempted to translate what she said into English. Having started to learn French at the beginning of Fifth Class, they were able to associate *verde y bianchi* with *vert* and *blanc*, while *azzurra* was linked to Spanish *azur*. In this way the pupils were able to identify the colours worn by each team. A speaker of Igbo asked how to say 'shorts' in Italian. When the SNA responded with *pantaloncini*, she said that *it sounds like French*. Another pupil compared *pantaloncini* to the Kurdish word for shorts, *panton*. A Romanian speaker explained that *pantalon sport* was the expression used in her language; she also commented on the similarity between Italian *dopo*, meaning 'after', and *după* in Romanian. She and the SNA agreed that in some respects Romanian and Italian are quite similar. A Polish speaker noted that *stadio olimpico a Roma* is similar to *stadion olimpijski* in Polish. The class worked out that the ball used in rugby is called *ovale* in Italian due to its oval shape, while *prendo coraggio* ('take courage') prompted a Romanian pupil to say that *prendo* means 'catch' in Romanian. A German speaker added that *coraggio* sounds like *courage*, and everyone agreed that the players would need to have courage during the match. Several pupils then used their home languages followed by translation into English to ask questions of the SNA. An Urdu speaker asked if the SNA liked rugby. The SNA answered in Irish before explaining how to ask the question in Italian: *Ti piace il rugby?* Further questions were asked in Kurdish, Amharic, Romanian and Malayalam. A speaker of Foula asked in Irish: *Cén t-am a bheidh an cluiche ar siúil?* ('What time will the match be on?').

In order to feed the enthusiasm generated by this brief exposure to Italian, the class teacher arranged for the Special Needs Assistant to return to the class with an Italian version of Aesop's fables, several of which she read to the class in the same way as the rugby reports.

Sixth Class (11+ years old)

Integrating French in the language of the classroom

In Chapter 2 we explained that when pupils begin to learn French, in Fifth Class, it is the sole focus of one lesson a week but is also drawn into the other work of the class. Rather than being treated as a pretext for 'fun learning' or mediated mostly through games, French is adopted as a new medium for engaging with curriculum content. At the same time, the learning of French is supported by the use of other languages. In Sixth Class, for example, a module on telling the time was taught in a way that required pupils to repeat target phrases in Irish as well as French, so that Irish provided a scaffold for practising new content in French. Sitting in a semicircle, the pupils took turns to ask and answer questions like 'What time is it? It is 3 o'clock'. Home languages were also used. At the beginning of the routine, each pupil said 'We are learning about time' in her home language, and when questions had been asked and answers given in French and Irish, home languages were added to the mix. The first pair of pupils chose to use Irish; subsequent pairs used English, Tagalog, Romanian, Albanian, Polish and French; and two pupils interacted with each other using Ukrainian and Slovakian.

Drawing home languages into the teaching of curriculum content

This is how one Sixth Class teacher described her approach to the use of home languages in her classroom:

> *I have twenty-one 11- and 12-year-olds in my class. Twenty of them are non-native speakers of English so only one of them has English as her home language. There is a large variety of home languages, so the pupils don't all speak the same 'other' language. For these children language is both an issue and not an issue. It's an issue in that coming here they have to learn English in order to access the curriculum. It's not an issue in that any language is just another language as far as they're concerned.*
>
> *In my teaching, I try to help them make connections in all areas of the curriculum. For example, if I'm teaching maths and we're doing shapes and I do something about the octagon or the dodecagon, I draw their attention to 'oct' at the beginning of 'octagon' or 'dodec' at the beginning of 'dodecagon' and ask them whether it reminds them of a word in one of the other languages they know. That helps them to figure out and remember how many sides the shape has.*

Introducing a lesson on bats

The same teacher helped her pupils to discover that knowing the names of animals in different languages can provide useful insights into their defining features. For homework, she gave them a text to read about bats and asked them to write down five facts in preparation for a class discussion the following day. Several pupils included the fact that the Irish word for bat is *ialtóg*. The teacher began the lesson by explaining that when she was a child she learned that the Irish for bat was *sciathán leathair*. Literally translated into English, this means 'leather wing', which tells us something about the appearance of the bat that we don't get from the English name. She asked if anyone knew the word for 'bat' in any other language. A French-speaking pupil knew *chauve-souris* and could explain that *souris* means 'mouse' but didn't know the meaning of *chauve*. Recourse to the dictionary revealed that it means 'bald', so the literal meaning of the French expression for bat is 'bald mouse'. A Ukrainian child then gave the name in Russian (*letuchaya mysh*/летучая мышь) and explained that it means 'flying mouse'. Just from reflecting on what it is called in three languages, the pupils learned that a bat flies, has leathery wings, looks like a mouse and appears to be bald. They made a further discovery when they read that most of the bats in Ireland are from the Vespertilionidae family. The teacher told them that one of the monastic offices is called Vespers. They looked this word up in their dictionaries and discovered that it means 'evening prayer', from which they deduced that bats fly in the evening. All of this information served as an advance organizer for a nature lesson on bats.

Translating a Latin carol

One autumn term the same Sixth Class teacher made a pact with her pupils not to mention Christmas before the beginning of December. The choir of which she was a member had been learning a Latin carol, 'Dormi Jesu', and she decided to see how much sense her pupils could make of the Latin text, drawing on their various plurilingual repertoires. She began by reminding them that a particular word for a big event in December was out of bounds, but for the purposes of the lesson they could refer to it using any language other than English. The sound of Romanian *Crăciun* was associated with the fact that Christmas is a 'Christian' festival, and French *Noël* was linked with Irish *Nollaig*. A Chinese pupil wrote the word for Christmas in Mandarin and attempted to explain the meaning of the characters used. The teacher then introduced the name of the carol and asked children to listen to the words as an aid to working out their meaning:

Dormi Jesu! Mater ridet
Quae tam dulcem somnum videt,
Dormi Jesu blandule!
Si non dormis, Mater plorat
Inter fila cantans orat
Blande, veni, somnule

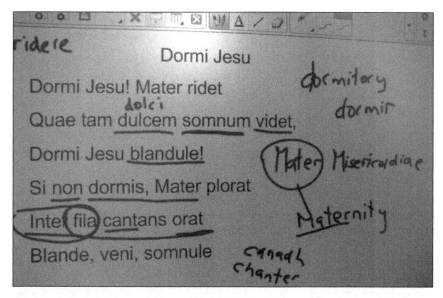

Figure 3.2 Interactive whiteboard: Sixth Class translates a Latin carol.

It took the class about forty minutes to translate the carol into English (Figure 3.2 shows the interactive whiteboard at the end of the process).

- *Jesu Dormi: Jesu* was immediately recognized and *dormi* was associated with the word for 'sleep' in Romanian; other pupils linked *dormi* to *dormitory* and French *dormir*, and the class decided that the carol is a lullaby.
- *Mater ridet: maternity* provided the meaning of *mater*, and the teacher explained that *ridere* means 'smile' in Italian.
- *Quae tam dulcem somnum videt*: a Romanian pupil said that *dulcem* is similar to Romanian *dulce* and Italian *dolci* meaning 'sweet'. In an effort to explain *somnum* the teacher pretended to be a somnambulist and a pupil provided *sleep*.
- *Dormi Jesu blandule: blandule* immediately evoked the translation *soft/not rough* from the Romanian pupil. Discussion then elicited *bland, plain, tasteless, soft, nondescript* and *unremarkable*.
- *Si non dormis Mater plorat*: a Russian speaker suggested *cry* for *plorat*, explaining that the Russian word *plakat*/плакать sounds similar to *plorat*. A Romanian pupil added that *ploaie* means 'rain' in Romanian, which led to French *pleut* and *pleurer*.

- *Inter fila cantans orat*: a pupil offered *singing* for *cantans*, referring to *choir* and Irish *canadh* as possible links; *inter* was associated with *inter-schools debate* and *interacting* with another school, and the teacher explained that *inter* in Latin can also mean 'while'. For *fila* one pupil offered Yoruba *fila* meaning 'hat', while another offered *feel* (the wool) and *filaments, threads*.
- *Blande, veni, somnule*: *veni* was identified as 'come' when the teacher prompted with *venir*, so the mother is saying 'come sweet sleep' to the baby.

Pupils were very engaged throughout the lesson, particularly when making links with their home languages and discovering that they were an asset when translating from Latin.

Clothes

A couple of months later, the teacher adopted a similar approach to exploring the topic of clothes. Again, pupils were highly motivated to participate and share the knowledge and insights they derived from their home language. One usually reticent child became particularly animated during this lesson, continually contributing with connections to her home language. The class compared the pronunciation and spelling of words for various items of clothing and footwear in different languages. A Ukrainian speaker noted that in her language the boots worn by Cossacks are *butsy*/буцси, which is pronounced like French *boite*. A Russian speaker said that *botinki*/ботинки has a different spelling from the Ukrainian word, although the sound is somewhat similar. A Polish speaker offered *kalosze* for galoshes or Wellington boots, while a Yoruba speaker compared Lithuanian *batai* with Yoruba *bata* – same sound, different spelling. A pupil from Benin offered *ebata*, a native English speaker said that her mother always said *galoshes* for *boots*, while another native English speaker asked for the Irish word for *boots* (*bútaisí*). As the discussion progressed the teacher recorded the various words used for different items of clothing and made a chart that the class used for subsequent reference (Figure 3.3). This was referred to at the end of the year by a Romanian pupil when she was interviewed by the principal:

> I think it's very surprising, between-language connectivity. We did a huge chart ... teacher started off ... we were learning clothes in French – 'pantalon' – then I said in Romanian it was 'pantaloni', then [we] made a huge chart with all different languages and most of them started with 'panta'.

Figure 3.3 Wall chart showing words for items of clothing in different languages (Sixth Class).

Food

In another Sixth Class, the teacher introduced the topic of food using a handout she had made with the names of various foodstuffs in English, Irish, French and Italian. The teacher read out the names in the first three languages and the Special Needs Assistant read the names in Italian, her native language. The class then made two different dishes and tasted both. Their follow-up task was to write out the ingredients and the method of cooking in their home language or one of the curriculum languages. (In this class, ELLs' home languages were Arabic, German, Hungarian, Italian, Kurdish, Malayalam, Romanian, Russian, Spanish, Tagalog.) A Kurdish pupil observed that it was easier to write the ingredients as there was generally only one word involved, whereas describing the method was more complicated. This activity prompted further comparisons between the languages present in the classroom. It was noted, for example, that *zucchini* or its equivalent is used in Italian, German, Hungarian, Yoruba and the Middle East, whereas French has *courgette*, Spanish *calabacín*, Romanian *dovlecel*, and Korean *aehoga*/서양 호박. The class further noted that for peppers Italian has *peperoni*, Romanian has *ardei* (which according to the Romanian speaker in the class means 'hot peppers') and Hungarian has *paprika*. Words for cheese were also compared: French *fromage*, English *cheese*, Italian *formaggio* (the SNA explained that *forma* means 'shape' or 'mould'), German *Käse*, Spanish *queso*, Irish *cáis*, Hungarian *sajt*, Russian *syr*/сыр, Malayalam *cīs*/ചീസ്, Korean *chijeu*/치즈, Yoruba *warankasi* and Romanian *brânză*.

Impact of use of home languages on Irish pupils' attitudes to the Irish language

In an interview with the principal, a Sixth Class teacher said that integrating English, Irish, French and the home languages of the classroom has highlighted two important issues for indigenous Irish children in Scoil Bhríde. First, they develop a heightened awareness that although they themselves are plurilingual, they live in a monolingual community, whereas many of their classmates use two or three languages outside school; and second, Irish is a medium of communication before it is a school subject. This latter consideration makes pupils more positive towards Irish, which in turn prompts them to use the language to express their own meanings. In response to the presence of other languages in the classroom, some Irish pupils use Google Translate to explore the content of their school work in another language, which gives them something different to bring to school.

What some of the pupils said

In discussion with the principal, some Sixth Class pupils said that knowing words in a variety of languages helped them to learn subjects like maths. An Irish child, for example, said that knowing that *ocht* (Irish) is linked to the word for eight in many languages helped her to remember how many sides an octagon has; and another native speaker of English claimed that knowing numbers in French made understanding maths easier. One Sixth Class teacher divided her class into ability-based groups for maths. As it happened, one group consisted entirely of Romanian pupils. The teacher noted that when given problems to solve, this group worked together in Romanian but had no difficulty in explaining their reasoning and their results in English.

A discussion that the principal had with a group of Sixth Class pupils revealed that Irish learners are increasingly aware of their monolingual origin and appreciate the educational value of plurilingualism. One pupil explained that she had

> *Irish and French, you know the way I don't have … Ukrainian, so when I go to school I usually speak Irish and French and then in the yard I sometimes hear* [other pupils] *speaking Polish and Yoruba and Benin and sometimes when I go home I try to say some of the words* [for my parents] *and they think it's nice the way that you can speak other languages and you can kind of pick it up.*

Another Irish pupil made the point that as she and her Irish classmates are native speakers of English, they can be helped by the presence in their class of speakers of other languages: *We can pick up things from other girls and … say when we're learning French, it would be easier for us to learn if we had other languages.* Describing herself as someone who had no other language, she asked why she should learn Irish *as no one speaks it anymore.* She was immediately challenged by a pupil from Benin, who said that people do use Irish. She was supported by a Yoruba speaker, who said that *when the teachers are talking* [Irish] *we can understand what they're saying.*

A Lithuanian speaker said that she enjoyed learning Irish, particularly when pupils got to talk about similarities with their own languages and the teacher wrote them down. She went on to say that *learning to write in another language helps you to improve in English.* A Chinese pupil explained that she was born in Ireland and she hated Mandarin while living there, but then hated the English language when her family returned to China. But now she said of her bilingual capabilities: *It feels really good and it's a bit special.* An Irish pupil added:

*When you hear someone speaking their own language it sounds so **nice** and you think you want to speak it too, so then speaking Irish, someone who doesn't know it thinks you can speak a nice language and it has really nice sounds. I like learning it because I have a language that's special to me as well, other than English and French.*

The Chinese pupil maintained that pupils should be able to choose whether or not to learn Irish. The Lithuanian speaker pointed out that *Irish ... is the original language of Ireland, so I think that they should still speak it and in some places in Ireland they still speak it and if you go there you won't know anything if you didn't learn Irish.* This was supported by a Polish pupil, who said that if Irish girls know Irish as well as English that makes them special too.

A Nigerian pupil said that her parents talk to each other in Igbo, but although she could understand everything they said, she didn't often speak the language herself. Besides using Irish at school, she used it at home when helping her siblings with their homework. She said that she had *friends who only speak Irish at home, so I just talk with them in Irish* when they are doing things together outside school.

Developing plurilingual repertoires

Throughout this book we use the term 'plurilingual' to refer to individuals who are able to communicate in two or more languages. In this we follow the Council of Europe's (not entirely consistent) practice of reserving 'multilingual' for communities and societies in which two or more languages are present. This distinction between the two terms usefully accommodates two sociolinguistic facts: individuals who have multiple languages may live in communities where a single language predominates, while individuals who live in communities with multiple languages may themselves have only one language. There is, however, more to the Council of Europe's concept of plurilingualism than a useful sociolinguistic distinction, and we conclude this chapter by briefly exploring the concept in the light of the varieties of classroom discourse developed by Scoil Bhríde and the emerging linguistic repertoires of its pupils.

At the beginning of the *Common European Framework of Reference for Languages* (CEFR), the Council of Europe's 'plurilingual approach' is summarized thus:

The plurilingual approach emphasises the fact that as an individual person's experience of language in its cultural contexts expands, from the language of the home to that of society at large and then to the languages of other peoples (whether learnt at school or college, or by direct experience), he or she does not keep these languages and cultures in strictly separated mental compartments, but rather builds up a communicative competence to which all knowledge and experience of language contributes and in which languages interrelate and interact. (Council of Europe 2001: 4)

Since the publication of the CEFR, the Council of Europe's work in language education has been founded on this definition. There are, however, at least three respects in which it is problematic. The first has to do with the contexts and dynamics of learning: 'from the language of the home to that of society at large and then to the languages of other peoples (whether learnt at school or college, or by direct experience)'. These words imply that all language learning is the same, regardless of where, when and how it takes place; developmental and 'naturalistic' modes of acquisition (learning the language of the home; learning the languages of other peoples by direct experience) are elided with instructed language acquisition (the languages of other peoples learnt at school or college). One of the foundational texts of the Council of Europe's project *Languages in Education, Languages for Education* claims that the plurilingual approach 'is not to be thought of as a new methodology for the teaching of languages' but rather as a 'change in perspective' (Cavalli et al. 2009: 7). But this contradicts the CEFR, which defines plurilingualism by contrasting it with (individual) 'multilingualism, … the knowledge of a number of languages' (Council of Europe 2001: 4). Given the definition of the plurilingual approach that follows (quoted above), this use of multilingualism is evidently intended to distinguish between the 'integrated' approach denoted by plurilingualism (however we decide to define 'integrated') and the tradition of teaching languages in isolation from one another. From a psycholinguistic point of view, the implication that different approaches to language curricula and language teaching result in different *kinds* rather than different *degrees* of proficiency is, to say the least, open to doubt. But the question remains: How can language teaching in formal educational contexts help to develop learners' plurilingual repertoires? How, in other words, can languages learnt at school or college be an integral part of learners' 'everyday lived language' (García 2017: 18) even as they are being learnt?

The answer to this question is disarmingly simple: by rooting the learning process in spontaneous and authentic use of the target language from the very beginning. The CEFR itself assumes that 'the language learner is in the process of becoming a language user' (Council of Europe 2001: 43). Accordingly, its descriptive scheme refers not to language learners but to user/learners whom it views as 'social agents': 'members of society who have tasks (not exclusively language-related) to accomplish in a given set of circumstances, in a specific environment and within a particular field of action' (Council of Europe 2001: 9). In the great majority of foreign language classrooms across the world, much more than a change of perspective is needed if language learners are to meet this description. It challenges us to develop approaches to teaching and learning that are not only grounded in target language use but engage learners' identities and agency and make use of their existing linguistic repertoires in order to extend them. This is precisely what happens in Scoil Bhríde, where the 'given set of circumstances' is defined by the linguistic diversity of the pupil cohort, the 'specific environment' is the classroom and its community of learners, and the 'particular field of action' is the Primary School Curriculum. Scoil Bhríde's pupils mostly become proficient in Irish and in due course French, and its ELLs become proficient in English. This happens not because they are taught these languages in any traditional sense, but as a result of their active involvement in classroom discourse that is conducted in English, has frequent recourse to Irish and (in Fifth and Sixth Class) French, draws continuously on ELLs' home languages in the ways we have illustrated, and thus helps pupils to develop plurilingual competence as they receive and process curriculum content.

The second problematic aspect of the CEFR's definition of the plurilingual approach has to do with its notion of 'a communicative competence to which all knowledge and experience of language contributes and in which languages interrelate and interact' (Council of Europe 2001: 4). This is clearly a close relative of the concept of linguistic multicompetence, originally defined by Vivian Cook as 'the compound state of a mind with two [or more] grammars' (1991: 112). But what exactly does the CEFR mean by the verbs 'interrelate' and 'interact'? This question encapsulates perhaps the biggest challenge that research into linguistic multicompetence faces. Cook (2002: 11) proposes an 'integration continuum' that runs from total separation of languages in the mind through various degrees of interconnection to total integration; and he suggests that this continuum applies across different aspects of language – phonology, grammar, semantics etc. According to this model, the degree to which different languages are integrated with one another in the individual user/learner's mind will be determined by the typological similarities and differences between them. The CEFR's lack of specificity on these matters threatens to create a great deal of confusion, especially regarding the relation (if any) between the involuntary way in which the mind stores and accesses multiple languages and the way in which languages should be included in curricula and taught in classrooms. The same confusion has arisen in much recent discussion of multicompetence. As Singleton (2016) has pointed out, despite a wealth of psycholinguistic research findings to the contrary, there is a widespread assumption that there are no boundaries between linguistic varieties in the mind. The waters are further muddied by sociolinguists who claim that 'standardized national languages' cannot be defined linguistically, in lexical or grammatical terms, and are thus not linguistic objects (Flores 2013), and by proponents of translanguaging who argue that the authority of national languages leads to the stigmatization of those, especially migrants, whose linguistic practices diverge from the majority (García 2017: 13; for a recent critique, see Cummins 2017).

Setting aside their doubtful validity as descriptions of linguistic and social reality, these views are likely to harm rather than assist immigrant communities. National languages are no doubt difficult to describe in detail and impossible to describe definitively, but their existence is beyond doubt; and it has always been one of the primary functions of education to develop in learners the highest possible levels of literacy, which means focusing on standard varieties. To adopt a different aim for immigrants would be to discriminate against them and thus to violate their human rights. It is undeniable that governments, schools and teachers around the world have frequently failed to ensure that immigrant learners have full linguistic access to education, and that has led to under-achievement, poor job prospects and marginalization. But we shall not remedy this failure by demonizing national languages and insisting that reality should be other than it is. Rather, we must develop a clearer understanding of the relation between communication and (language) learning, and the ways in which learners can extend their linguistic repertoire by making use of the languages they already know. For Scoil Bhríde's teachers, English, Irish, French and ELLs' home languages are discrete. Some home languages are closely related, like Russian, Ukrainian, Polish and Czech; others are typologically distant from one another, like French and Chinese, or Italian and Malayalam; but for purposes of classroom use, each of them is distinct. We have no easy way of knowing how and to what extent the languages in each pupil's repertoire 'interrelate and interact' in her mind. But the use of multiple languages in classroom discourse *always* serves a learning purpose that coincides with curriculum goals and is focused on English or Irish or French or pupils' home languages.

The third problematic aspect of the CEFR's definition of the plurilingual approach is its reference to 'an individual person's experience of language *in its cultural contexts'*, because this seems to imply that learning a new language necessarily entails learning a new culture. A child's acquisition of the language of the home is certainly part of a larger process of socialization and enculturation; his or her developing linguistic proficiency increasingly reflects – is indeed rooted in – the social and cultural practices of the home, the local community and society at large. Similarly, learning a foreign language 'by direct experience' is a matter of living as a member of a community in which the target language is the medium of everyday life; and in this case too, language learning has an unavoidable cultural component. But what about languages that are learnt 'at school or college', especially if learning takes place at a distance from communities of native speakers? As the examples presented in this chapter show, when such learning is rooted in language use, the various languages in play contribute to the development of a learning culture – the term 'community of practice' (Lave and Wenger 1991, Wenger 1998) seems especially apt – in which classroom discourse mediates between curriculum content and the developing plurilingual repertoires of the pupils. ELLs are encouraged to contribute fragments of their home cultures – songs, traditional stories, recipes, family traditions, interesting domestic or social practices and so on. But those fragments add variety, colour and novelty to the gradually expanding stock of knowledge and experience that constitutes the emerging culture of the individual classroom. They may be experienced as new and different, but they are valued for the enrichment they bring and not treated as markers of 'otherness'.

Conclusion

In this chapter we have been concerned with the role that home languages play in oral classroom communication in Scoil Bhríde. In a situation of extreme linguistic diversity, the teacher does not know her pupils' home languages (exceptions may be languages the teacher learnt at school or college, usually French, German, Spanish or Italian). This means that home languages cannot be used in reciprocal communication between teacher and pupils. They can, however, fulfil two important functions in the ongoing learning conversation: they can be used to show the rest of the class how each home language present expresses particular meanings, and they can be drawn on as a source of linguistic information and intuition. Both functions encourage pupils to make comparisons and contrasts between languages; and we hypothesize that constant reference to home languages ensures that they are activated in the minds of their speakers and thus available to support the cognitive processes of learning. All Scoil Bhríde's pupils, including native Irish pupils from English-speaking families, are emergent plurilinguals: all the languages in each pupil's repertoire are an integral part of her 'everyday lived language' (García 2017: 18). By reflecting on the Council of Europe's plurilingual approach as defined in the CEFR, we have sought to indicate how a refined version of the approach might help to shape innovative pedagogical practice. This is something to which we return in Chapter 6.

Classroom talk frames and shapes learning activities, but from the earliest stages of primary education, speech is related to writing – as we have insisted, the development of the highest possible levels of literacy is one of the principal aims of education. In the next chapter we explore the development of pupils' plurilingual literacy.

4

The Development of Plurilingual Literacy

In this chapter we are concerned with the development of pupils' plurilingual literacy. We begin by summarizing the trajectory of literacy development described in the Primary School Curriculum (PSC); we then provide examples of pupils' writing in English, Irish, French and home languages, and we conclude the chapter by returning to the concept of translanguaging and considering the contribution that writing in multiple languages makes to pupils' language awareness and their sense of identity.

The Primary School Curriculum and the development of writing skills

In the PSC, the development of literacy skills in English-medium schools belongs to the teaching of English (Government of Ireland 1999b). For the four curriculum bands (Junior and Senior Infants; First and Second Class; Third and Fourth Class; Fifth and Sixth Class) more than 150 goals are listed under four headings: Receptiveness to language, Competence and confidence in using language; Developing cognitive abilities through language; and Emotional and imaginative development through language. Some goals recur in each strand, for example: providing a classroom environment that encourages writing and affirming pupils' work by displaying it in the classroom; other goals are assigned to more than one heading. In the necessarily selective summary that follows we focus on those goals that best reflect the trajectory of development illustrated by the examples we present later in the chapter.

Under *Receptiveness to language*, the overall goal is to create and foster the impulse to write. In Junior and Senior Infants this entails providing pupils with a print-rich environment and giving them frequent opportunities to write ('scribbling, making attempts at writing, letters and symbols, captions, words and sentences') for different audiences ('oneself, teacher, other children, family, visitors'). In First and Second Class, the teacher should model writing stories, encourage pupils to seek her help in achieving accuracy, explore with them how stories are structured, and let them choose topics to write about and experience writing as a collaborative process. In Third and Fourth Class, the teacher should model writing in different genres – 'writing about a personal experience, writing a letter, writing a description' – and allow her pupils to choose the audience for which to write and the subject and form of their writing. In Fifth and Sixth Class, pupils should express and communicate reactions to reading experiences, experience interesting and relevant writing challenges, and write for an increasingly varied audience.

Under *Competence and confidence in using language*, the overall goal is to develop the ability to write independently. In Junior and Senior Infants, pupils should 'learn to form and name individual letters', 'understand the left–right, top–bottom orientation of writing', write their name, copy letters and words, become aware of capital letters and the full stop, and 'begin to develop conventional spelling of simple words'. In First and Second Class, pupils should 'experience an abundance of oral language activity when preparing a writing task', 'realize that first attempts at writing are not necessarily the finished product and learn to undertake second drafts', 'understand that the conventions of punctuation help to make meaning clearer', 'spell words in a recognizable way based on an awareness of the most common spelling strings and patterns', and 'use approximate spelling as an interim measure in mastering the conventions of spelling'. In Third and Fourth Class, pupils should 'gradually extend the period over which a writing effort is sustained', 'experience varied and consistent oral language activity as a preparation for writing', 'develop an appreciation of how the intended audience should influence the nature of a piece of writing', and 'learn to write with increasing grammatical accuracy through the process of revision and editing'. In Fifth and Sixth Class, pupils should 'write for a sustained length of time', 'write, without redrafting, on a given or chosen topic within certain time constraints', 'use dictionaries and thesauruses to extend and develop vocabulary and spelling', 'explore the possibilities of syntax and sentence structure in reading and writing', and 'take part in co-operative writing activities'.

Under *Developing cognitive abilities through language*, the overall goal is to learn how to clarify thought through writing. In Junior and Senior Infants, pupils should learn to add a name, caption or sentence to a picture they have drawn. In First and Second Class, they should write about something that has been learned, write a simple sentence and add words to extend its meaning, and listen to a story and write down questions to ask about it. In Third and Fourth Class, pupils should read a story and summarize it in their own words, write about an idea to explain it to someone else, write about ideas encountered in other areas of the curriculum, and write down directions on how to perform a particular process. In Fifth and Sixth Class, pupils should explore the differences between written and spoken language, use writing to reflect on and analyse ideas, express and communicate new learning, use notes to summarize reading material, and argue the case in writing for a point of view with which they agree or disagree.

Finally, under *Emotional and imaginative development through writing*, the overall goal is to develop emotional and imaginative life through writing. In Junior and Senior Infants pupils should draw and write about feelings ('happiness, sadness, love, fear'), likes and dislikes, and sensory experiences ('hot, cold, bright, dark, sweet, sour'). In First and Second Class, pupils should express feelings in writing ('happiness, sadness, excitement, pride, anticipation'), write about experiences ('enjoyable, funny, annoying, frightening'), and express in writing likes and dislikes about events and characters in stories and poems. In Third and Fourth Class, pupils should express their reactions to particular experiences in writing, write about experiences and feelings in diary form, write extended stories in book form, and express in writing their reactions to poems and personal reading. In Fifth and Sixth Class, pupils should analyse in writing their reactions to personal experiences, express in writing their reactions to the experiences of others, keep a personal diary, and express and analyse their reactions to poems.

As this summary indicates, in Irish primary schools learning to write is closely associated with self-expression. From an early age, pupils produce stories, diaries, autobiographical texts, poems etc. with gradually increasing linguistic and structural complexity. The PSC expects that writing activities will be framed by exploratory classroom talk and modelled by the teacher. The teacher usually does this by writing on the board, often negotiating the content of what she writes with her pupils; that explains why members of the same class often produce closely similar texts. When pupils read aloud the texts they have written, in whatever language, they feed into further exploratory talk. At the same time, most writing tasks require individual effort and the exercise of creative agency. Learning to write opens up a new world of cognitive and communicative potential that many five- and six-year-olds are keen to explore for themselves outside school, compiling word lists, labelling drawings, writing stories and so on. The individual pupil's ability to create written records is the beginning of critical thinking and lays the foundations for autonomous learning.

The PSC for Irish in English-medium schools specifies many of the same goals as the PSC for English, but it places greater emphasis on listening and speaking than on reading and writing: formal reading in Irish is not expected to begin until Second Class, and the development of what the curriculum calls 'higher reading skills' is saved for the middle classes. In Scoil Bhríde, however, Irish is part of the print-rich environment provided in the Infant classrooms, and Irish is included along with English in pupils' early writing activities. This is partly a consequence of the school's long-established practice of including Irish in classroom discourse as an alternative medium of communication. But it is also a necessary precondition for the inclusion of ELLs' home languages in their early literacy development; for if Irish were allowed to lag significantly behind English, the early inclusion of ELLs' home languages in their literacy development could be seen as discriminating against Irish pupils. It would also work against the development of integrated plurilingual repertoires as described in Chapter 3.

As we noted in Chapter 1, language education professionals in Ireland have been arguing for an integrated language curriculum for more than thirty years. The most recent version of this argument is developed in *Towards an Integrated Language Curriculum in Early Childhood and Primary Education*, a research report by Pádraig Ó Duibhir and Jim Cummins commissioned by the National Council for Curriculum and Assessment (Ó Duibhir and Cummins 2012). Ó Duibhir and Cummins base their argument on Cummins's interdependence hypothesis, which claims that when children learn to read and write in (say) English, they acquire generic skills and learning strategies that they can transfer to other languages. The interdependence hypothesis influenced the new Primary Language Curriculum, introduced for the first two curriculum bands in 2017/2018 (by which time most of the data presented in this book had been collected). The new curriculum envisages interdependence between English and Irish. In its present form it acknowledges the presence of other languages in classrooms but has nothing to say about how they might be included in curriculum delivery; we understand, however, that this limitation is to be addressed in a revision of the curriculum (see also Chapter 6, p. 166 below).

Scoil Bhríde's integrated approach to language education assumes that the processes posited by the interdependence hypothesis operate bi-, even multidirectionally. In Chapter 3 we argued that ELLs' home languages can serve three functions in classroom discourse: as the medium of reciprocal communication between speakers of the same or closely related languages, for purposes of non-reciprocal display (e.g. ELLs can show the rest of the class how to count in their home language), and as a source of intuitive linguistic knowledge that individual pupils can make available to the teacher and the rest of the class. We hypothesize that when these functions are given free rein, home languages remain activated in the minds of ELLs and support the cognitive processes that produce learning, and as they develop proficiency in English and Irish, ELLs gradually transfer cognitive processes to those languages. The inclusion of home languages in the writing activities of the classroom, by contrast, is motivated by the assumption that literacy skills acquired in English can be transferred more or less immediately to Irish and ELLs' home languages, and in due course to French. There are, however, some counter examples – witness the Bosnian pupil whose reading in English improved dramatically once she learnt to read in Bosnian (see Chapter 3, p. 66), and the Hungarian pupil who came to Scoil Bhríde in the final term of Senior Infants and transferred her writing skills in Hungarian to English and Irish (Chapter 2, p. 33).

Some examples of pupils' developing plurilingual writing skills

In Junior Infants pupils learn to recognize simple words and phrases and to form the letters of the alphabet, but it is in Senior Infants that most of them begin to use writing to express meaning, and it is from that year that our earliest examples are taken. The educational publisher Scholastic supports primary schools' efforts to encourage creative writing by printing collections of pupils' work under the title *We Are Writers!* Scoil Bhríde took advantage of this service in 2013, and we conclude our account of the development of writing from First to Sixth Class with one or two examples of the work ELLs contributed to this publication. Throughout the book we use pseudonyms when we name individual pupils. In all other cases we reproduce pupils' work without correction; the texts from *We Are Writers!* were lightly copy-edited prior to publication.

Senior Infants (5+ years old)

From the beginning of Junior Infants, pupils gradually become aware of the plurilingual repertoires of their classmates, but this is based on the spoken language. In Senior Infants they begin to use the written language to refer to themselves, their likes and dislikes, often in combination with drawings, and here too plurilingual repertoires are drawn into the work of the classroom. For example, pupils may draw pictures of fruit, vegetables, healthy food or what they like to eat, adding appropriate labels. In class they do this in English, and for homework ELLs add labels in their home language, while Irish pupils add labels in Irish (Figure 4.1). Some parents of ELLs write down the words or phrases their

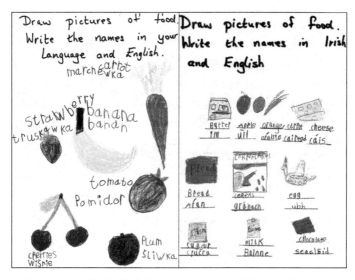

Figure 4.1 Drawings of food labelled in two languages (Senior Infants, 5+ years old).

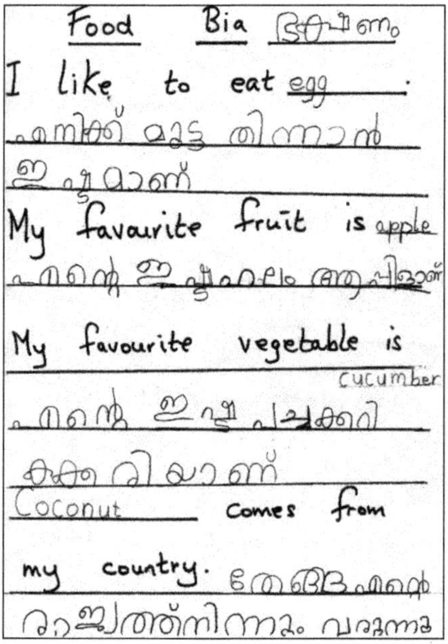

Figure 4.2 Text about food completed in English and translated into Malayalam (Senior Infants, 5+ years old).

daughter needs in her home language and she copies them; others dictate, one letter at a time. The next day pupils share the results of their homework with the rest of the class, reading their labels aloud in English, Irish and home languages. In terms of providing cognitive support for learning, this early inclusion of home languages in the written work of the class is closely similar to the oral use of multiple languages when learning how to count or do simple sums, as described in Chapter 3. Treating Irish as the home language of English-speaking Irish pupils ensures that they too are challenged to produce texts in two languages and thus secure parity of esteem with their ELL classmates. Interestingly, some Irish parents have expressed a renewed interest in learning Irish for their own sake as well as to support their daughters' learning.

In due course pupils produce simple texts following templates provided by the teacher. This may entail completing a series of sentences by adding an appropriate word or phrase, as in Figure 4.2; alternatively, pupils may copy sentences from the board (Figure 4.3). In either case, ELLs add a version of the

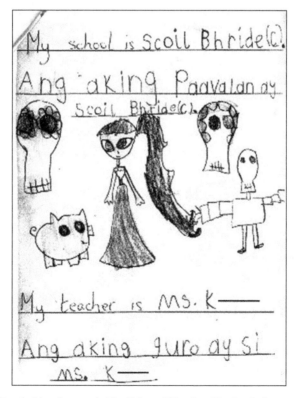

Figure 4.3 Simple identity text in English and Tagalog (Senior Infants, 5+ years old).

text in their home language (Malayalam in Figure 4.2, Tagalog in Figure 4.3), again with parental support. Even at this early stage, knowing that their home language is an area in which they are expert is a powerful motivator and stimulus to further learning.

First Class (6+ years old)

Writing stories in two languages

Aware that much of the language ELLs must learn in order to survive at school is very different from the language used in writing fiction, the language support teacher decided to explore the demands of story writing during three consecutive small-group sessions. As always, these included native English speakers as well as ELLs because all children benefit from the extended opportunity for interaction afforded by working in small groups. The teacher began the first lesson by asking her pupils what is involved in writing a story in English; she then raised the question of writing the story in a different language. One pupil was concerned to know how this would happen if the child did not know how to write in her home language. The group agreed that she could ask a parent or appropriate adult to help her. The content of the story would be decided by the child, but the adult could help with spelling or, if necessary, with writing the entire story in the home language. Another pupil then asked about children who do not have two languages. Discussion led to the realization that all the children and the teacher had access to a second language: Irish. The meaning of the word 'translate' was then considered and the teacher invited each pupil to name the language into which her story would be translated.

In the second lesson the teacher asked the group which words they must think about when writing a story. A Bangla speaker answered: *Who, what, when, where, how and why.* The teacher then asked the pupils to name the story that they planned to write and asked them if they were the original authors. A child whose home language was Isoko answered: *'Goldilocks and the Three Bears'*, and the group agreed that they were not the original authors. A Polish speaker explained that they would rewrite the story, using their own words and making it shorter. The teacher then asked them to identify the steps involved in writing the story. The Isoko speaker said that they needed to talk before writing, and the Bangla speaker added that they had also *discussed and described* what they would write.

In the third lesson the teacher summarized how the children had written their story and revisited some of the vocabulary they had used:

Teacher:	She went into the house without doing something. Bella
Bella:	*Without asking permission*
Teacher:	*What does asking permission mean, Nicki?*
Nicki:	*It means that you're not asking if you can do that*
Teacher:	*Exactly. And then there was another word that somebody came up with down here* [points to a word on the whiteboard]. *Who can read it?*
Anya:	*Returned*
Teacher:	*Returned. Why did we use the word 'returned'? … Nicki, what does it mean?*
Nicki:	*Because the Three Bears returned*
Teacher:	*Yes, what does 'returned' mean? What is that word? What does 'returned' mean, Eva?*
Eva:	*Em, like you're going on a walk and then you came back?*

The teacher then asked for a volunteer to read the story from the whiteboard, once again drawing pupils' attention to the words identified at the beginning of the second lesson. Figure 4.4 shows part of the story as written by one pupil, in English and Congolese French.

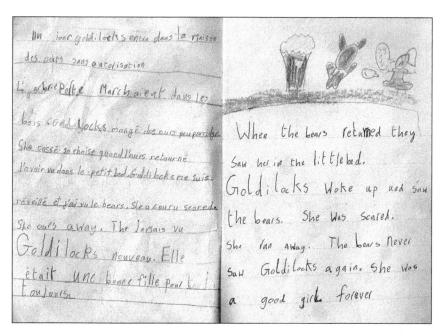

Figure 4.4 Part of 'Goldilocks and the Three Bears' in English and Congolese French (First Class, 6+ years old).

How ELLs in First Class said they learned to write in their home language

A pupil of Spanish/Irish parentage wrote Spanish unaided in class and then translated what she had written, pointing to each sentence in turn: *That one says my hair is brown. I have a nice friend. My Mam is nice to me.* When asked who had helped her learn to write in Spanish, she said: *I already knew … my Granny showed me when I was three and she started writing my first letter and then I just started writing sentences in Spanish.* Another Second Class pupil who was in her third month in Scoil Bhríde, having arrived from Israel the previous September, explained how she learned to write in English and in Hebrew: *My Mam learned me* [to write English] *and* [I learned to write in Hebrew] *when I was at school in Israel.*

We Are Writers!

Our first example from the book *We Are Writers!* is by a First Class pupil who started at Scoil Bhríde in Junior Infants with no English. Her parents were strongly committed to speaking Spanish at home. When the pupil wrote this poem, she was in her third year at Scoil Bhríde.

Big Cats

Big cats are wild animals.
They are very different to cats you have at home.
They are not pets.
They are predators and live in the wild.
They are carnivores which means they eat meat.
They have sharp claws and big jaws.
You can see them in zoos.
Here are some examples of big cats: tigers, lions, cheetahs and pumas.
Never go near big cats.
You never know if they are hungry or not!

Our second example, written by a pupil whose home language is Malayalam, is another compilation of facts, this time about the planets and space:

The Universe

The universe is made up of eight planets. They are Mercury, Venus, Earth, Mars,
Saturn, Uranus and Neptune. They all orbit the sun. Comets also orbit the sun.
On the planet Venus there is a landscape of rolling plains, mountains and volcanoes.
Mars is very hot and it has a place called Mariner Valley.
Jupiter has four moons called Ganymede, Calisto, Io and Europa.

Saturn's rings are made out of rock and ice.

Neptune has many storms and the Roman god of the sea is called Neptune.

We live on planet Earth.

Pluto was the ninth planet a long time ago. Now it has disappeared and there are eight planets in the universe.

When you throw a ball into the air gravity pulls it down. There is no gravity on the moon so everything floats.

The Andromeda Galaxy is far away. Its light takes two million years to reach us on earth.

I love learning about space.

Second Class (7+ years old)

In Second Class, teachers introduce a more disciplined approach to written composition in English. Pupils choose a topic, write a first draft, present it to the teacher for correction, revise the draft and then read their composition aloud to the class. Parents continue to make an essential contribution to the writing of dual-language texts, which gradually become more elaborate as pupils' ability to produce written text in English increases. The requirement that they read their work aloud in a combination of languages – English, Irish and/or a home language – reminds pupils that they are always writing for an audience. Referring to themselves as authors and having their written work valued and displayed in the classroom undoubtedly motivates them to greater efforts and encourages autonomous learning. As their literacy skills in their home language increase, so does their awareness that they possess linguistic knowledge and skills that are unique to them or that they share with a minority of other pupils. This too contributes to the growth of self-esteem.

Interactive preparation for creative writing

The approach to story writing introduced by the language support teacher in First Class is also used by the class teacher in Second Class. A brainstorming session determines the general theme of their story; then the teacher asks individual pupils about sub-themes and characters in an effort to help them clarify and develop their thoughts. She uses whatever opportunities present themselves to draw attention to similarities between languages; for example, a Bangla speaker is writing about a girl with magic shoes and the teacher comments on the similarity between the English word *shoes* and its Bangla equivalent, *jutā*. Another pupil translates orally into her home language, Hungarian, what she has written in English, and the teacher points to the similarity between the English word *cardigan* and its Hungarian equivalent *kardigán*. A Spanish speaker explains that she knows how to say what she wants to say in Spanish but is unsure about spelling. Some children make a written note of their ideas in both English and their home language.

'The Leprikon and the Dragon'

When interviewed by her class teacher, a Russian speaker explains the procedures involved in story writing: she first chooses a topic and then writes it on a piece of paper using the words she has written as part of her initial brainstorming; next she brings it to her teacher who *puts a line that it's a mistake and you make sure you make your capital letters right, like, names or places*; finally she writes the finished story *slowly and neatly* on another piece of paper. She gives a brief outline of her story for young children, 'The Leprikon [leprechaun] and the Dragon', explaining that she intended to write about a leprechaun but as the story progressed she *fitted in* a dragon. She says that her favourite part of the story is the funniest and happens when the leprechaun and the dragon go to heaven. When asked why she likes creative writing, she replies: *I like closing my eyes and imagining all the story … I like writing a lot … but the first page I write fast, like, to not forget it but on the other page I write it neatly and all of that.*

The Leprikon and the Dragon

> *Once upon a time there lived a leprikon. He lived* [sic] *to play but all he had is a pot of gold and a cat named Puss. He was black and soft. One day the leprikon was looking for his pot of gold. He couldint find it. He looked out the window. He saw a dragon with his pot. He was very angry. He went to the dragon's cave and stole the pot of gold. When the dragon got angry too, he went to the fields where the leprikon was with the pot of gold. They fighted. they for a long time in the fields fighted on until they were dead. A lot of people found them lying dead. When the leprikon and the Dragon were in heaven they promised they will never fight again.*

'The Viking who wanted a pet'

A Spanish speaker outlined her approach: *First you do a brainstorm and you write your topic, and maybe you could write as many words as you can that kind of describe the story, and then after you're finished your brainstorm you do your first draft.* The teacher asks what is in the first draft, to which she replies: *Writing.* The pupil identifies correction as the next step and explains that *you go through the story and maybe if a … you can change sentences if they don't really make sense, you can change it … bring it to the teacher … read it to her.* In the second draft there is *some writing and maybe you could change some of the spelling mistakes … you could change a bit of the story,* and finally *you read it to the class.*

The Viking who wanted a pet

Once upon a time, a long time ago, there was a Viking. He had always wanted a pet. And do you know what pet he wanted? He didn't want a dog or a cat or a hamster. He wanted a dinosaur! One day he was outside playing with his friends. 'David, come in' said his sister Sarah. 'It's raining!' 'Coming' said David. 'I want a pet' said David. 'Ok' said Sarah. 'Let's go to the pet store.' So they went. 'Would you like a goldfish? 'No' said David. 'I want a dinosaur' said David. 'A dinosaur?' said Sarah. 'Dinosaurs are extinct' said Sarah. 'You can't have a dinosaur.' 'What else would you like?' said Sarah. 'I don't know' said David. 'What about a cat?' 'NO' said David. 'Let's go home and think about it' said Sarah. So they went. When they got home David thought. Suddenly he screamed 'I want [a] dinosaur.' 'Sshh! said Sarah. The next day they went to the pet shop again. David looked around. 'Look' said David a dinosaur. 'It's not a dinosaur it's a lizard.' 'What's that' said David. 'It's a parrot' said Sarah. 'Do you know what' said David. Sarah stepped forward hoping that he would not say he wanted a dinosaur. 'I want a parrot' said David. 'Ok' said Sarah. 'Can we have this parrot?' said Sarah. Yes said the shopkeeper as he gave some parrot food and a cage, when they got home Sarah got two small bowls and filled one with water and the other with parrot food. She put them in the cage and then she put the parrot in. I will call you Polly said David. And every day he came to play with Polly and help Sarah with the feeding. The End.

What some Second Class pupils said about learning to write in their home language

One pupil reads, in English and Russian, from the book she has written herself and in which she has covered a wide range of topics – herself, her family, favourite food, animals, television programmes, school, gardening and much more. She says that she speaks Russian with her parents and English with her older sister who is in Fifth Class and *learns her new things*. She explains that she wrote her book in school and at home. While she can read Russian, she says that her mother *wrote it in Russian but I did everything myself and I made it up*. When asked if she likes working with her mother she answers: *I like doing things by myself but not, like, Russian. I do Russian with my Mam but I like doing everything else myself*.

A Latvian pupil reads from the book she has written, first in English and then in Latvian. She explains that she and her parents speak Latvian at home, but she got no help when writing Latvian: she *just guessed how to write it*. She says that her parents praised her Latvian writing when she showed it to them. She likes spelling long words, and both her class teacher and the language support teacher agree that she has good memory skills. When asked why she chose to write about rainbows, she answers that it is because of the colours. She can name the colours of the rainbow without hesitation in English and Latvian.

A Polish pupil reads from the book she has written in English and Polish. She explains that she wrote the English text in school and copied her mother's translation of the text into Polish. She says she can read Polish but is still learning to write it so needs help. She also says that because she uses English in school, she sometimes forgets how to speak in Polish.

The example of Hanna

Hanna, whose home language is Hungarian, came to Scoil Bhríde late in the Senior Infant year with no knowledge of English. At first, she appeared to make very slow progress and alternated between clinging and withdrawn behaviour. At the beginning of Second Class, after almost fourteen months, she made a breakthrough into writing in English, Irish and Hungarian. Having visited a farm on a school tour, she wrote her impressions in English that evening. The following day she read her text aloud to the language support teacher, who transcribed it and made a number of corrections. Both texts are shown in Figure 4.5. Hanna is still a long way behind her peers, but she is showing signs of confidence in producing fluent discourse, however deficient her morphosyntax may be. Interestingly, at this time Hanna started to become very interested in the grammatical differences between languages, asking why sentences in Irish sometimes begin with 'Is í' and sometimes with 'Is é'. When it was explained that some words are feminine

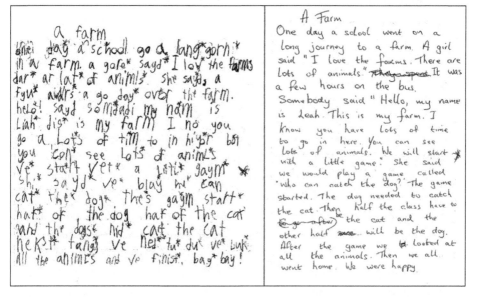

Figure 4.5 Report of a visit to a farm written by a Hungarian pupil (Second Class, 7+ years old) and transcribed by teacher when read aloud by pupil.

and others masculine, she expressed amazement that inanimate objects could be described in this manner: *How can this be?* Her reaction is not surprising: Hungarian lacks grammatical gender and gender-specific pronouns.

The Second Class diary

In an effort to establish links between classroom learning and his pupils' lives outside school, one Second Class teacher introduced a class diary, an A4 book with board covers. Each day a different pupil took the diary home and wrote in English and their home language about what they did after school. Again, many pupils needed help from their parents to write in their home language. Each day the pupil who had taken the diary home the previous day read aloud what she had written for her classmates. The pupils responded very positively to this initiative, taking particular pride in reading aloud in their home language. The parents of the only Irish child in the class were very enthusiastic about the diary, reporting that they were happy to use this initiative to refresh their own knowledge of the Irish language. In effect, they were learning with their child (Figure 4.6).

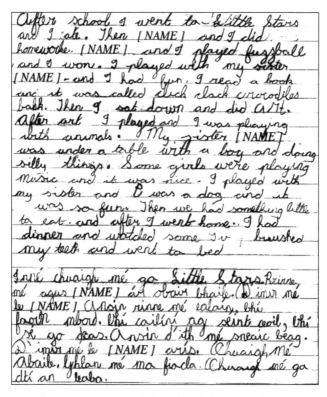

Figure 4.6 Dual-language text in English and Irish (Second Class, 7+ years old). This pupil was the only Irish girl in her class.

We Are Writers!

Our Second Class example from *We Are Writers!* is by a pupil whose home language is Yoruba.

Autumn

A *Actually pretty nice and cosy*
U *Umbrellas are needed a lot*
T *The leaves fall from the trees*
U *Under the sun it is windy*
M *Many people like autumn*
N *Nobody hates Autumn*

Third Class (8+ years old)

Texts in three languages

By Third Class some ELLs can write in their home language without parental support. They also begin to write texts in three languages: English, Irish and their home language. Hanna, referred to in the previous section, became an enthusiastic writer in Irish, English and Hungarian. When asked which language she chose to write in first, she answered: *Gaeilge* [Irish] … *because I just like the language.* Hanna provides us with two examples of texts written in Irish, English and Hungarian. Referring to the first example, she explained that she discussed and wrote the Irish text in the language support class and the English and Hungarian texts at home. When asked to read the texts aloud in class, she read Hungarian first, Irish second and English third.

> *Bhí mé sa phairc inné. Bhí mé ag luascadh ar an luascán. Tá ag Daidí ag icspheil. Tá Mamaí ag imirt leadóige. Tá Heni ag scátáil. Tá cat ag siúl. Feicim an eitleog agus a loch. Feicim Heni agus madra ag súgradh. Feicim mé ar gráinneog agus iorra rua.*

> *I am in the park. I'm swinging on the swing. Dad [is] basketballing. Mum is tennising. Leni's skating. The cat is walking. I see the kite and the lake. I see Leni and a dog playing. I see a hachog [hedgehog] and a squerrel [squirrel].*

> *Én most a parkland vagyok. Hintazok a hintán. Ara kosár labdocik. Anya keniszerzik. Leni gökouzik. A macska sétál. látam a sárkanyt és a tavat. látam Lenit és egy kutyat jatscani. latok egy sünt és egy mokut.*

The second trio of texts retains Hanna's titles. For homework the teacher had asked the class to write a short text in English, encouraging ELLs to add a version in their home language. Hanna also chose to write an Irish version, and her title is designed to remind her teacher that this is extra work freely undertaken.

Not (Homework)

Bhí mé sa ghairdín. Bhí mé ag luascadh ar an luascán. Hanna arsa Mamí, Bhí ar an pancóga sa chistin. Rith mé sa chistin. Bhí mamí subh sa pancoga agus Rollaigh sí suas na pancóga. Ith mé sa pancóga agus ól mé. Rith mé sa ghairdín agus leamh ar an luascán. Bhí Mamí uachta reoite sa ghairdín. Is maith lime uachta reoite. Hanna arsa an Leni. Rith mé sa Leni. Rith mé sa ghairdín arís. Bhí uachta reoite ag imithe.

In English

I'm in the garden. I'm swinging on the swing. Hanna, said Mum there pancac in the cicen. Mum puted jam in my pancec and then she rolld the pancac. I ate all of the pancac and I drank. I ran to the garden a read on the swing. Mum briot ice cream to the garden. I like ice cream. Hanna said Leni. I ran to Leni. I ran to the garden again. My ice cream was melted.

In Hungary

A kertben uagyak. Hintazok a hintán. Hanna manta anya uan palacsinta a kanyhorba. Anya lekvart rakot a palacsintámba és fel gargete a palacsintát. Megetem az egész palacsintát és itam. A kertben futatam és olvastam a hintan. Anya faggt hazot a kertbe. Szeretem a fagyit. Hanna monta Leni. Oda futatam Lenihez. Visca futatam a kertbe. A faggim elolvat.

For purposes of comparison, here are three texts written by a Filipino pupil. She wrote the English and Irish texts unaided, but her parents helped her with the Tagalog text:

Bhí mé sa bhaile. Tá Mamaí agus Daidí sa seomra suí. Tá Daidí ar an ríomhaire agus bhí Mamaí ag scríobh ar an leabhar. Tá mo deartháir ina chodhladh sa seomra codlata. Bhí mé sa gháirdín agus bhí mé ag luascadh ar an luascán. Agus ansin faoin duilleoga tá an grainneog! 'gráinneog!' dúirt mé. Tá mé agus an gráinneog ag súgradh ar an luascán arís sa gháirdín.

I was at home. Mammy and Daddy are in the living room. Daddy is on the computer and Mammy is writing on the book. My brother is sleeping in his bedroom. I was in the garden and I was swinging on the swings. And then under the leafs there was a hedgehog! 'Hedgehog!' I said. Me and the hedgehog were playing on the swing in the garden again.

Ako ay nasa bahay. Si Mama at si Papa nasa silid tanggapan. Gumagamit ng kumpyuter si Papa at sumusulat sa Mama sa libro. Ang kuya ko ay natutulog sa kanyang kwarto. Ako ay nasa hardin at naglalaro sa pag-indayog. At pagkatapos ang nasa ilalim ng dahoon ay parkupino! 'parkupino!' sabi ko. Ako at ang parkupino ay naglaro sa pag-indayog sa hardin ulit.

This pupil's English text could easily have been written by a native speaker; Hanna's English texts, on the other hand, are clearly at an earlier stage of development, though they show that she has made significant progress since First Class (cf. her report on the farm visit in Figure 4.5).

Irish children write texts in three languages

As we have seen, Irish pupils earn parity of esteem by writing dual-language texts in English and Irish to set beside the texts that ELLs produce in English and their home language. But what are they to do when ELLs start to produce texts in three languages? Some of them get help from parents, older siblings or a neighbour to produce text in a third language. One pupil, for example, presented work in English, Irish and Spanish:

Teacher: *How were you able to write it in Spanish?*
Pupil: *My Nanna helped me and my cousin helped me with this* [points to labelled drawings]
Teacher: *And why did you pick Spanish?*
Pupil: *Because my ... nobody else in my family knew how to speak another language*
Teacher: *Oh right! And what attracted you to Spanish rather than French or German or Mandarin or some other language?*
Pupil: *I just thought it would be nice and ... yeah technically just nice*
Teacher: *And would you like to be able to speak another language?*
Pupil: *Yeah*

Collaborative writing

Dual-language texts are sometimes written collaboratively. When more than one home language is involved, the text may be written first in English and then successive paragraphs are written in different home languages. Figure 4.7 shows a story about a snowman written in Romanian and English by two Third Class pupils.

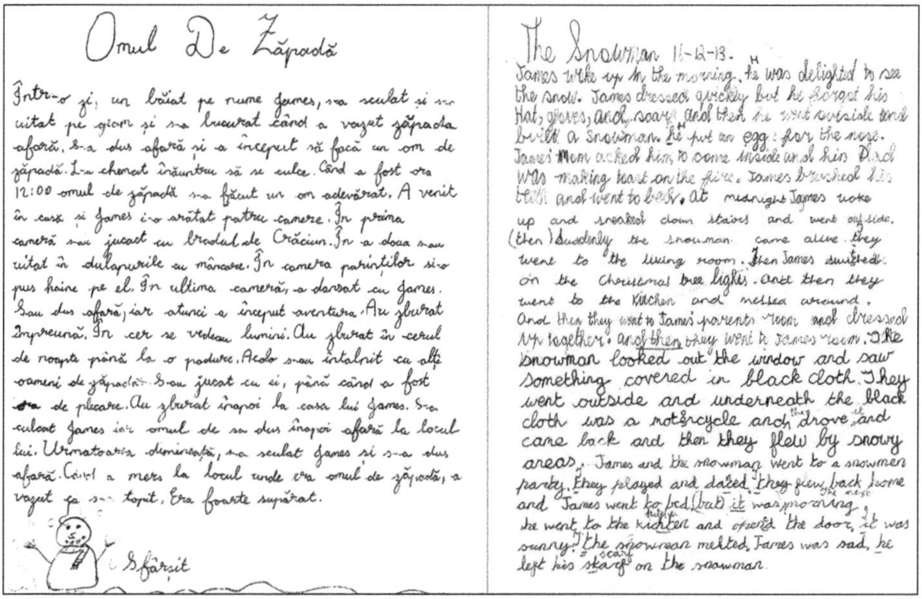

Omul De Zăpadă

Într-o zi, un băiat pe nume James, s-a sculat și s-a uitat pe geam și s-a bucurat când a vazut zăpada afară. S-a dus afară și a început să facă un om de zăpadă. L-a chemat înăuntru să se culce. Când a fost ora 12:00 omul de zăpadă s-a făcut un om adevărat. A venit în casă și James i-o arătat patru camere. În prima cameră s-au jucat cu bradul de Crăciun. În a doua s-au uitat în dulapurile cu mâncare. În camera părinților si-o pus haine pe el. În ultima cameră, a dansat cu James. S-au dus afară, iar atunci a început aventura. Au zburat împreună. În cer se vedeau lumini. Au zburat în cerul de noapte până la o padure. Acolo s-au întalnit cu alți oameni de zăpadă. S-au jucat cu ei, până când a fost ora de plecare. Au zburat înapoi la casa lui James. S-a culcat James iar omul de sa dus înapoi afară la locul lui. Urmatoarea dimineață, s-a sculat James și s-a dus afară. Când a mers la locul unde era omul de zăpadă, a vazut ca s-a topit. Era foarte supărat.

Sfârșit

The Snowman 11-12-13.

James woke up in the morning. He was delighted to see the snow. James dressed quickly but he forgot his Hat, gloves, and scarf and then he went outside and built a snowman. He put an egg for the nose. James' Mom asked him to come inside and his Dad was making toast on the fire. James brushed his teeth and went to bed. at midnight James woke up and sneaked down stairs and went outside. (then) Suddenly the snowman came alive. they went to the living room. Then James switched on the Christmas tree lights. and then they went to the Kitchen and messed around. And then they went to James's parents room and dressed up together. and then they went to James room. The snowman looked out the window and saw something covered in black cloth. They went outside and underneath the black cloth was a motorcycle and they drove it and came back and then they flew by snowy areas. James and the snowman went to a snowmen party. They played and danced. They flew back home and James went to bed. (but) it was the next morning. he went to the kitchen and opened the door, it was sunny. The snowman melted. James was sad. he left his scarf on the snowman.

Figure 4.7 Story about a snowman written collaboratively in Romanian and English by Third Class pupils (8+ years old). The English text has been written by different hands.

We Are Writers!

Our Third Class example from *We Are Writers!* is a story written in English and Romanian:

The Giant's Last Journey

Once upon a time there was a terrible giant called Scamper. He was very angry and naughty.

One day he decided to go into the village. He squashed a horse, and everyone kept saying 'Naughty giant'.

Then a clever girl remembered that she had a sleeping potion. So she put it into the jelly. Then the big giant came and started to eat the jelly. He quickly fell asleep.

Then all the people that lived in the village came to help. They all put the giant on the wooden raft. They pushed Scamper into the sea and he floated away while sleeping. Everyone was cheering and waving tissues.

A fost odată că niciodată un uriaș teribil care îl chema Scamper. El a fost foarte rău și nervos!

El a decis să meargă într-un lac. Uriașul a sărit pe case. Toată lumea tot âi spunea uriaș rău. Dupaea o fată deșteaptă și-a amintit ca a avut o porțiunie de adormit după acea fata deștiaptă a pus porțiunia în măncarea lui. Când uriașul a mâncat o cât ai zice peşte a picat pe jos să doarmă. După acea toţi oameni care aveau casele distruse din causa uriaşului au ajutato să puna uriaşul pe o scândură. Au înpins pe Scamperm în ocean. El plutea pe apă şi toţi strigau şi fluturau şerveţele.

Fourth Class (9+ years old)

Adopting a collaborative approach to writing in different genres has proved to be a very effective way of pushing children to use more complex language in language support classes. In this relaxed setting, the more linguistically advanced pupils can contribute vocabulary that they might be reluctant to use in the mainstream classroom, and this supports the development of their less advanced peers. One language support teacher wanted to focus on the differences between factual reporting and creative fiction. She illustrated the former by recounting an accident that had befallen one of the teachers when she was trying to cook an egg in the microwave in the staffroom. The teacher involved was their own class teacher, so the pupils listened with rapt attention and had no difficulty recalling and discussing the sequence of events and accompanying details. They were able to reconstruct the report, taking turns to narrate the successive steps in its unfolding. Even though the group comprised only six pupils and there was no acoustic need for amplification, they used a microphone to deliver their contribution: the teacher had discovered that using a microphone increased both their confidence and their engagement.

Switching to creative fiction, the language support teacher showed the children a poster depicting a boy and a house and containing the opening words of a story:

> *Jim ducked down. 'I don't like the sound of that,' he said to himself. He stood there listening. He could hear creaking.*

Starting with these sentences, the group gradually developed the story, suggesting ideas, discussing possibilities and constructing sentences. When they were happy with their efforts the language support teacher wrote the story in a large book:

> *Jim ducked down. 'I don't like the sound of that,' he said to himself. He stood there listening. He could hear creaking. The gate was moving. He pushed it open slowly and he crept up to the front door. He opened the door slowly. It creaked. Jim was so scared. He wanted to run home. But he also wanted to see …*
>
> *He peeked in. It was so dark. There was dust everywhere. There were lots of spider webs. All over the place! Suddenly he heard a noise – a terrifying noise! A*

horrible scream followed by sobbing. He looked around. What could he do? He ran up the stairs. The noise was coming after him. Closer and closer. He tried to run silently but then … Bang! He fell and down, down he fell … into a horrible scary basement. His leg was bleeding. He was shaking. He began to cry. He looked around. There was a big black box in front of him. Into the box went Jim. Closer and closer came the noise … Oh no …!

It was a big bright open room. It was magic. Puff! Jim disappeared and in a minute he was back at his own home.

*I'm **never** going into empty houses again! Ever, thought Jim.*

The pupils were then asked to write the part of the story that they liked best. Having constructed the story through the medium of English, they were free to write this in the language(s) of their choice. The following day, pupils read their favourite section of the story to their classmates in their home language.

Development of vocabulary and longer texts produced

In Fourth Class, the English texts produced by native and non-native speakers alike – homework but also unaided spontaneous writing – provide ample evidence of an increasingly diverse vocabulary and an ability to use more complex structures. Pupils' written work in Irish and in their home languages shows similar development. The following two stories were written, unaided, at the beginning of Fourth Class, by pupils for whom Irish was their third language:

Sá Phairc

Inniu an Mháirt. Inné an Luan. Amárach an Cheadaoin. An Mháirt chuaigh mé go dtí an phairc. Bhí mo mhamaí agus mo dheirfiúr agus mo mhadra in aice liom. Bhí mé ag rothaíocht agus thit mé ar an talamh. Bhris mé mo chos, mo lámh agus mo rúitín. Rith mo mhamaí agus mo dheirfiúr agus mo mhadra chugam. Ghlaoigh mo mhamaí ar an dhochtúir. Dúirt an dhochtúir 'go raibh sé ag teacht'. Tar éis tamaill chuaigh mé go dtí an ospidéal leis an dhochtúir. Thug an dhochtúir buuidéal leighis do mo mhamaí. chuaigh mé abhaile. An Chéadaoin tháinig an dhochtúir go dtí mo theach. 'Conas tá tú Nóra' arsa an dhochtúir. Dúirt mé ' taim níos fearr' agus thug an dhochtúir buidéal leighis orm. Ar a naoi a chlog bhí mé ina chodladh).

[Our translation:

In the Park

Today is Tuesday. Yesterday was Monday. Tomorrow will be Wednesday. I went to the park on Tuesday. My mammy, my brother and my dog were with me. I was cycling and I fell on the ground. I broke my foot, my hand and my ankle. My mammy, my brother and my dog ran to me. My mammy called the doctor. The doctor said he was coming. After a while I went to the hospital with the doctor. The doctor gave (a bottle of) medicine to my mammy. I went home. On Wednesday the doctor came to my house. 'How are you, Nicole?' said the doctor. I said 'I am better' and the doctor gave me medicine. After a while I read. At nine o'clock I was asleep.]

Mo Bhreithlá

Bhí mo bhriethlá inniu. Chuigh mé ar scoil. Scríobh mé i mo chóipleabhar agus léamh mé sceal. Ar a trí a clog chuigh mé abhaile. Doscail mé an doras agus chuir mé mo mhála ar an tolg. Shuigh mé ar an gcathaoir agus rinne mé an obair bhaile. Dhún mé an leabhar ar a cúig a clog. Shiúil mamaí sa seomra suí. Bhí sí ag sásta. D'fheach sí amach an fhinneog. An maith leat dul ag siúil sa phairc? Dúirt mé, ceart go leor agus chuigh mé, mamaí agus mo dheartháir sa phairc. Thug mé aran do na lacha. Chonaic mé an fear agus bhí sé ag canadh. D'éist mé leis ar gceol. Bhí sé go hálainn. Ghlaigh mamaí orm. Chuigh mé abhaile ar a sé a clog. Bhí ocras orm ansin. Thosaigh Mamaí ag ullmhú an dinnéir. Tar éis tamall, bhí mo dinnéar reidh. D'ith mé scealloga, citseap, prataí agus borgaire. Ní maith liom an prataí ach bhí sé go deas. Dól mé liomanaid freisin. Fuair Mamaí glothach agus uachtar-reoite sa chuisneoir, bhí sé go blasta! Ar a seacht a clog, bhí mé i mo chodladh sa leaba.

[Our translation:

My Birthday

My birthday was today. I went to school. I wrote in my copy and I read a story. At three o'clock I went home. I opened the door and put my schoolbag on the sofa. I sat on the chair and did my homework. I shut the book at five o'clock. Mammy walked into the sitting room. She was happy. She looked out the window. Would you like to walk in the park? I said I would and Mammy, my brother and I went to the park. I gave bread to the ducks. I saw a man singing. I listened to the music. It was beautiful. Mammy called me. I went home at six o'clock. I was hungry then. Mammy began preparing the dinner. After a while the dinner was ready. I ate chips, ketchup, potatoes and a burger. I don't like potatoes but they were nice. I drank lemonade as well. Mammy took jelly and ice-cream from the fridge. It was tasty. At seven o'clock I was asleep in bed.]

One Fourth Class teacher collected many examples of poetry and stories that pupils wrote spontaneously in English, Irish and home languages as the Christmas holidays approached. A speaker of Urdu wrote a bilingual poem in English and Irish; a Filipino pupil translated a Christmas carol into Tagalog; a Romanian pupil filled six pages of her copybook with a story in English in which several of the characters speak Romanian (Figure 4.8); a Kurdish pupil wrote a

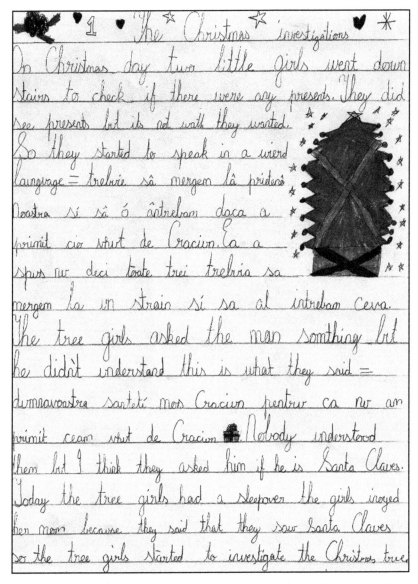

Figure 4.8 First page of a six-page Christmas story in English and Romanian (Fourth Class, 9+ years old).

story in which the two principal characters speak in several languages; an Irish pupil wrote in English and Spanish, a language she liked and was learning with help from a neighbour; and a German speaker wrote a story in English and Irish about what happened to an Irish child who didn't know English when she attended school in England (Figure 4.9).

Figure 4.9 A Christmas story that uses English and Irish (Fourth Class, 9+ years old).

We Are Writers!

Our Fourth Class example from *We Are Writers!* was written by a pupil whose home language is Malayalam and who came to Scoil Bhríde as a Junior Infant. She was chosen to read her story at the book launch. When asked by the master of ceremonies why she wanted to write in Irish, she replied: *I just felt inspired and I really wanted to write in Irish because I know how to write in English but I really wanted to try Irish.* When interviewed with a group of her classmates, she told Déirdre Kirwan that learning Irish was fun. When she first came to Ireland as a child she thought that English was the only language people spoke: *So when they introduced Irish I thought it was interesting to know another language besides English. It sounded a bit like Malayalam* (though she quickly realized that it wasn't the same). She believed that having more than one language improves your *ability to learn languages: When you go to different countries you'll know more, and you'll be happy with what you've got. If you want to talk to a person, you'll have a lot of languages in your head; it improves your stamina and your abilities for learning languages.*

Conas Atá Tú?

Tá mé go hiontach go raibh maith agat.

   Chuaigh mé go dtí siopa na mbuataisí ar an Luan. Cheannaigh mé buataisí dubha agus bhí siad go deas.

Tar éis tamaill, chuaigh me go Penney's. Cheannaigh me sparán, bábóg, muince agus gúna bándearg.

Tar éis tamaill, shiúil mé agus Mamaí go Burger King. D'ith mé borgaire agus sceallóga. D'ól me cóc freisin. Bhí an-spórt againn.

Ach! Ar an Déardaoin, bhí mé tinn!

Shuigh mé ar an gcathaoir. Scríobh mé scéal. Shiúil mé ar mo mhála. Ní fhaca mé an peann. Thit mé ar an úrlár. Bhí mo shrón ag cur fola.

'A Mhamaí!'

Rith Mamaí isteach sa seomra suí.

Ghlaoigh sí ar an dochtúir. Tháinig an dochtúir go dtí an teach.

'Ó, a Ria! An bhfuil do shrón ag cur fola?'

'Tá mo shrón ag cur fola agus tá pian i mo shrón freisin. Bhrúigh mé mo shrón.'

Shiúil an dochtúir go dtí an tolg. Ní fhaca sé an mála. Thit sé ar an úrlár.

'Ó! Tá pian i mo chos,' arsa an dochtúir.

Bhí Mamaí crosta.

'A Ria! Cuir an mála sin sa seomra codlata anois.'

'Tá brón orm a Mhamaí.'

'Déan deifir Ria.'

Tar éis tamaill, rinne Mamaí tae. Thug Mamaí tae don dochtúir.

'Go raibh maith agat,' arsa an dochtúir.

Bhí náire orm.

Bhí an Déardaoin go huafásach!

[Our translation:

How are you?

I went to the shoe shop on Monday.

I bought black boots and they were nice.

After a while I went to Penny's. I bought a purse, a doll, a necklace and a pink dress.

After a while Mammy and I walked to Burger King. I ate a burger and chips. I drank Coke as well. We really enjoyed ourselves.

But! On Thursday I was sick!

I sat on a chair. I wrote a story. I walked on my bag. I didn't see the pen. I fell on the floor. My nose was bleeding.

'Mammy!'

Mammy ran into the sitting room.

She called the doctor. The doctor called to the house.

'Oh Ria! Is your nose bleeding?'

'My nose is bleeding and it's painful as well because I banged it.'

The doctor walked over to the couch. He didn't see the bag. He fell on the floor.

'Oh! I've a pain in my foot,' said the doctor.

Mammy was cross.

'Ria! Put that bag in the bedroom now!'

'I'm sorry Mammy.'

'Hurry up Ria!'

After a while Mammy made tea. Mammy gave tea to the doctor.

'Thank you,' said the doctor.

I was ashamed.

It was a dreadful Thursday!]

Fifth Class (10+ years old)

French is introduced in Fifth Class and immediately takes its place alongside English, Irish and ELLs' home languages. Learning how to describe the weather in French, based on modelling by the teacher, is reinforced by the production of texts in three or four languages:

Le temps

Au nord, il pleut, il y a des nuages, il y a du vent, il fait froid et il fait mauvais.

Sa tuaiscesrt, tá sé ag cur báistí, tá sé fuar, tá an talamh fluich agus tá sé scamallach. Tá sé gaofar agus tá an spéir dorcha. Níl tintreach agus toirneach ann ach níl sé te.

In the north, it's raining, it's cold and damp, the ground is soaking and the clouds are dark and the wind is strong.

Au nord il pleut
Sa tuaisceart tá sé fliuch
In north it is raining
In nord plouă.

A l'oest il y a du vent.
San iarthar tá sé gaofar.
In west it is windy.
In vest este vânt.

Au sud il fait beau.

Sa deisceart tá an ghrian ag taitneamh.

In sought it is sunny and cloudy.

In sud este inorat cu soare

A l'est est nuggeux

San oir-thear tá sé ag scamallach

French was also included in a module on the topic 'My house': pupils described their homes in English, Irish, home languages and French (Figure 4.10). What

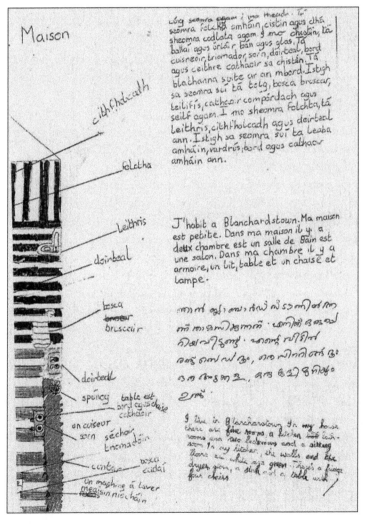

Figure 4.10 'My house' described in four languages: Irish, French, Malayalam, English (Fifth Class, 10+ years old).

they wrote in French was negotiated in interaction with the teacher in the same way as English and Irish texts had been negotiated since First Class.

We Are Writers!

The Fifth Class example from *We Are Writers!* is by a pupil who enrolled in Senior Infants when she arrived in Ireland from China. She spoke Cantonese at home, where she also learned to write Chinese. Her text is one of the longest in the book, and it shows a well-developed capacity for sustained narrative invention. Clearly, her proficiency in English will be no obstacle to her continued educational success.

My nightmare

'Mum, can I go to the fortune-teller please?' I pleaded, on arrival at the carnival.

'Oh, alright. But you must meet me back at the parking lot in half an hour' said Mum.

After that Mum went to the coffee shop and I went to the fortune-teller. When I arrived there, I saw nobody at the front entrance and I thought it was a bit strange. When I went in I saw an old lady with a big, black clock behind her.

'No wonder nobody else came!' I muttered to myself.

'Now please sit down and put your hand out in front of the crystal' said the old lady.

I did as I was told. Then the old lady looked closely at the crystal.

'I can see your future very clearly but you will find out when it is the time for you to rest' said the old lady slowly.

I didn't know what she meant and I thought it was just a waste of time but I said thank you anyway and I just went off. I looked at my watch for the time and then I just realised that I had forgotten to pay the old lady. When I went back I couldn't see the fortune-teller's tent and I thought my eyes were playing tricks on me.

After all the confusion, I went to the parking lot. Mum was waiting impatiently for me. Mum asked me loads of questions like: Where were you? Didn't I tell you to meet me at the parking lot in an hour? – all of these questions run through Mum's head when she thinks I might be lost.

When we got back home we had our dinner and, in a little while, we brushed our teeth and Mum tucked me in. We both said our good nights and then we turned off the light. When I fell asleep, I started dreaming. I was dreaming that I was spinning round and round until I landed in a classroom ...

Then I realised that it was my classroom. It was just the same. All of my classmates were sitting down doing their work while the teacher was writing on the chalkboard. Our teacher told us that she was going down to the staffroom for a quick coffee. All of us were just doing our work until a little while later when one of the boys said that teacher was taking a long time.

He tried to open the door but he said it was locked. We thought the teacher was just messing with us and we started to laugh and then we decided to keep on doing our work until our teacher came back. But she didn't come back ... We waited a whole hour but she still didn't come back.

Suddenly we realised that ten of our classmates were missing and all of us were searching for them. One of the girls screamed. We went into the bathroom and found a girl crying. The ten missing classmates were lying dead on the floor with blood dripping everywhere on the wall. We got such a fright that nearly all of us fell on top of each other.

I found a note on the mirror saying that the person would kill ten of us each hour. All of us got really scared when I read it out – after all, ten of our classmates had died! We all began to say a prayer. There were only thirteen of us left. We knew that we would have to keep a close eye on ourselves and others.

Another hour went by and another ten classmates were found dead in the same bathroom. There were only three of us left. I found another note on the mirror saying that the person would kill each person, one each hour. We all knew the person was catching up on us. Sooner or later we would have to prevent the murder from happening.

One of us would die unless we found out who was doing these murders. We thought it must be one of us but we just laughed. There was me, my best friend, Emerald and one of my oldest friends, Joyce. We were all good friends and we didn't want anything to happen to each other.

After telling stories to each other, an hour went by. We held our hands tightly together, feeling something would happen in any moment. Suddenly Joyce disappeared. We had a terrible feeling running down our spine that the murderer was getting closer.

Suddenly the murderer appeared. The murderer looked like Joyce. Then, to my horror, I realised that it was Joyce.

'Why do you want to kill everyone?' I asked, scared and crying at the same time. She didn't say anything. Then she started screaming and then she turned and disappeared.

It was a happy and a sad ending for us. But what had happened to our teacher? The door wasn't locked anymore and both of us ran to the staffroom. We couldn't see our teacher but we heard mumbling from the closet. We went over to the closet and found our teacher tied to a chair. We untied her and told her all about what had happened. I couldn't believe that Joyce would do such a bad thing.

Afterwards, I woke up from the nightmare. Now I know what the old lady meant. I was still shocked after that nightmare. But what if the old lady was right? What if my nightmare did come true?

Nobody really knows the real future …

Sixth Class (11+ years old)

A new way of using French words, a new kind of translanguaging

In Sixth Class, French continues to be fully integrated in classroom discourse. The well-developed habit of comparing languages makes the pupils aware of the many French words that are part of everyday English, and this is something they are encouraged to explore for themselves by writing an English text that contains as many French words as possible. In this way they can embed French words in discourse that is significantly beyond anything they can produce in French. Here are two examples:

Madame *and her* **fiancé** *went to the* **café. Madame** *ordered* **café au lait** *and a* **baguette.** *Her* fiancé *got* **crème du lait** *and a* **croissant. Madame** *said, '***Bon Appetit!***'*

After that, another woman gave a **brochure** *about the new* **manicure** *shop across the road.* **Madame** *was so excited but her* **fiancé** *wasn't! So he decided to buy her a* **bouquet** *of flowers while* **Madame** *was getting her nails done.*

When they were both finished, they met at a **restaurant. Madame** *was very happy. She then decided to open her very own* **boutique.** *It was called* **Madame's Boutique.** *Her store was* **unique.** *She gave strangers* **brochures** *of her* **boutique** *and it was successful.* **Madame** *and her* **fiancé** *were very happy.*

Every Monday **Madame** *went to* **ballet** *lessons in a studio. There was a* **cuisine** *next to her* **boutique.** *The* **chef** *was called* **Alexandre.** *He was very strict chef.*

One lovely day in Paris a rich, **chic madame** *went to the* **haute couture boutique.** *She bought many* **chic,** *colourful new outfits she also bought a bright, pink dress for a wedding that she was going to go to. She did not want to* **camouflage** *with the wedding scenery which was white!*

She then went to get her **manicure, pedicure** *and hair done. After an hour* **madame** *became hungry and went to an expensive* **restaurant** *and she bought a* **café au lait** *and a lovely* **souflée.** *After her meal she paid the* **Chef** *and took one of the* **restaurant's brochures.**

On the way home she met the bride's **fiancé.** *He gave her an invitation and she filled in the* **RSVP. Madame** *came home and got changed. She put on her* **tutu** *and went to teach her* **ballet** *class. She got a new pair of* **ballet** *shoes. She really* *loved* **ballet**. *For her dinner she ate an* **omelette** *and* **baguette** *because she was on a diet. Then she went to sleep in her* **unique**, *hotel-like bed. Her dog went to sleep with her in her* **haute couture** *pyjamas. She turned off her* **antique** *night stand lamp.*

Producing a coherent multilingual text

Another writing activity that is used at this level arose by chance. One morning a Sixth Class teacher had to deal with an unexpected visit from a parent. The previous evening her pupils had visited the post-primary school to which they would be moving at the beginning of the next school year. She asked them to occupy themselves by writing an account of their visit in a language or languages of their choice while she dealt with the parent. Many of the pupils responded by writing in English, Irish, French and their home language, producing coherent text that switches between languages without mixing them at phrase or sentence level. Here are two examples:

Cuairt ar an Meánscoil

Bhí mé ag an Meánscoil aréir. Chuaigh me agus Ana agus páistí ó rang go rang. We went to the science room and the woman was asking us what do we know about volcanoes. Chuaigh mé agus páistí don rang Béarla agus bhí said ag déanamh an dráma Romeo agus Julliet. Then we went to French class and the lady asked us: Comment tu t'appelle? I said: Je m'appelle Duska and she said: Trés bien! Then we could get lollipop or a French flag. Fuair mé agus Ana an bratach Francach. After that we went to Music room and they were telling us about the school. Chuaigh mé agus páistí go dtí an rang Ealaíne agus bhí said ag péinteáil. Potom ma zacala boliet hlava takze sme museli íst s mamou a so sestrou domov.

(Irish, English, French, Slovakian)

Cuairt ar an Meánscoil

Chuaigh mé agus mo chlann go dtí Pobal Scoil Mhin. Talagang yumao sa gabi. Nous avons vu beaucoup filles e garcons. Thosaigh an phríomhoide ag caint. The whole room started to quiet down. We were told that all the sixth class children were to make their way to the door. Ensuite, une fille a amenée nous dans une piece. Thosaigh said ag scoilt ar na páistí. Si Rabia, si Duska, at si Ana at ako nag paghati-hatiin sa isang grupo. We went into one of the English Classes and we did a Volcano Quiz. Une femme a demandé une question difficile et facile a propos de volcan sur le tableau. We also saw a bit of Romeo and Juliet. Four of my neighbours were part of the play.

(English, Irish, French, Tagalog)

The Sixth Class fashion show

Shortly before the end of the summer term, having recently completed a module on clothes, one Sixth Class persuaded their teacher to allow them to organize a fashion show. The teacher imposed one condition: all languages available to the pupils must play a role. The pupils were happy to take full responsibility for the show, acting as models and commentators, providing background music and ensuring that each outfit worn by the models was described in two or three languages (English, Irish or French and at least one home language). After the fashion show, the teacher suggested that each pupil should invent a model and write a short text about her in three or more languages. Marceline (Figure 4.11)

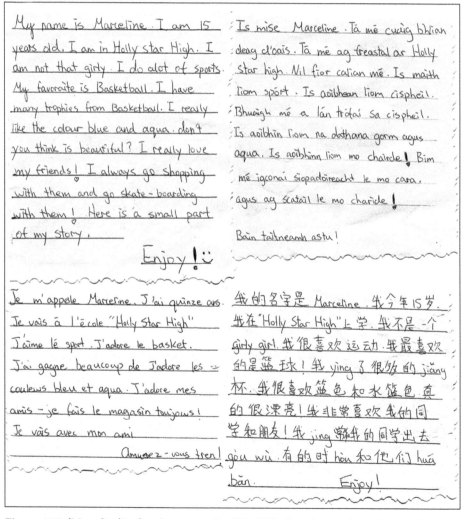

Figure 4.11 'Marceline' in four languages: English, Irish, French, Mandarin (Sixth Class, 11+ years old).

is one example. The teacher commented on the high level of pupil engagement in the fashion show project and the large amount of independent work undertaken.

Other multilingual writing activities

Another Sixth Class teacher entered her pupils in the annual *Write a Book* project run by the local Teacher Education Centre, encouraging them to write stories collaboratively in their home languages as well as English. Several groups decided to retell Irish legends in two languages, while another pupil made a dictionary of words and phrases from her mother's language, Chichewa. She had not learned Chichewa herself but had become interested in it when she came to Scoil Bhríde and experienced the inclusive language environment there.

Another Sixth Class produced a multilingual book entitled 'Languages Are Fun! A Class Book of Many Languages'. There were twenty-six pupils in the class with fifteen languages between them (including English, Irish and French learnt at school). Their teacher encouraged each of them to contribute to the book which includes such items as: 'Basic Tagalog for tourists'; 'Mamos Rankos (Mothers' Hands)', a poem in Lithuanian with an English translation; word lists on a variety of topics in various languages, with English translations; identity texts written by two Irish pupils (L1 English), one in Danish and English, the other in Italian and English; a text written in Mandarin accompanied by a Mandarin/English glossary designed to help the reader to decipher the text (an English translation is available but hidden by a flap of paper); a Nigerian legend about a tortoise written in Yoruba and English; a short history of Romania in Romanian and English (Figure 4.12); and the *Madame* stories written in English with French words (see above).

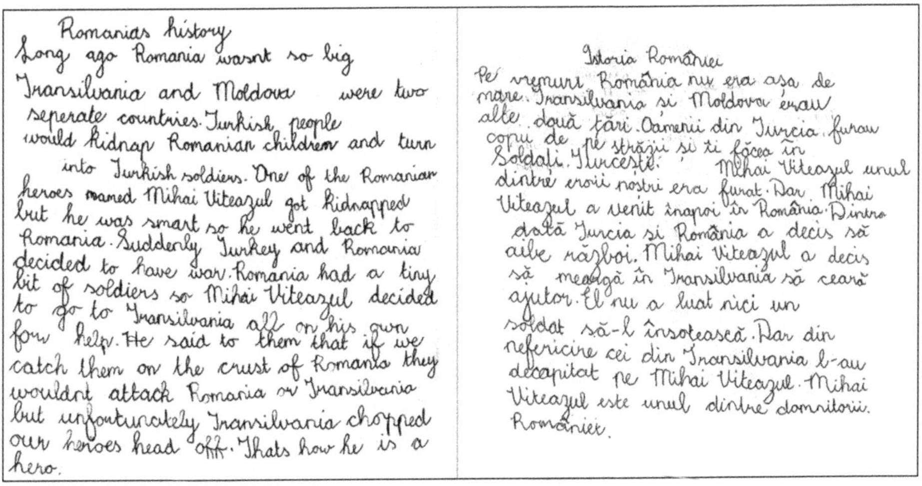

Romanias history
Long ago Romania wasnt so big
Transilvania and Moldova were two
seperate countries. Turkish people
would kidnap Romanian children and turn
into Turkish soldiers. One of the Romanian
heroes named Mihai Viteazul got kidnapped
but he was smart so he went back to
Romania. Suddenly Turkey and Romania
decided to have war. Romania had a tiny
bit of soldiers so Mihai Viteazul decided
to go to Transilvania all on his own
for help. He said to them that if we
catch them on the crust of Romania they
wouldnt attack Romania or Transilvania
but unfortunately Transilvania chopped
our heroes head off. Thats how he is a
hero.

Istoria României
Pe vremuri România nu era așa de
mare. Transilvania și Moldova erau
alte două țări. Oamenii din Turcia furau
copii de pe străzi și îi făcea în
Soldați Turcești. Mihai Viteazul unul
dintre eroii noștri era furat. Dar Mihai
Viteazul a venit înapoi în România. Dintr-o
dată Turcia și România a decis să
aibe război. Mihai Viteazul a decis
să meargă în Transilvania să ceară
ajutor. El nu a luat nici un
soldat să-l însoțească. Dar din
nefericire cei din Transilvania l-au
decapitat pe Mihai Viteazul. Mihai
Viteazul este unul dintre domnitorii
României.

Figure 4.12 Dual-language text on Romanian history (Sixth Class, 11+ years old).

We Are Writers!

Our first Sixth Class example from *We Are Writers!* is by a pupil whose home language is Tagalog. Before coming to Ireland, she had attended playschool in the Philippines and had no hesitation in using Tagalog when she was enrolled in Scoil Bhríde in Junior Infants. After three months, Tagalog was interspersed with occasional words in English, and from there she made rapid progress. Before the end of the year, she was able to describe how ships go looking for whales and other creatures, and her growing proficiency in English was matched by her confidence in asking the teacher questions. When she was in First Class, an older Tagalog-speaking pupil visited her class to read aloud work that she had written in Tagalog; she reacted with pleased surprise: *that's **my** language.* By the time this pupil was in Sixth Class, poetry was her favourite form of writing, and she wrote a poem for *We Are Writers!* It shows a remarkable command of English vocabulary for a twelve-year-old, whatever her language background.

Dear Autumn

A season of ecstasy, romance and misery
Bursting with suspicion and trustworthiness,
Thou cannot tell what is and what is not,
For the world is filled with guilt and innocence.

Come dear friend of the mellowing tree,
Maturing him now to praise and enlighten,
One's born days with swelled fruits and their ripeness,
Nourished with His words, not of Satan's

As the petals fall one by one,
Each representing a saddened heart,
For Hardship and Agony have beaten Joviality,
As the leaves and the branches break apart.

The evergreen tree stood grand and tall
For nothing did it lack.
The couple divorced – the bush who mourned
For its own baby berries back.

When you get that sentimental feeling,
The winds join a choir with the leaves,
The couple commits their undenying love
As they sit under the ivy thatched eaves.

The scarlet sun disappears beneath the horizon,
Leaving a faint stream of light,
The moon surfaces and removes its veil,
Revealing its beauty to Autumn's night.

A time of harvest for the season to come,
As Hallowe'en drew nearer and nearer.
Pumpkins and corns grew on their stalks,
Before the weather gets drearier.

Who hath not seen the oft amid thy store,
For swallows just left their nests?
I'll let you do your seasonal work,
For my dear Autumn friend knows best.

The pupil read her poem at the book launch and was then interviewed by the master of ceremonies:

Master of ceremonies: *This is a very interesting poem. There is some very serious language in it. Where did you get the idea to use this kind of language?*

Pupil: *Well, I got it from Keats' poem 'Autumn'.*

Master of ceremonies: *It's extraordinary that you should have used Keats as your inspiration. How did you find the poetry of Keats? Who told you to read it or where did you read it?*

Pupil: *This poem was for a competition in our class. Whoever had the best Autumn poem was given this box with letters in it, and I actually hadn't read any autumn poems before, so I decided to look some up on the internet and the first one that came up was Keats' Autumn, and as I read it, like, its words, it made me smile as in really happy because of the way he expressed his feelings towards autumn.*

Our second Sixth Class example from *We Are Writers!* is by a pupil whose home language is Polish. When she enrolled in Scoil Bhríde as a Junior Infant, no member of her family was proficient in English, and not having attended playschool, she had no previous experience of English. To begin with, she was very quiet and was not easily drawn into classroom interactions. But she listened attentively, and as time went on she developed the confidence to make contributions that were important to her. By the time she was in Sixth Class she was fully proficient in English as this example shows:

All Good Things Come to a Dreadful End …

There he lay, too weak to even eat his supper. My eyes were red and puffy, my heart stung. I felt as if someone had jabbed a sword through it. My throat was dry and I didn't have the energy to do anything. Why me? Why us …?

I looked at the elderly dog. Every time I did, I felt a mild rush of happiness, but it was immediately dragged away by a rush of sadness. I sat in the kitchen crying softly. I looked at the table, where a few of my tears lay. They were so small compared to how large they felt and their heaviness when they came out of my eyes and slid along my cheeks …

Suddenly I heard a noise and the poor fellow limped into the room and leaned against the wall for support. He stared at me with his big brown eyes. We were staring at each other for a few short moments. His eyes could speak a language we both understood. I tried to force a smile but it wouldn't come and everything turned blurry again. All I heard was when he slid a bit lower and squealed softly.

I walked up to him, gently forcing every step. Why was it so hard to approach him? I knelt down beside him and touched his head with great care. I lowered my head and he lifted his nose up to me. Another big tear flew down my face and he licked my cheek. I sobbed even louder and gave him an extremely fragile hug. With all his might, he dragged his paw up. I was speechless.

I was suddenly slapped with memories of us together. I remembered the first time I met him when he sank his nails into my shoulders … when he was hyper all the time, more energetic every second … Those days seemed far away now …but I would always be with him and he with me.

As he gave me his last glance ever and slowly put his head down I felt the biggest stab of all.

'Good boy,' I whispered, 'Sleep tight my little angel.'

This text too was read aloud at the book launch and its author was interviewed by the master of ceremonies:

Master of ceremonies: *Will you tell me a little bit about how you were inspired to write this story and I think this might be a sad bit.*

Pupil: *When my hamster died.*

Master of ceremonies: *And when your hamster died, how long ago was that?*

Pupil: *A year or two ago.*

Master of ceremonies: *How quickly after your hamster died, how quickly did you decide, I'm going to write this story down?*

Pupil: *A few months.*

Master of ceremonies: *So, was it churning around in your head before you wrote it?*

Pupil: *Yeah.*

Master of ceremonies: *At what point did you think, I'm going to take up my pencil now and write it. What made you do that?*

Pupil: *Well I just wanted to get it out onto paper.*

Master of ceremonies: *'I wanted to get it out onto paper', a thing I hear regularly on the radio, so that's how a writer starts.*

Plurilingual literacy and the development of language awareness

Scoil Bhríde's integrated approach to language education assumes that ELLs' proficiency in spoken English will develop from their involvement in interactive classroom discourse that also includes Irish, their home languages and French. From Junior Infants on, this process is supported by reading and writing. As we have seen, the PSC expects teachers to model writing for their pupils. This has two important consequences: even in the earliest stages, most of what pupils write is *discourse* that has a meaning beyond its constituent words and phrases, and concern for orthographic correctness provides an age-appropriate focus on linguistic form. Pupils become proficient in writing English by writing English, and the same is true for Irish, for French in Fifth and Sixth Class, and for ELLs' home languages. The crucial difference between English, Irish and French on the one hand and home languages on the other is, of course, that whereas the teacher models the texts she wants her pupils to produce in curriculum languages, ELLs must depend on other resources to acquire literacy in their home language. Some are helped by their parents and/or older siblings; others attend weekend schools organized by immigrant communities to support the development of children's home language literacy. Reading books in their home language, whether provided by their parents or borrowed from the school library, is also an essential support.

The examples we have given of parallel texts in three or four languages recall the pedagogical practice of 'translanguaging' as it was developed in Wales in the 1980s (Lewis, Jones and Baker 2012: 643). At that time few resources were available in Welsh, so textbooks in English were used in Welsh-immersion programmes but classroom activities were carried out in Welsh (Williams 2002: 36). In this way content was communicated and processed in both languages. Translanguaging in this sense entails the use of one language to reinforce another in order to increase understanding and expand the learner's capacity in both languages (Williams 2002: 40). This mutual reinforcement moves backwards and forwards between oral and written modes; learners listen and speak in language A in order to read and write in language B, and vice versa.

In Scoil Bhríde the use of multiple languages to express the same or closely similar meaning has led to a greater appreciation of the cognitive function of literacy. We noted in our introduction to this chapter that the PSC expects teachers to focus on listening and speaking when teaching Irish to the junior grades (this is in part a hangover from audiolingual doctrine, strongly favoured in the 1960s, according to which learners should listen and speak before they read and write). One experienced teacher had this to say when she was asked about the relation between speaking and writing:

> *A number of years ago if you had asked me about this I would have had a different answer because I would have said … written work, no, the oral is the most important …. [But now] I think that if they form their thoughts with pen and paper first, it gives them the confidence then to go and speak. So at home they would put together their three or their thirty-three or whatever number of sentences, and the next day they don't open the copybook, I just ask the question or say tell me the story, tell me about …, and because they've already gone through that process of putting it together they then have that bank of ideas rather than just standing up and going … I can't think. So the thinking is done with pen and paper and then the speaking is done without any reference to any written word and I do think that really helps to gain confidence going forward.*

The continuous production of text in English, Irish and home languages also helps to explain the high levels of language awareness acquired by Scoil Bhríde's pupils. Since the 1970s, the Canadian scholar David Olson has argued that literacy entails much more than the transcription of speech (1979, 1994, 1995, 2016): it adds a distinctive dimension to human cognition, and because it makes language visible, it is the source of our awareness of linguistic form. In Chapter 3 we offered numerous examples of the linguistic comparisons and contrasts that pupils are able to draw. Many of them would be much less likely to arise without the continuous production of written text, and thus focus on orthographic form, in multiple languages, like the following example. When one Sixth Class pupil drew attention to the *sz* combination of letters in Hungarian, a German-speaking pupil explained how this affects pronunciation: *it's the same in German, where you have 'ch' but you say 'sch'* [both clusters pronounced as in English] … *and do you remember when we were doing the homophones and we had the same words like I said with the three words 'cherry', 'church' and 'kitchen', you have 'Kirsche', 'Kirche' and 'Küche'*. Homophones are not a topic of discussion in most Irish primary schools.

Conclusion

Scoil Bhríde began to draw immigrant pupils' home languages into the life of the classroom and of the wider school community because the principal and her colleagues recognized that each ELL's home language is central to her identity; it is impossible to affirm her identity without at the same time affirming her language. The same recognition motivates the use that Canadian teachers have made of 'identity texts', in which minoritized students' identities are reflected back to them in a positive light. They have found that identity affirmation encourages and supports literacy engagement and thus begins to address a major cause of educational underachievement (Cummins and Early 2011, Cummins et al. 2015). Scoil Bhríde's inclusion of home languages in the writing activities of the classroom has a similar motivating effect. As some of the examples we have included in this chapter show, pupils often undertake more written work than their teacher asks of them. Self-generated work of this kind is evidence of an emerging capacity for autonomous learning. From an early age, many pupils become so interested in exploring the languages they know and are learning that they undertake ambitious learning activities in their own time and quite independently of the teacher's initiatives. This phenomenon throws important new light on the concept of language learner autonomy and we discuss it in detail in Chapter 5.

5

Plurilingual Learning and the Development of Learner Autonomy

In Chapter 3 we showed how the inclusion of home languages in the life of the classroom encourages ELLs to use their primary cognitive tool to support their learning and at the same time helps all pupils to develop high levels of language awareness. The examples we gave support the view that the use of home languages fosters ELLs' self-esteem by bringing their 'action knowledge' (Barnes 1976) into interaction with school knowledge, or curriculum content, and allowing them to make an individual and unique contribution to the learning of the class as a whole. In our introduction to Chapter 4 we pointed out that the Irish Primary School Curriculum (PSC) associates learning to write with a developing capacity for self-expression, and we argued that the individual pupil's ability to create written records is an essential tool of critical thinking and lays the foundations for autonomous learning. Highly prized as educational goals, critical thinking and autonomous learning are among the principles that underpin the PSC: 'higher-order thinking and problem-solving skills should be developed' (Government of Ireland 1999a: 9), and 'the child is an active agent in his or her learning' (Government of Ireland 1999a: 8). The examples we gave of pupils' developing plurilingual literacy included many instances of work they had undertaken spontaneously and on their own initiative. Repeatedly producing written text beyond what the teacher requires (in one case always labelling it 'not homework') is evidence not only of a commitment to personal learning but of a determination to exercise control. In this chapter we explore further the link between the use of home languages at school and pupils' developing capacity for autonomous learning. We begin by exploring the concept of learner autonomy as it has been elaborated in relation to the learning of foreign languages; we go on to consider some of the ways in which classroom practice at Scoil Bhríde encourages learners to reflect, and provide examples of pupils' autonomous learning initiatives; and we conclude the chapter by discussing the implications of the examples we have presented for our understanding of the concepts of plurilingualism, plurilingual education and language learner autonomy.

The theory and practice of learner autonomy in foreign language learning

The concept of learner autonomy has been associated with language learning since 1979, when the Council of Europe published Henri Holec's report *Autonomy and Foreign Language Learning* (cited here as Holec 1981). Holec defined learner autonomy as 'the ability to take charge of one's own learning' (Holec 1981: 3), which entails determining objectives, specifying the content of learning and its progression, selecting learning materials and techniques, monitoring the learning process, and evaluating learning outcomes (Holec 1981: 3, 9). According to this definition, learner autonomy is a capacity for self-instruction, and the terms of the definition imply that it can be developed and exploited in relation to any curriculum subject or skill set. Essentially concerned with how learning is organized, this version of learner autonomy has nothing to say about the impact that the exercise of learner agency may have on learning outcomes and achievement. Indeed, according to Holec, the development of proficiency in a foreign language is quite separate from the development of the ability to manage one's own learning (Holec 1981: 23). The underlying assumption is that learners in formal education are non-autonomous and teacher-dependent. They may be content to remain in this state and still achieve their learning objectives, but if they become autonomous, they will be able to manage without a teacher.

A rather different understanding of learner autonomy emerged in the late 1970s in the Nordic countries, especially Denmark; the paradigm case is the classroom of Leni Dam, who taught English to young teenagers (for a detailed account of Dam's work, see Little, Dam and Legenhausen 2017). Dam first developed her version of learner autonomy in response to the Danish education authorities' policy of differentiation, according to which it was the duty of schools to provide a learning environment in which all learners could thrive according to their individual interests and abilities. She was strongly influenced by Barnes's (1976) distinction between 'action knowledge', which includes learners' interests and abilities, and school knowledge (it is worth noting that Barnes's book was published in Danish translation as early as 1977). Whereas Holec's version of learner autonomy assumes that learners start from a position of non-autonomy,

Dam's version acknowledges that they are used to being autonomous in their lives outside the classroom. Accordingly, the teacher's task is to harness her learners' capacity for autonomous behaviour and focus it on the business of language learning. In other words, autonomy is the cause as well as the outcome of successful learning. The growth in learners' ability to manage their own learning does not lead to a dilution or diminution of the teacher's role; she has an enduring responsibility for maintaining the learning dynamic of the classroom.

Within the framework provided by the official curriculum, Dam required her learners to set their own goals, choose their own learning activities and materials, monitor the learning process, and evaluate learning outcomes. But from the very first lesson she expected them to do these things as far as possible in and through the target language: she used English for *all* classroom communication, and she expected her learners to make every effort to respond to her in English. Especially in the early stages, target language use was strongly dependent on teacher modelling and scaffolding, in writing as well as speech. Oral communication was also strongly interactive: as much importance was attached to effective collaboration as to individual effort. The learning activities in which learners engaged always took account of curricular requirements, but they also connected with their wider interests. In this way their cognitive but also their emotional and volitional resources were fully invested in their language learning. The requirement that they exercise agency in planning, implementing, monitoring and evaluating successive phases of learning helped them to develop metacognitive as well as communicative proficiency in English.

The management of individual and group learning depended on two tools, logbooks and posters. Learners used their logbooks to keep a record of each lesson, note new words as they encountered them, write the texts they produced individually, and regularly evaluate their learning progress. Posters, written in real time by the teacher in interaction with the class, were used for a wide variety of purposes – for example, to compile a list of new vocabulary, record the features of a good conversation, keep track of project work, and evaluate a phase of learning. Learning activities were of two broad kinds, analytic and creative. Analytic activities focused on learning bits of the language; for example, learners supported their learning of vocabulary and idioms by making word cards, picture dominoes, picture lotto and board games. Creative activities included stories, poems, plays and projects, sometimes produced individually and sometimes collaboratively.

This version of learner autonomy is more radical than Holec's because it embodies a theory of language learning. It claims that the most beneficial language learning environments are those in which, from the beginning, the target language is the principal channel of the learners' agency: the communicative and metacognitive medium through which, individually and collaboratively, they plan, execute, monitor and evaluate their own learning. To put the matter more simply, the development of proficiency depends on the learner's agentive use of the target language, where 'agentive' implies full involvement in planning, implementing, monitoring and evaluating learning. Evidence in support of this claim came from a four-year study carried out by Leni Dam and Lienhard Legenhausen in the 1990s. The study compared the learning achievement of one of Dam's mixed-ability classes with that of a class of learners in a German *Gymnasium* who were learning English from a communicative textbook. Dam's learners outperformed their German peers by a significant margin in the acquisition of vocabulary, grammar and pragmatic competence; they also revealed a capacity for spontaneous oral interaction that contrasted strongly with the German learners' halting efforts to build conversation using half-remembered chunks from textbook dialogues. This result is hardly surprising: Dam's approach ensured that English was part of her learners' 'everyday lived language' (García 2017: 18), whereas the textbook-based approach of the German classroom did not (for a detailed account of this research, see Little, Dam and Legenhausen 2017, Chapter 5).

The growth of autonomy in Scoil Bhríde's pupils

There are three obvious differences between Leni Dam's classroom and Scoil Bhríde. First, Dam was concerned exclusively with English as a foreign language and all her learners experienced the same pedagogical approach and followed a similar trajectory of English language development. Scoil Bhríde's teachers, on the other hand, vary in their pedagogical preferences, and although English is the principal focus of language support classes, it is also the principal medium of curriculum learning. Secondly, Dam's pupils ranged in age from 10+ to 15+ years. When they began to learn English, they had already completed the first three primary grades, they were familiar with school as a social environment, and they had acquired basic literacy skills in Danish. Scoil Bhríde's pupils, by contrast, range in age from 4+ to 11+ years; to begin with, school is new to them and ELLs cannot use literacy skills of any kind to support their early learning of English. Thirdly, from the beginning Dam's approach to language teaching requires her learners to set their own goals, select learning activities and materials, and evaluate the learning process and its outcomes. It's certainly possible to take account of the interests and preferences of very young learners, but they cannot be expected to take explicit control of their learning until they are fully habituated to school life and the routines of the classroom. As we noted in Chapter 2, Scoil Bhríde's integrated approach to language education developed partly under the impact of David Little's work on learner autonomy. On the wall of one Sixth Class classroom he noticed a quotation from his 1991 book on learner autonomy (strongly influenced by the work of Leni Dam); Déirdre Kirwan had given a copy of the quotation to all teachers. In this particular classroom the teacher told him she used it to discuss her pupils' learning with them. But by no means all of the teachers think of their work in terms associated with learner autonomy. Some of them use the WALT ('We are learning to …') and WILF ('What I'm looking for') strategies to make learning intentions and success criteria explicit to their pupils, but others don't.

At the same time, there are some striking similarities. Dam exploited her learners' action knowledge to stimulate their interest in learning English, and Scoil Bhríde encourages ELLs to use their home languages (the medium in which they mostly acquire and use action knowledge outside school) as a way of engaging with curriculum learning. Dam didn't attempt to 'teach' English in any traditional sense; rather, from the first lesson she used modelling and scaffolding techniques to support her learners' efforts to use English for their own communicative purposes. In much the same way, Scoil Bhríde's teachers help ELLs to develop proficiency in English not by 'teaching' them the language but by engaging them in the interactive use of English in language support lessons and the mainstream classroom. Grammar is not taught in the way it traditionally has been in foreign language classrooms, though there is inevitably a focus on form when pupils learn to write in English and Irish. Dam established a strong symbiosis between speaking and writing: her learners used writing to support speaking, and they interacted with one another orally in order to generate written text. As we saw in Chapter 4, in Scoil Bhríde writing is the mode in which ELLs can use their home languages productively, and their texts are validated when they read them aloud to the rest of the class and explain what they mean.

There are similarities too between the primary instruments of learning. The copybooks in which Scoil Bhríde's pupils write texts in multiple languages perform some of the same functions as Leni Dam's logbooks. The reflective and evaluative dimensions may not be present, but copybooks no less than logbooks cumulatively capture the emerging linguistic identity of the individual pupil. And in Scoil Bhríde as in Dam's classroom, posters on the classroom wall support learning in a multitude of ways. Sometimes posters are written in real time by the teacher in interaction with the pupils, sometimes teachers prepare them in advance, and sometimes they are commercially produced. But wherever they come from, they make language as well as curriculum content visible and provide a focus for reflection of various kinds.

In general, as we saw in Chapter 2, the ethos of the PSC is strongly learner-centred, and it shares many underlying principles with Leni Dam's version of learner autonomy. The teacher's understanding of her role, the engagement of learners in reflective discussion and self-assessment sow the seeds from which autonomous learning initiatives grow.

The teacher's role

In a classroom that encourages autonomous learning the teacher is open and flexible, ready to allow pupils to contribute freely to the flow of interactive classroom talk and to adjust lesson plans to accommodate unforeseen developments. A Sixth Class teacher made the point that if the school encourages ELLs to use their home languages, it is important to let them express themselves freely regarding their linguistic intuitions and observations:

> If the teacher creates an atmosphere where it is acceptable for a child to interrupt the plan of the lesson and say: 'In my language we say such and such a thing...', that makes a huge difference, and then the teacher can stand back and they learn from each other and the teacher learns as well.

This often causes the lesson to take an unexpected turn, but unexpected turns are usually beneficial:

> I ask them if there is a similar word in any other language, and that usually results in a discussion about the names of the various different things in the other languages that are in the classroom, which can mean that we go off on a tangent, but it usually benefits them in some way.

The development and exploitation of this kind of language awareness is woven into every aspect of classroom discourse, irrespective of the subject that is being taught. When ELLs take their home language as their starting point, their identity and action knowledge are brought into play. The same Sixth Class teacher went on to say that when pupils begin to find their own connections, *the teacher can stand back and it just happens, it takes off*. This creates an effective launch pad for autonomous learning. It is worth pointing out that this exploratory approach to the languages present in the classroom is entirely consistent with the ethos of the PSC, which emphasizes the importance of establishing links between all areas of learning (Government of Ireland 1999a: 24, 25).

Another Sixth Class teacher explained that as a result of exposure to the home languages in her class, she was learning from her pupils:

> *I have learned many words in other languages and I'm keeping my own language notebook for my own research. It has definitely broadened my horizons and I think that one of the huge things that has come out of this is that we have become familiar with and accustomed to looking at the links between languages, and the girls do it now as an almost automatic response. Every time we learn a new word I can see them making the links and they're very enthusiastic about languages and about learning about other cultures and countries.*

This teacher argued that the inclusion of home languages was helping her pupils to take ownership of their own learning, while the relaxed style of classroom interaction meant that they were ready to look for help when they needed it. She explained that learning had become a partnership and her pupils had readily helped her with an action research project that was part of her postgraduate studies on school leadership:

> *I have been able to integrate what we are doing with senior level with my own studies. With action research it involves looking at something and then seeing how we can change it for the better, and the children have been very proactive in that and I have to say it has been a pleasure to carry out this project with them.*

In the autonomy-oriented foreign language classroom, language learning proceeds from collaborative interaction that is driven by the initiatives taken by the learners themselves and caught in a recursive cycle of reflection: planning, monitoring, evaluation. Documentation of the learning process and its outcomes plays an essential role. At the end of each learning cycle, self- and peer-assessment seek to identify strengths and weaknesses as a basis for planning the next cycle. Thus, the methods of the autonomy-oriented language classroom have much in common with the techniques of action research (Burns 1999, 2009) and exploratory practice (Hanks 2017). The same is true of the senior classes in Scoil Bhríde. The same Sixth Class teacher noted that her pupils were developing the ability to transfer their skills to other areas of learning. She also confirmed that the pupils themselves were making links between languages and undertaking to write in their home language, without being asked to, in addition to doing their assigned tasks in English, Irish and French; necessarily, all writing in home languages was done independently of the teacher.

Reflection

Openness to contributions from pupils leads to free-flowing discussion, which leads naturally to evaluative reflection. Especially when home languages are in focus, reflection stimulates the growth of self-awareness, while the habit of evaluative reflection helps to develop pupils' critical capacity. In due course these provide a basis for formal and explicit self-assessment.

Self-awareness

Our first example of reflective talk that encourages self-awareness comes from Second Class (pupils aged seven and eight). They have been using the United Nations Charter for Children as the basis for exploring the rights and responsibilities of being a global citizen when one is under eighteen. To sum up their discussion pupils volunteer to name a right and its accompanying responsibility in English and in their home language. Where a speaker has difficulty translating into her home language, another speaker of that language provides assistance. A Polish speaker offers the right to play and the responsibility to include others in her play, while a Bosnian speaker offers the right of all children to be safe and the responsibility to take care not to undermine the safety of others. A Latvian speaker says that all children have the right to learn and the responsibility not to disturb others when they are trying to learn.

From a very young age many pupils are able to describe how they understand and/or speak various languages, even though they have not yet learnt to read and write them. For example, a Slovak speaker in Second Class says:

> *I speak normally Slovakian ... we speak in school and on yard we speak* [English] *... and then ... Polish because I understand Poland because it's similar and sometimes we speak together and ... and next I ... Irish because sometimes we speak in classrooms and* [the Irish textbook].

She goes on to explain that sometimes she and a Polish-speaking pupil talk to each other in their respective home languages: *Yeah ... I speak Slovakian, she speaks Polish and we understand each other*. She agrees that this means that she understands Polish. When asked where she uses Slovakian she says: *I speak Slovakian at home and when we come to Slovakian so then we speak Slovakian*. When asked where she uses English she says: *In school, when we play on yard and yeah with teacher*. She also says she uses Irish in school and explains that *sometimes when teachers come we say 'Dia dhuit fáilte romhat isteach'*. She agrees that she can speak and understand all the languages she has mentioned and can *write some, some in Irish like 'is maith leat'. I can write some sentences, and English I normally write, and Slovakian I really good, I really know how to write that, and Polish no, I just understand.*

A Lithuanian speaker who has recently turned eight explains that she knows *Lithuanian the most, the second one I know English, the third one Irish, a teeny bit of Russian, and only one or two words of French.* She says that *because my Mam always speaks Lithuanian and I can understand it and she l- … teached me how to speak.* She explains that she started to learn English by watching *loads of videos* that are chosen by her mother and are about *how to speak English and they translate it in different languages and what they mean.* She enjoys watching them because when she gets bored she can listen to them in other languages for enjoyment. She says that she has learned Irish from her teacher. While *all her family* speaks Russian, neither she nor her minder understands Russian, although she herself *can speak some words.* She can also read and write Lithuanian, English and *a little bit of Irish.*

As pupils progress through the school, their views are sought on their education generally and how they feel about learning in a multilingual environment. In 2013/2014, for example, Déirdre Kirwan interviewed a group of seven Fourth Class learners whose home languages (and ages) were English (11:8), German (10:1), Igbo (10:2), Kurdish (10:10), Malayalam (10:11), Polish (10:3) and Romanian (10:8). What they had to say reveals an acute awareness of their linguistic identity; it is also clear that they themselves take various initiatives to develop literate proficiency in their home languages.

When asked if she reads Polish at home, the Polish pupil says that she does but admits to having some problems with this *'cause I live here long time and Polish is kind of difficult* [to read]. She says that *writing is easy because I'm used to the alphabet and everything because I went to* [Polish] *school in Ireland so I kind of learned it.* Her first choice of language in which to read is English because *it's too tricky in Polish.* When she says that she would like to be better at reading Polish, the German speaker points out that there are dual-language books in the school library and *if you're reading in Polish and you get stuck you just look at the English words.* The Romanian speaker recommends

> *an app that you can have on your phone or your iPad, it's a reading app and you just plug your earphones in and listen to stories and they could be in Romanian and English and the sight-read tells you to say it all over again, and if you say it wrong you have to listen again.*

She explains that you can read the words as you listen to the story. The German speaker then explains how Duolingo[1] works. The Malayalam speaker suggests that getting books from the library and reading with parental help is a way of improving home language reading skills.

All these pupils have access to reading material in their L1 at home. Two of them, however, make the point that there are no books in Romanian and Kurdish in the school library. Another says that when she is reading library books, she sometimes tries to translate them into her home language in her head. When she has a problem with a word she asks for help at home, and she has recently begun to bring a dual-language dictionary to school as it helps to improve her translating skills. She adds that another good way to improve home language proficiency is to visit the country where it is spoken. The Malayalam speaker explains that when she was a small child her parents read legends from their country to her. She remembers these stories very well and they have helped with her vocabulary development. The Kurdish pupil explains that she attends Kurdish school for two hours on Saturdays and there she learns poems, stories and new words. She sometimes incorporates her knowledge of Kurdish in school projects, getting help at home when she needs it.

Critical evaluation

By the time pupils are in Sixth Class critical evaluation is a fully integrated part of regular classroom discourse and they need little encouragement to exercise their critical faculty. One Sixth Class teacher asked her pupils to write a letter expressing their thoughts on Scoil Bhríde's integrated approach to language learning. Four of the five letters expressed dissatisfaction with the textbook used to teach Irish:

> *I prefer French to Irish because I find more interesting were has* [whereas] [the textbook] *is downright boring … I would get rid of the textbook for good, even take it off the Education board for all of Dublin.* (Yoruba speaker)

> *One thing I don't like doing is* [the textbook]. *In my opinion it is very boring and useless. The stories written in the book are very easy and have the answers written everywhere.* (Polish speaker)

> *I don't like the book it's boring I'd rather do it orally.* (Arabic speaker)

---

[1]   https://www.duolingo.com

What I don't like about is that the textbook is boring and heavy. (Lithuanian speaker)

The last of these pupils was keen to explain that it was not Irish itself that she found boring but the textbook: *I would prefer Irish because I like the way some words sound, and for me it's easy to remember even though it is complicated.* These reflections show that when pupils are fully engaged in classroom learning, used to taking their own learning initiatives and making full and flexible communicative and cognitive use of the languages available to them, traditional textbooks and workbooks can be an obstacle to enjoyable learning.

Self-assessment

In Fifth Class, pupils are introduced to self-assessment that focuses on the language skills of listening, speaking, reading and writing. Scoil Bhríde's practice grew out of the school's earlier use of the European Language Portfolio (see Chapter 1, pp. 19–20 above), which includes checklists of 'I can' descriptors linked to the language activities and proficiency levels of the *Common European Framework of Reference for Languages*. Pupils write their self-assessment claims on paper leaves which they attach to a languages tree pinned to the classroom wall. The tree has four branches, one for each of the language skills, while its roots – a feature suggested by the pupils – are the various home languages present in the class (Figure 5.1). Scoil Bhríde's tree was inspired by David Little's description of the tree that a Czech primary teacher devised to use with the ELP model for primary language learners in the Czech Republic. This version had five main branches, for reading, listening, spoken interaction, spoken production and writing, and each main branch had a separate smaller branch for each of the ELP's 'I can' descriptors for CEFR level A1. This provided a clear focus and constraint that Scoil Bhríde's tree lacked (this problem was discussed in the record of the principal's meeting with Fifth and Sixth Class teachers quoted in Chapter 2, p. 36 above).

The pupils nevertheless developed a clear and cogent understanding of the concept and practice of self-assessment. A Polish pupil in Sixth Class, for example, offered this explanation:

It's called self-assessment ... it's like we quiz ourselves to see if we understand the different languages in French, Irish, English and our own language, and we have questions and we have to answer them and see if we understand them and then we put them up on our language tree.

When asked why self-assessment is important, a pupil whose home language is Tagalog, replied:

Figure 5.1 Sixth Class languages tree used for self-assessment (11+ years old).

Even though the teachers teach us, we still have a job to do and it's to learn it, and we can learn it ourselves like when we're talking about something where a particular word comes up … in some other language that word is similar to that language and we just jot it down in our little blue notebooks … to make some links about it.

A native speaker of English believed that

self-assessment is really good, you learn more in it and you can ask questions with your partner and test each other in what questions you can say and read, it's really fun and it's better than doing [the Irish workbook].

A Ukrainian speaker explained how the language tree is used in self-assessment:

On our language tree we have four parts, the listening part, the speaking part, the reading part and the writing part. For every one we have four leaves, so for the individual one we have a separate sentence and we say that we can read it or write it or speak it or eh, like understand it when teacher says it to us. And that's the language tree. And we also have our roots which are all the … first languages in our class and there's more than twelve of them.

Teachers encourage autonomous learning

The learner-centred ethos of the PSC envisages modes of work that allow learners to make individual contributions within the framework of teacher-directed activity. As we have pointed out several times, the use of home languages in the classroom and the practice of drawing comparisons between languages presuppose that ELLs will be encouraged to contribute spontaneously to teacher-led classroom discourse. They are also given many other opportunities to make individual contributions to teacher-directed activity, as the following examples show.

First Class pupils collect examples of their written work in personal books

Children are regularly encouraged to discuss and write about topics in which they have a particular interest and about events at school in which they have been involved. One First Class teacher gave added impetus to this activity by having each of her pupils collect a selection of her written work in a book for which she designed an attractive cover. The topics chosen were: Myself, Our School, Our School Garden, All about Everything, My Favourite Animal, and Hobbies. Pupils took great pride in this unaided writing. As they had often written on the topic Myself, many of them produced texts in English, Irish and their home language.

They enjoyed reading their books aloud to their peers, and this gave them a sense of writing for an audience, which is one of the stated curriculum goals (see Chapter 4, p. 88 above). Here are two examples.

Example 1 – English, Irish, Polish

My name is Emma. Mam na imię Emma. Emma is ainm dom. I have one sister. Her name is Anna. She is one years old. She is smaller than me. Mam jedną siostrę. Nazywa się Anna. Ma jeden rok. Ona jest mniejsza niż ja.

Our school. We planted radishes in spring. Then the plants are growing. The potatoes are growing at the moment. They going to be ready to eat in October. The sunflowers are growing too. I love summer.

All about me. My name is Emma. I am in First Class. I will be eight next month. I will like reading books and playing watching monsters computer game. My best friend is Lily. We love to play together. I love my family my Mam Dad and my little sister.

Garden is a place for vegetables and fruit and trees. In our school garden we grow radishes and a sunflower. We can eat the sunflower and potato and the scarecrow is very good because he scares the crows.

Example 2 – English, Irish, Russian

My name is Natasha. Natasha is ainm dom. Меня зовут Natasha. I am seven years old.

I'm from Latvia. My birthday is the 5th of November.

Our school garden. This year we have a new school building and new garden. In our school garden we are growing vegetables and flowers. Our flowers have roots under them. Our vegetables are called radishes carrots and potatoes.

The teacher told a Polish pupil that by listening to her reading from her book she had learned a Polish word, *lubya* ('like'). She checked the word with the pupil and asked how she would say *I like the garden* in Polish. The pupil provided a translation and helped the teacher to repeat the sentence. They then translated the sentence into Irish. By presenting herself as a learner the teacher gave this pupil a teaching role; experience of teaching as well as learning encourages learners to take their own learning initiatives.

Debating in Third Class

Fifth and Sixth Class founded a debating society that aroused the interest of younger pupils. A language support teacher decided to exploit this by giving the Third Class pupils in her language groups opportunities to hold debates in English on topics of interest to them. Teams were formed, and the teacher explained the basic rules of debating. Here are some of the points made by pupils when arguing the proposition 'Children should not get homework':

I think homework is good because when you're older you're not going to know anything. (Hungarian 1)

I think homework is good because if you're doing homework and your mam has something to do you are saying 'no I'm doing my homework'. (Latvian)

I think homework is good because you work hard. (Hebrew)

I think homework is terrible because you might promise your little brother or sister something but you can't because you're doing your homework. (English/Isoko)

I think homework is terrible because if you promise your friend that you will go outside and meet them and then you had to do your homework and then your friend will say why are you not playing with me because you are doing your homework. (Tagalog)

I think homework is bad because you worked hard in all of school and then finish your homework there not allowed to go outside because it's all dark. (Hungarian 2)

Third Class pupils' survey of their parents

Also in Third Class, the class teacher and language support teacher encouraged pupils to interview their parents, asking them about their cultural background and their views on living in Ireland, and then to get their parents to interview them. As one pupil explained to Déirdre Kirwan: *You interview your parents and your parents interview you about your home country and Ireland.* Apart from some help with spelling, the survey questions were the unaided work of the pupils.

Questions asked by the pupils:

What is your full name?
What is the name of the country you were born in?
What languages do you speak?
How many people in your family?
Where did you go to school in _____?
How did you go to school?
Describe how life is different in your country to life in Ireland.
Can you remember the name of any special song or poem or story from your country?
Can you tell me about it?

Questions asked by the parents:

> *Tell me about what you enjoy doing in school and why?*
> *Tell me about your friends.*
> *What do you want to be when you grow up and why?*
> *Tell me about your home country.*
> *Can you remember the name of any special song, poem, story from Ireland?*
> *Can you tell me about it?*

Because of the sensitive situation of some immigrant families, participation in this project was voluntary. Almost all pupils wrote their questions in English and their home language; answers were reported in English. Here are four examples:

Example 1 – Spanish and English

My name is [name deleted]. *I go to SBC. I am in Third Class. My favourite subject is Irish because I like the stories. I also really like Art and PE. My teacher is* [name deleted]. *I am eager to go to the library.*

Parent answers: *Spanish and English. Four. San José de* [unclear]. *By car. Weather warm and here it is a bit cold. Il niño* [unclear]. *The song is about how Jesus is alive.*

Pupil answers: *She likes art because it's fun and she really likes painting. She has lots of friends. They are …. I want to be a designer because I am creative. Caracas is the capital and 28 million people live in Venezuela. The Children of Lir. It's about a woman called Aoife who turns Lir's children into swans.*

Example 2 – English and Irish

I like yard time. Is maith liom súgradh. My best friend is [name deleted]. *Is í* [name deleted] *mo chara. I don't like homework. Ní maith liom obair bhaile.*

Parent answers: *Ireland. English. Eight. He walked. Not much technology. The Children of Lir. It was about children who belonged to Lir. Their mother died so Lir married Aoife. She put a spell on the children and turned them into swans and that is why you can't kill a swan.*

Pupil answers: *PE because I learn sports. My friends are funny and caring. A vet because I like animals. Ireland is big and beautiful. St. Patrick. It was about a man who was kidnapped and took to Ireland. He showed the … a man and picked up a shamrock and said in the name of the Father, and of the Son and of the Holy Spirit. Amen.*

Example 3 – English and Urdu
I go to Scoil Bhríde. I am anxious to do the St Patrick's project. Our school is huge. I like to do cross-country running. My teacher's name is [name deleted]. *My best friend is* [name deleted].

Parent answers: *Pakistan. English, Urdu and French. Ten. It is very hot in Pakistan. The national anthem. This song is about the Pakistani flag and the people that live in the country.*

Pupil answers: *I like to do Art, Maths, Handwriting and after school activities. My friends are [names deleted]. They are really nice. I want to be a doctor so I can help to cure people. Pakistan is good at cricket and sport. The Children of Lir. This story is about a king called Lir whose wife …*

Example 4 – English and Tagalog

I go to Scoil Bhríde. I am eager to learn well. My favourite subjects are English and Maths. I like making new friends. What I like most is playing in school.

Parent answers: *In the Philippines. Tagalog and English. Six in my family. [unclear] is the school that I go to in college. By jeep. You can't go to school when there's a flood or a storm.*

The Sixth Class language box

An increase in the work undertaken by pupils autonomously prompted a Sixth Class teacher to introduce a language box. This was situated in an accessible area of the senior corridor and children from all classes were invited to contribute, for example, their favourite recipes written in various languages (Figure 5.2), free

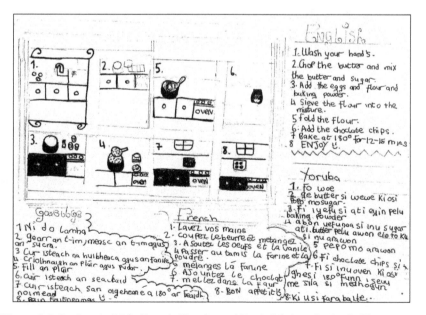

Figure 5.2 Recipes in Irish, French, Yoruba and English left in the Sixth Class language box (11+ years old).

writing in languages of choice, and personal profiles, one of which used twenty-three languages: Afrikaans, Albanian, Arabic, Basque, Bosnian, Bulgarian, Catalan, Cebuano, Chichewa, Croatian, Czech, Dutch, Esperanto, Hmong, Indonesian, Italian, Kazakh, Maltese, Portuguese, Slovak, Uzbek, Vietnamese, Welsh.

Pupil initiatives support classroom learning

From regularly engaging in learning activities that go beyond the teacher's requirements, it's a short step to autonomously undertaking initiatives that complement the work of the classroom in a variety of ways.

'It's a Small World'

A Second Class teacher celebrated European Day of Languages by teaching her class the Disney song 'It's a Small World After All'. This gave the pupils the idea of translating the chorus into all the home languages of the class and learning to sing it together in all those languages, as the teacher and pupils explained to Déirdre Kirwan:

> **DK:**   *Can you explain exactly how it happened?*
>
> **Teacher:**   *Exactly how it happened? Well, it started on European Languages Day, didn't it girls?*
>
> **Pupils:**   *Yes*
>
> **Teacher:**   *… where we learnt the song in English and then the girls said even though it is such a small world, we've brought the small world into our classroom with all these different languages, so they said why don't we sing this in all of our languages? So I said fine. Everybody went home, they translated into their own language, that was on Friday and they came back in on Monday and a few girls had remembered to do it. As the week went on everybody came in with it in their own language and we put it together and this is what we got.*
>
> **DK:**   *And did you tell me that the girls were practising this out in the yard and everything?*
>
> **Teacher:**   *They practised it more in the yard than we did in the classroom. I couldn't believe one day when we came in and everybody was able to sing it in everybody's language. It wasn't just in their own language. They had been listening to each other on the yard.*
>
> **Irish pupil:**   *… I started singing it in all the different languages.*
>
> **DK:**   *Isn't that fantastic!*

Irish pupil: *First I sang it in English, then Irish, then Polish, and then I sang a bit of it in Tagalog*

DK: *Who actually came up with the idea? … Was it as a result of European Day of Languages?*

Teacher: *Well, I think we were celebrating all of our languages that day anyway, so the idea just kind of formed itself*

DK: *Excellent. Very good. That's great. And there's a new language in this class that we didn't have last year. Does anybody know which language it is?*

Pupils: *Italian*

DK: *Italian! And how do we sing the verse in Italian?*

Pupils: [All sing chorus in Italian]

DK: *Excellent! Well do you know something? I can definitely tell you that there's no other Second Class in Ireland where the girls can sing the verse of a song or the chorus of a song in eleven different languages. So you are all unique. What are you?*

Pupils: *Unique*

DK: *You're unique.* [to pupil with her hand up] *Yes, what did you want to say to me?*

Pupil (L1: Konkani):   *We have two other languages but we wasn't able to get them.*

DK: *Oh! Not to worry. I mean eleven is quite good really I think.* [to another pupil with her hand up] *Were you going to say something?*

Pupil (L1: Yoruba):   *We're missing three languages.*

The twelve languages in which the class learnt the chorus were English, Irish, Yoruba, Polish, Romanian, Indonesian, Italian, Malayalam, Bosnian, Latvian, Tagalog and Tamil.

Word lists

In Third Class, pupils often take the initiative in compiling lists of words in various languages, using them to identify similarities and differences between languages. They derive great satisfaction from sharing their knowledge with teachers, the principal, visitors and anyone else who has time to listen to them. Birthday and Christmas cards are sometimes written to friends and teachers in languages that are not taught in school, and pupils' projects increasingly contain sections devoted to languages. One child collected information on traditional breakfasts in nineteen countries and included the names of some foods in the language of their country. Other pupils are keen to share what they can say in languages they are learning outside school – an Irish child who is learning

French from her grandmother, a Polish child who has learned to speak a little Korean from a computer game, English-speaking children who begin to write for themselves in their preferred additional language. The autonomous compilation of word lists continues through the senior classes.

The lure of Christmas

Festivals receive all due attention in Irish primary schools – St Patrick's Day, Halloween and above all Christmas. Perhaps because these festivals are an important part of life in the wider community, their approach stimulates pupils to undertake a variety of autonomous learning activities. In Fourth Class, for example, a Romanian speaker wrote a long story (six pages in her copybook) entitled 'The Christmas Investigation', mostly in English but including some Romanian; a native-born Irish pupil wrote an account of her holiday, 'Christmas in Spain', in English and Spanish; a Filipino pupil compiled a Christmas word list in English, Irish and Visayan; and another Filipino pupil translated an English poem into Tagalog. Figure 5.3 shows a Fourth Class pupil's dual-language story entitled 'Christmas'.

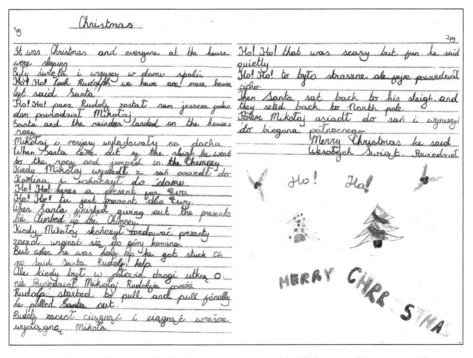

Figure 5.3 Fourth Class pupil's dual-language story entitled 'Christmas' (9+ years old).

Writing for pleasure

Many pupils write extensively for enjoyment. A Filipino pupil in Third Class, decided to keep a diary *for fun ... filled with stories*, writing it in Irish in the person of her dog, Oliver (Figure 5.4); her confidence and fluency are reflected in her handwriting. Another Third Class pupil wrote part of her homework in Spanish because no one in her family knew the language and she wanted to learn it; she got help from a Venezuelan classmate. Many pupils keep a diary and/or write stories outside school, often in more than one language. A Romanian pupil in Fifth Class, kept a diary in English and Romanian; she included words in five additional languages for which she provided an English translation at the side

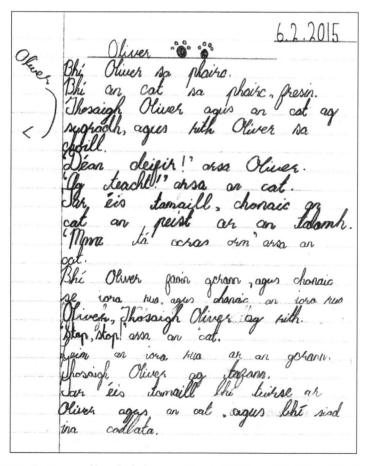

Figure 5.4 First page of her dog's diary, written in Irish by a Third Class Filipino pupil (8+ years old).

of the page as a reference for herself (Figure 5.5). She explained that *teacher said if you could add some languages, so I said to do it like this and I asked people for words* [in their language] *and then I put it together*. In addition to Romanian, English, Irish and French, this pupil said she also knew *a bit of Polish and a bit of Iraq and some Spanish*. She liked using different languages when writing because *it's good that I learn a lot of languages and it makes it sound better*. Another Fifth Class pupil whose family came from Benin wrote an admiring profile of her class teacher in French, taking the opportunity to include some words that had not yet come up in class (Figure 5.6).

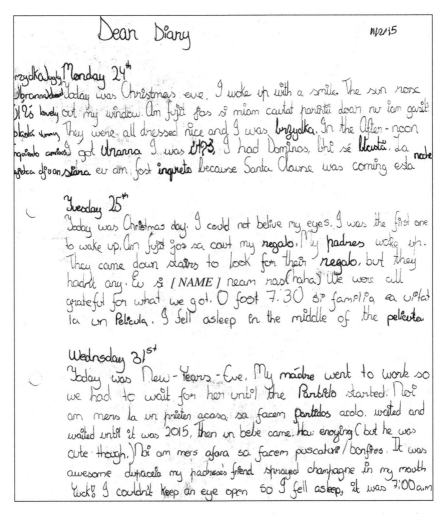

Figure 5.5 Extract from diary written in English and Romanian, with words in other languages, by Fifth Class pupil (10+ years old).

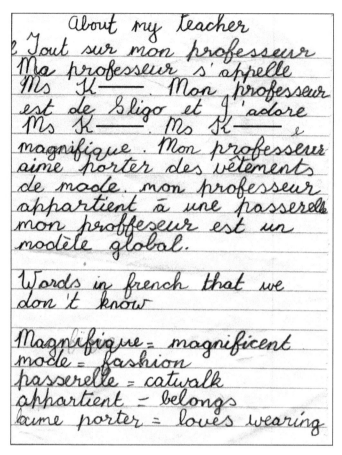

Figure 5.6 Fifth Class pupil's description of her teacher – the pupil's family came from Benin (10+ years old).

Sixth Class: shopping for clothes

Towards the end of morning school one day, a Sixth Class discussion of similarities and differences between languages had touched on the issue of inter-comprehension between closely related languages. During their lunch break two pupils, one from Poland and the other from Ukraine, devised a short sketch to demonstrate the close similarity between words for various items of clothing in the two languages; the Polish pupil played the shopkeeper and the Ukrainian the customer. Shortly before the beginning of afternoon school they presented themselves at the principal's office and offered to perform the sketch so that she could video-record it (senior pupils were well aware of her research interest in the implementation of the school's language policy). The Polish and Ukrainian pupils were assisted by a Romanian and a native-born Irish pupil, the former acting as clothes rack and the latter holding a prompt card. At the end of the performance Déirdre Kirwan recorded this interview with the four pupils.

DK:	*OK girls, that was really good, and you made that up during lunchtime, did you?*
Pupils:	*Yeah*
DK:	*So tell me about it now*
Pupil 1:	*It's a shop, and me and Katja can communicate with each other very easily while she's talking in Ukrainian and I'm talking in Polish and she just comes in and she asks me for different sorts of clothing and I tell her where they are and how much they cost*
Pupil 2:	*And Polish and Ukrainian are really similar, like some words are very similar to each other, so we really understand each other*
DK:	*So can you give me some examples in terms of the clothes you were talking about there*
Pupil 1:	*bluza*
Pupil 2:	*bluzka ... kurtka*
Pupil 1:	*kurtka*
Pupil 2:	*škarpetki*
Pupil 1:	*skarpety*
Pupil 2:	*piżami*
Pupil 1:	*piżama*
DK:	*That's obviously pyjamas*
Both:	*Yes*

A Sixth Class pupil teaches a Yoruba song to Junior Infants

A Sixth Class pupil from Nigeria taught her classmates a traditional Yoruba song, 'Under the Orange Tree', which she translated into English (Figure 5.7). She was then invited to teach the song to a Junior Infants class where some of the pupils also spoke Yoruba. This pupil had come to Scoil Bhríde in Fourth Class, having previously attended a school where the use of home languages was forbidden. Scoil Bhríde's approach to language education had given her an interest in exploring her own language and culture, which she did with help from her mother. The experience of teaching 'Under the Orange Tree' to Junior Infants was very affirming for her, drawing attention to her Nigerian identity and enhancing her self-confidence, which was evident in her increasingly assured body language. Her interest and motivation communicated itself to a wide range of people, including other pupils who spoke Yoruba at home and pupils who were inspired to explore their own linguistic and cultural

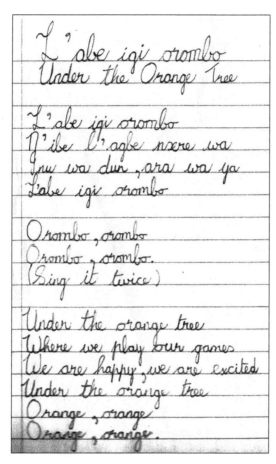

Figure 5.7 'Under the Orange Tree', a Yoruba song translated into English by a Sixth Class Nigerian pupil (11+ years old) and taught to a class of Junior Infants.

backgrounds. Teachers too were influenced by this example, which made visible the positive outcomes to be gained when an interdependent relationship is established between school knowledge and pupils' action knowledge (Barnes 1976: 81).

Autonomous learning beyond the curriculum and the classroom

The Fifth Class fashion show

A group of five pupils in Fifth Class, devised their own fashion show, entitled 'Linguistic Fashion', during play time. Their home languages were Amharic,

Foula, German, Romanian and Igbo. Two pupils acted as presenters. The first presenter, whose home language was Amharic, spoke in French; the second provided a translation into her home language, German. The first model, whose home language was Igbo, used Irish and Igbo to describe her outfit. In Amharic the first presenter asked the second model, a Romanian speaker, to describe what she was wearing, repeating the question in French: *Qu'est ce que tu portes?* The model answered: *Je porte des pantalons noirs, t-shirt rose, Convers vert et bleu.* The second presenter translated this into German. Switching to Irish, both presenters introduced the third participant as *an mainicín is fearr sa tír* ('the best model in the country'). She described her outfit in her home language, Foula, and English. Using French and German respectively, the two presenters then invited the audience to say whether the outfits on display were *à la mode* or *mal*. As a finale, all five pupils used all the languages at their disposal to express their appreciation of the audience. The fashion show was performed first for the rest of the class and then for all pupils and their parents as part of the school's International Day celebration.

Pupils themselves promote home languages

A pupil in Sixth Class had been born in South Africa. Her home language was English, but realizing that Scoil Bhríde valued all languages, she began to take an interest in her mother's first language, Chichewa. She created a diary in the shape of a heart and recorded English words from A to Z with their equivalents in Chichewa. She dedicated her dictionary to her mother, her teacher and her classmates.

Two Nigerian girls devised a plan to encourage more pupils to learn and speak their respective home languages:

1. *Make a poster to encourage people to speak their own language.*
2. *Knit an L for Languages and get teacher to sew it.*
3. *Get girls who can speak their language and teach the people who can't. In the yard. Like a Yoruba who can speak it and the girls who can't can learn from the girl who can speak it.*
4. *We'll see how it works out.*

One of these pupils had taught 'Under the Orange Tree' to Junior Infants (Figure 5.7 above). She summed up her feelings about Yoruba and Scoil Bhríde's language policy in the text reproduced in Figure 5.8; she also devised a poster on the theme 'A Child without a Language Is a Child without a Soul' (Figure 5.9). She explained that her family wanted her to speak Yoruba

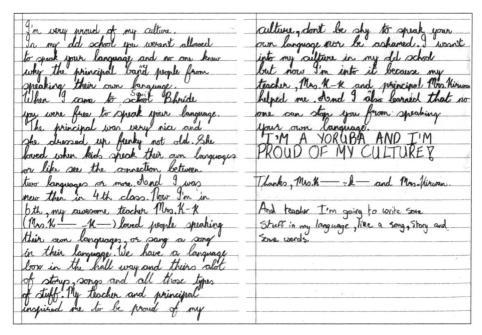

I'm very proud of my culture.
In my old school you weren't allowed
to speak your language and no one knew
why the principal banned people from
speaking their own language.
When I came to school Bhríde
you were free to speak your language.
The principal was very nice and
she dressed up funky not old. She
loved when kids speak their own languages
or like see the connection between
two languages or more. And I was
new then in 4th class. Now I'm in
6th, my awesome teacher Mrs. K-K
(Mrs. K—— -K—) loved people speaking
their own languages, or sang a song
in their language. We have a language
box in the hall way and theirs alot
of storys, songs and all those types
of stuff. My teacher and principal
inspired me to be proud of my

culture, don't be shy to speak your
own language nor be ashamed. I wasn't
into my culture in my old school
but now I'm into it because my
teacher, Mrs. K-K and principal Mrs. Kirwan
helped me. And I also learned that no
one can stop you from speaking
your own language.
I'M A YORUBA AND I'M
PROUD OF MY CULTURE!

Thanks, Mrs. K—— -k— and Mrs. Kirwan.

And teacher I'm going to write some
stuff in my language, like a song, story and
some words.

Figure 5.8 A Sixth Class pupil's expression of her pride in her Yoruba identity (11+ years old).

Figure 5.9 A Sixth Class Nigerian pupil's poster proclaiming the importance of home languages (11+ years old).

at home, but she had never done so. Then one day her grandfather phoned and she spoke to him in Yoruba. She explained to her surprised family that a classmate had helped her to learn the language and she had been inspired by Scoil Bhríde, where pupils are free to speak their home languages; now her mother was helping her to become more proficient in Yoruba by watching Nigerian cartoons. This pupil said she liked the fact that when new pupils come to the school they are supported in learning English *and* their home language; she gave the example of a Romanian speaker in her former school who had forgotten her home language and was now a monolingual speaker of English. She made the point that *if you don't know your language future generations won't know it and your tradition, your culture is gone.* When she came to Scoil Bhríde in Fourth Class and heard other pupils speaking their home languages she wanted to learn Yoruba: *When I started to learn different languages it made my heart feel warm, so I wanted to learn it as well ... it gave me this sort of spark inside.*

Pupils learn non-curricular languages

Scoil Bhríde's language policy means that throughout the school, pupils learn and use fragments of one another's home languages. Especially in the senior classes, moreover, it is by no means uncommon for pupils to find ways of learning languages that are not included in the curriculum. For example, one child, a native speaker of English, produced a simple identity text in Italian (Figure 5.10). She received help from her father, who had learned Italian for a short time when he was in school; she also asked the special needs assistant, who is Italian, for help with pronunciation. She was very happy to read her Italian text aloud to her classmates, the principal and anyone else who was prepared to listen. A pupil whose home language is Yoruba became interested in learning Korean. She watched YouTube presentations to help her and confidently announced in Korean: *Hi, my name's Odile. How are you?* A Filipino pupil's interest in Japanese prompted her to learn how to pronounce a number of phrases in the language, and a Romanian speaker wrote an identity text in twenty-four languages, getting help from school friends for some of the languages and using Google Translate for others.

When Déirdre Kirwan retired, every pupil in the school wrote her a letter of thanks and good wishes; many pupils wrote in two languages. A pupil whose home language is Yoruba wrote in Spanish and English (Figure 5.11). This is her explanation of how she went about learning Spanish on her own:

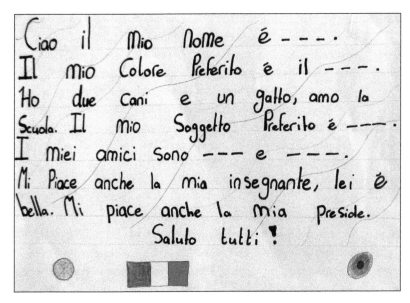

Figure 5.10 Simple identity text written in Italian by Sixth Class Irish pupil (11+ years old).

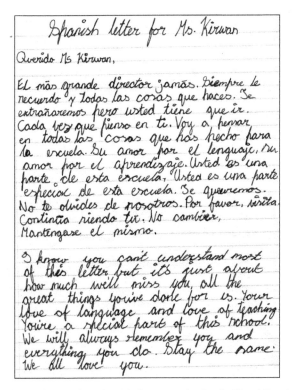

Figure 5.11 Letter in Spanish and English written by Sixth Class Nigerian pupil (11+ years old) who taught herself Spanish.

DK: *You wrote me a beautiful letter. The first half of it was in Spanish and
the second half of it was in English. What I'm intrigued about is that you
wrote the first half of it in Spanish, but you don't learn Spanish in school.*

Pupil: *Yeah. I just love the Spanish culture because Spanish people are so free
and fun, and their language, I feel that it's really beautiful being able to
speak that language. I speak Yoruba and I love to be able to speak other
languages because I love going to other countries and seeing the nature
in that country and the culture that they have in that country, so Spain
is one of my main countries that I love very much.*

DK: *And that encouraged you to learn the language.*

Pupil: *Yeah.*

DK: *What I want to know is, how did you learn it?*

Pupil: *Well em the school library has two Spanish books that I think would be
easy for starting off so em there's a CD in one of them so the guy in the
CD taught me a few words of how to say hello, where you're from, where
you live and stuff like that, and em then I have a book like if I want to
say what a chair is in Spanish or I want to put chair into a sentence,
then I got a verbal book to learn my nouns and proverbs and stuff like
that, and eh I'm thinking of getting a class as well and I'm doing Spanish
in secondary school.*

DK: *Oh excellent. Well, you'll be well ahead of the posse. So essentially
you learned it from two books that were there to teach people to learn
Spanish and you found them in the school library.*

Pupil: *Yeah.*

DK: *Did you use the internet?*

Pupil: *If I want to do something quick like let's say eh a sentence in Spanish I
use Google Translate, but usually I use my own words and then I see if
Google Translate can get it right or not, to see if I actually want to use
Google Translate ... I use Babel and the online translating for like for to
teach you and I have Five Thousand Words in Spanish.*

DK: *What's Five Thousand Words in Spanish?*

Pupil: *It's like ... it teaches you how to speak about your family, places, how to
speak in restaurants in Spanish, how to ask for directions and it gives
you quizzes as well to see if you're doing well or if you should go back to
another lesson.*

DK: *Is that a book or is it on the internet?*

Pupil: *It's on the internet.*

At the end of Chapter 2 we quoted what some of Scoil Bhríde's pupils said
about the school's approach to language education. The examples of autonomous
language learning initiatives we have brought together in this chapter provide

further confirmation of the school's success: outside as well as inside school pupils are ever ready for new linguistic challenges. As a Romanian pupil said: *It's like you're cool if you know so many languages ... and my best friend is Polish, so when I visit her house everyone there speaks Polish and I get better every time I can speak it, and when she comes to my house she learns* [Romanian]. A native-born Irish pupil identified the true nature of Scoil Bhríde's educational purpose and achievement when she remarked: *It's not really about which language you're learning, it's like how to learn a language.* Learning *how* to learn, in other words, is an essential part of all learning, as the PSC insists (Government of Ireland 1999a: 7).

Learner autonomy and plurilingualism

Although it was elaborated in relation to foreign language learning, the version of learner autonomy summarized at the beginning of this chapter drew much of its theoretical underpinning not from research into second language acquisition but from investigations of classroom discourse enacted in the language of schooling. The work of Douglas Barnes (1976) was foundational, while additional insights came from such researchers as Robin Alexander (2008), Neil Mercer and Karen Littleton (Mercer 1995, 2000, Mercer and Littleton 2007), and Gordon Wells (2009). The dialogic view of classroom discourse that underlies this research assigns a central role to learner agency in the interactive processes of learning, and that is the essence of learner autonomy. The dialogic view also emphasizes the role that the learner's existing knowledge plays in the acquisition of new knowledge. Crucially, existing knowledge includes the learner's action knowledge, and as we pointed out in Chapter 2 (pp. 38–9 above), according to this understanding of learning, the goal of education is to present and mediate school knowledge, or curriculum content, in such a way that it enlarges and refines learners' action knowledge.

In the version of language learner autonomy described in detail by Little, Dam and Legenhausen (2017), learners are required to set their own learning targets and select learning activities and materials. In order to do this, they must bring their action knowledge into play: pursuit of individual and group interests is what drives their learning forward. This goes a long way towards disposing of the motivational problem that is often identified as one of the principal barriers to language learning success. From the beginning, the target language is as far as possible the medium of all classroom discourse, metacognitive as well as communicative. Nevertheless, the learners' first language is overwhelmingly the medium of their action knowledge. Danish inevitably 'interferes' with their attempts to speak and write English, and it is ever-present as a source of (mostly unconscious) knowledge about language use in the social context of the classroom. Danish, in other words, is the soil in which learners' proficiency in English grows. In Scoil Bhríde, ELLs' home languages play the same role in relation to English, Irish and French. This establishes an explicit relation between learning at school and pupils' lives outside school, which also has an impact on native-born Irish pupils whose home language is English. The readiness with which pupils take autonomous learning initiatives is evidence of the strong motivational advantage as well as the general educational benefit that accrues from encouraging the use of home languages in the classroom.

The widespread development of a capacity for autonomous learning in Scoil Bhríde's pupils adds a further dimension to our understanding of plurilingual education. By definition, all the languages in a plurilingual repertoire are available for immediate, spontaneous use in appropriate communicative contexts (cf. our discussion in Chapter 3, pp. 81–2 above). Because each language is a fully integrated part of the individual learner/user's everyday lived language, it is available as a channel of her agency. In a foreign language classroom, this effect is achieved by ensuring that the target language is the dominant medium of learning; in Scoil Bhríde, on the other hand, home language use plays a central role in the development of fully integrated plurilingual repertoires. Both approaches exploit the capacity for autonomous behaviour that learners bring with them to school; both approaches, in other words, use autonomy to develop autonomy. As defined by the CEFR, plurilingual education fosters the learner's capacity to use two or more languages agentively in order to perform tasks (CEFR 2.1; Council of Europe 2001: 9). The Council of Europe's various publications on the topic say very little about practical pedagogy; Scoil Bhríde's experience, however, suggests that the ability to exercise agency in language use may be a direct consequence of exercising agency in language learning and vice versa.

Conclusion

We explained in Chapter 2 that Scoil Bhríde was first motivated to develop its distinctive approach to language education because it wished to include ELLs as fully as possible in the life of the school, which entailed allowing them to make use of the language that was central to their identity and their primary cognitive tool. We concluded that chapter by providing evidence of the success of the approach and its generally positive reception by teachers and pupils. Chapters 3, 4 and 5 have offered a detailed description of the approach from the perspectives of classroom discourse, plurilingual literacy development and autonomous learning. We conclude our description of Scoil Bhríde's integrated approach to language education by making the following claims:

1. The educational inclusion of immigrant learners is most likely to succeed if they are encouraged to use their home languages at school, inside as well as outside the classroom.
2. The use of home languages in the classroom facilitates comparison between languages, which is likely to foster the development of unusually high levels of language awareness in all learners.
3. As they develop literacy in the language of schooling and curriculum languages, immigrant pupils should be encouraged to transfer their literacy skills to their home languages. In order to succeed, this requires effective school–home liaison.
4. Taken together, these pedagogical practices arouse in pupils a level of interest in language and language learning that is likely to manifest itself in ambitious autonomous learning initiatives related to language.

It remains to consider the implications of these claims for broader contexts of language education.

6

Implications and Consequences

We began this book by summarizing the background to our study: the pattern of recent immigration to Ireland and the official educational response to the challenge of linguistic diversity in a country that is officially bilingual but for most practical purposes monolingual. We then described the distinctive approach to language education developed by one primary school, Scoil Bhríde (Cailíní), Blanchardstown, in order to accommodate an unusually diverse pupil cohort. Essentially, the approach grew out of the decision to encourage pupils from immigrant families to use their home languages inside as well as outside the classroom and as far as possible to include those languages in pupils' literacy development. Evolving over more than two decades, the approach has generated high levels of language awareness and enthusiasm for language learning; the constant reference to home languages in the discourse of the classroom has evidently had a positive impact on native-born Irish pupils' attitude to Irish as their 'home language', and from an early age, pupils have shown an unusual willingness to undertake ambitious language learning projects of their own. The success of the approach is confirmed not only by the many examples of classroom interaction and pupils' written work we have presented in previous chapters: the school performs consistently above the national average in the standardized tests that all pupils, including ELLs, take annually from First to Sixth Class.

In Chapter 3 we considered the ways in which home languages are included in classroom interaction and contribute to the learning of *all* pupils, concluding the chapter by arguing that Scoil Bhríde's approach is a convincing example of 'plurilingual education' as promoted by the Council of Europe. In Chapter 4 we explained how home languages are included in ELLs' literacy development, which leads them to produce parallel texts in three or four languages. English and Irish are taught by involving pupils in interactive communication and providing extensive modelling to support the production of written texts;

the only consistent focus on linguistic form arises from a general concern for orthographic accuracy. Supported by their reading, pupils' prolific writing in multiple languages evidently helps them to develop a sense of what is linguistically and discursively appropriate in the texts they produce. In Chapter 5 we explored the generally reflective approach to teaching and learning that arises from the constant reference to home languages in classroom interaction and described various autonomous learning initiatives undertaken by pupils individually and collaboratively. Originally, Scoil Bhríde's decision to include home languages in their pupils' education was designed to acknowledge their linguistic identity and encourage them to use their home language as a cognitive tool. We have also cited evidence, however, especially in Chapter 5, to show that the approach encouraged some pupils to take a more positive attitude to their home language and the culture associated with it.

As Chapter 2 made clear, Scoil Bhríde's approach arose in circumstances of increasing linguistic diversity – by 2015, 80 per cent of the pupils came from immigrant families and between them they had fifty-one home languages. This prompted Déirdre Kirwan to seek a response to the challenge this posed, first by attending the in-service seminars provided by Integrate Ireland Language and Training (IILT) and using the tools and supports IILT developed, and then by undertaking PhD research that investigated evolving practice at various levels of the school. Her interest and commitment were shared by Scoil Bhríde's teachers, who from the early 2000s onwards were all teaching classes that included a growing number of ELLs. In other words, Scoil Bhríde developed its distinctive approach in response to a distinctive though constantly evolving situation, and the successful implementation of the approach was due to a strongly collaborative ethos among the teaching staff. This prompts questions about sustainability. Since 2008, when IILT ceased to exist, schools have largely been left to find their own solutions to the challenge of educating a linguistically diverse population. This prompts questions about the generalizability of Scoil Bhríde's approach and its implications for teacher education. The first three sections of this chapter address these questions.

As Chapter 2 also made clear, Scoil Bhríde's approach was shaped by a concern to take seriously the child-centred ethos of the Primary School Curriculum and implement principles of inclusive pedagogy. It was not driven by hypotheses drawn from theories of second language acquisition, and there was never any attempt to subject it to empirical investigation of the kind undertaken by second language acquisition research. Its successes were, however, extensively documented in a variety of ways: video recordings of classroom interactions, pupil presentations, and interviews with teachers and pupils; teachers' records of especially memorable pupil contributions and successful lessons; examples of pupils' written work. That documentation provided the basis for the 'thick description' we have elaborated in this book. Our descriptions and interpretations of classroom practice and pupils' learning nevertheless raise questions that invite further investigation, and the final section of the chapter identifies the most obvious of them and offers some concluding thoughts on 'plurilingual and intercultural education'.

Sustainability

Scoil Bríde's approach developed over two decades as the linguistic diversity of the school's pupil cohort gradually increased. In the mid-1990s the school had a handful of immigrant pupils; by the school year 2003/2004, 20 per cent of the pupil cohort came from immigrant families, and over the next twelve years that percentage increased fourfold. By then, the great majority of ELLs entering the school were Junior Infants born in Ireland. The flexibility of the approach is guaranteed by the last of the five principles on which it is founded: teacher autonomy. Teachers are expected to respect and implement the school's language policy (see Appendix), but the precise relation between policy and pedagogical practice in their classroom is for them to determine. It is nevertheless clear from the examples presented in Chapters 2–5 that the approach achieved a high degree of coherence, largely because teachers were prepared to share their experience with one another and forge a common response to the challenges they faced. By the time Déirdre Kirwan retired, in 2015, the approach was fundamental to all the school's activities and gave it a unique character. There were two potential threats to its sustainability: a sudden change in the linguistic profile of the pupil cohort and significant turnover of teaching staff. To date there is no indication that the percentage of ELLs and the number of home languages present in the school are likely to diminish, but the second threat became a reality in 2015. The principal retired, and four teachers (approximately 25 per cent of the teaching staff) who had played a central role in the development and implementation of the school's language policy were themselves appointed to principalships; one of them took over from Déirdre Kirwan and the rest moved to other schools. The approach nevertheless survives, and newly qualified teachers continue to be inducted into modes of classroom practice for which their pre-service education did little to prepare them.

The question of sustainability also arises for the individual pupil. By the time most of Scoil Bhríde's ELLs move on to post-primary school, they have native or near-native literate proficiency in English and are also confident communicators in Irish and French with age-appropriate levels of literacy to match. In September 2013 Scoil Bhríde moved into new buildings adjacent to the old ones. A week after the primary term began, a Filipino pupil who had been in Sixth Class the previous year came to visit. She called first to the principal's office, greeting her in Irish and telling her about her new school, also in Irish: the fact that she had a different teacher for each subject instead of just one class teacher as at Scoil Bhríde, the different subjects she would be studying and so on. She then asked if she could visit her Sixth Class teacher and have a look around the new school. As the principal showed her the way to her former teacher's classroom, the conversation continued in Irish, turning to the new building and what people thought of it. Altogether it lasted approximately twelve minutes and showed that the former pupil had not lost her ability to communicate spontaneously and fluently in Irish.

This example suggests that if Scoil Bhríde's pupils experience difficulties coping with the post-primary curriculum, those difficulties are unlikely to be linguistic in origin. The continuation of their language education, however, may be very different from what they have experienced so far. For example, the minority of students who come to post-primary education with some proficiency in French pose a challenge to teachers who are used to teaching classes of complete beginners. In one school the French teacher used students from Scoil Bhríde to support their peers in group work, but in another school, students from Scoil Bhríde were sent to the library during French classes until such time as the rest of the class caught up with them. As for Irish, many of Scoil Bhríde's former pupils have reported that at post-primary school they are taught Irish through English and are rarely if ever challenged to use the language for purposes of spontaneous communication. To date, the concept of plurilingual education has made little impact on the Irish post-primary sector, and this can only be counted a loss for students whose primary education has made them efficient plurilingual communicators and pluriliterate learners.

Generalizability

Scoil Bhríde does not enjoy special status. Like all other primary schools in Ireland, it is entitled to additional resources to provide English language support for ELLs and learning support for pupils with learning difficulties. But its approach to language education evolved without the added stimulus of targeted funding or the status of a special project. And although the school took advantage of the resources developed by IILT and benefited from Déirdre Kirwan's PhD research, most of the teachers included ELLs' home languages in the life of the classroom simply by drawing on their pedagogical experience, intuitions and instincts. These considerations prompt the question: to what extent is Scoil Bhríde's approach generalizable to other schools? If one school can organize teaching and learning in this way, why can't other schools follow suit? The situation is, however, less straightforward than this question implies.

Scoil Bhríde's approach evolved in response to a gradual increase in the percentage of ELLs attending the school and a corresponding diversification of the linguistic profile of the pupil cohort. Given the school's openness to the use of ELLs' home languages, it is tempting to argue that at any stage between the late 1990s and 2015, the role of those languages in classroom discourse reflected the limits of the possible. According to Scoil Bhríde's experience, activities that are feasible when 80 per cent of the pupils in a class are ELLs remain feasible when the percentage drops to 60 and then to 40. But common sense suggests that sooner or later a point will be reached when the number of ELLs and the diversity of home languages are no longer large enough to support this version of the plurilingual approach. One way of maintaining the approach and generalizing it across the primary sector would be to assign the role of educating ELLs to particular schools, thus ensuring a minimum percentage of ELLs and diversity of home languages in the pupil cohort of those schools. But it is a long-established policy that primary schools admit pupils from their local area, which means that the linguistic profile of the pupil population is largely a matter of chance, and any attempt to change this policy would encounter strong opposition.

Another way of approaching the issue of generalizability is to focus on the pivotal role that Irish has played in Scoil Bhríde. On the one hand, Irish is a new language for all pupils, native-born Irish as well as ELLs; on the other hand, its role in Ireland's national identity is confirmed when Irish pupils claim it as their 'home language'. Seen in this way, Irish is the common L2 glue that bonds together the various languages in each pupil's plurilingual repertoire. The many examples we have given show how, from the beginning of Junior Infants, an English-medium primary school can use Irish as an alternative (though necessarily subordinate) medium of classroom communication. By processing curriculum content bilingually in dual-language texts, pupils gradually develop biliteracy and in due course high levels of fluency in speaking and writing Irish. If all primary schools approached the teaching of Irish in this way, encouraging pupils from an early age to compare and contrast features of English and Irish, it should be possible to include ELLs' home languages in this process, whatever their number in a given classroom.

There is already official support for this kind of approach to the teaching of English and Irish. The new Primary Language Curriculum, introduced in 2017/2018 for the four years from Junior Infants to Second Class, 'integrates English and Irish and includes all children and the language knowledge and experiences that children bring to school' (Department of Education and Skills 2015: 7). In its present form this new curriculum gives the strong impression that English and Irish should be integrated in a closed system, but it is currently being revised to take account of ELLs' home languages. The strategy document *Languages Connect*, moreover, acknowledges 'the need for an integrated policy covering all aspects of languages in the education system' (Department of Education and Skills 2017a: 6). It also includes the languages of immigrants among Ireland's strengths and announces plans to provide for those languages in the curriculum. The accompanying implementation plan promises to develop guidelines for teaching children with a home language other than Irish or English (Department of Education and Skills 2017b: 16). It adds that 'guidelines and good practice exemplars will be developed and made available to principals, teachers and parents on their role in supporting an intercultural dimension and promoting the home language, where the home language is neither Irish nor English' (Department of Education and Skills 2017b: 17). This addition is referenced to an article by Déirdre Kirwan (Kirwan 2015). These developments give cause to hope that Irish primary education is moving towards the more general adoption of a plurilingual approach such as we have described in this book.

Meanwhile, however, the 1996 version of the Department's circular on the granting of exemption from Irish remains in force (Circular 12/96; Department of Education and Science 1996), allowing that 'pupils from abroad, who have no understanding of English when enrolled, would be required to study one language only, Irish or English'. In other words, such pupils need not learn Irish if they enrol in an English-medium school or English if they enrol in an Irish-medium school. This even-handed policy fails to explain what kind of lives will be lived by immigrants to Ireland who learn only Irish; in any case, as Scoil Bhríde's experience shows, the policy imposes an unnecessary limitation on the language education of primary pupils from immigrant families.

The question also arises: would it be possible to transplant Scoil Bhríde's approach to primary schools in another jurisdiction? Assuming the absence of insuperable political obstacles and a culture of collaboration among teachers, our answer is yes; although bearing in mind the pivotal role played by Irish in Scoil Bhríde, implementation would be greatly facilitated if all pupils, native-born and immigrant, were learning a common second or foreign language from an early age. In non-English-speaking countries, the practice of teaching English to very young learners could well provide the L2 glue that Irish provides in Ireland.

In the previous section we offered anecdotal evidence to suggest that Scoil Bhríde's pupils are likely to have a very different experience of language education when they make the transition to post-primary level. Admittedly, structural features of post-primary education make it more difficult to respond to the challenges posed by linguistic diversity and convert it into educational capital. For one thing, whereas the primary curriculum is holistic in conception and implementation, the post-primary curriculum is divided into different subjects, most of which are taught without reference to one another. As a consequence, communication and collaboration among teachers tend to be much less frequent than at primary level. For another thing, whereas primary schools are centrally concerned with developing pupils' literacy and equipping them in due course to meet the challenges of post-primary and tertiary education, post-primary schools tend to treat the language of schooling as transparent. No doubt there are exceptions, but in post-primary education generally there is no sense that each teacher is a language teacher, responsible for introducing students to the terminology, genres and text types that are fundamental to the practice and development of their discipline (cf. the documents and resources developed by the Council of Europe's project on Languages of Schooling).[1] Without such a sense there is little chance that a plurilingual approach will be adopted at post-primary level in Ireland.

The role of teacher education

Current preparation to meet the challenges of linguistic diversity

Informal enquiries suggest that programmes of primary teacher education in Ireland and the UK address the challenges of linguistic diversity in two ways.

---

[1] https://www.coe.int/en/web/language-policy/languages-of-schooling

EAL and the needs of ELLs are included as a sub-theme of other areas – for example, in modules on literacy, supporting learners with difficulties, or the use of information technologies to provide differentiated instruction; in addition, many programmes also offer elective modules on EAL. This optionality is commonly defended by pointing out that immigrant populations are not evenly distributed so that many teachers will never be required to manage linguistically diverse classes. Such a defence loses plausibility, however, as our societies become more diverse. In any case, even recently qualified teachers at Scoil Bhríde report that their pre-service education left them unprepared to manage linguistic diversity in their classrooms.

In Chapter 1 we summarized the official response to the growth of linguistic diversity in Irish schools: additional resources were provided to help pupils and students from immigrant families to become proficient in English as the language of schooling. IILT's *English Language Proficiency Benchmarks* (IILT 2003a, 2003b) were designed not as separate curricula but as a means of gauging and describing the extent to which individual ELLs could participate in mainstream curriculum learning at different levels of proficiency in English; the *Benchmarks* assumed close collaboration between English language support teachers and class or subject teachers. But notwithstanding the relation of the *Benchmarks* to the curriculum and the fact that IILT's in-service seminars repeatedly emphasized the importance of maintaining home languages, official policy as well as practice in the majority of schools implied that ELLs posed a problem to be solved by assimilating them as quickly as possible into the monolingual discourse of English-medium schooling. The more we treat EAL and the needs of ELLs as a special case to be remedied, the more we run the risk of replacing the reciprocity of integration with the one-way process of assimilation.

The report *English as an Additional Language in Undergraduate Teacher Education Programmes in Ireland* (Bracken et al., n.d.) is based on a 2009 survey of students at two colleges of education, one in Ireland and the other in Northern Ireland. Its overall finding is that there is a need to 'strengthen student teacher capacities in providing for the teaching and learning of pupils with EAL requirements' (Bracken et al.: 36). Accordingly, the first of the report's recommendations is that 'all student teachers should be provided with more than a basic introduction to the knowledge and skills which inform good practice in contexts of linguistic diversity' (Bracken et al.: 36). But what are the knowledge and skills to which they should be introduced? And what exactly is good practice in contexts of linguistic diversity? The report does not tell us, but it cites one student teacher as saying:

We should do TEFL in college as part of the course as I feel it is very important nowadays. It would also be a huge benefit to us when looking for jobs. I feel that if it was part of the course it would be of more benefit to us and we would understand it. I do not feel prepared at all to teach English as a foreign language. (Bracken et al., n.d.: 33)

It is a sad reflection on the course this student was following that he could equate meeting the needs of ELLs with teaching English as a foreign language. In any case, Scoil Bhríde's experience suggests that the answers to our questions lie not in additional training to teach EAL but rather in a new exploration of the relation between language and learning and the very nature of learning itself.

A new focus on the relation between language and learning

Scoil Bhríde's decision to encourage ELLs to use their home languages in the classroom as well as in the yard was prompted by a recognition that pupils from immigrant families cannot be fully included in the life of the school if they are required to leave their home language at the school gate. Each pupil's home language is, after all, central to her identity, her sense of herself as an individual in relation to other individuals; it is also the default medium of her discursive thinking and thus her primary cognitive tool. At the beginning of Chapter 3 we distinguished between teaching as transmission and teaching as exploration and interpretation. Teaching as transmission assumes that the school's task is to fill empty vessels with knowledge; teaching as exploration and interpretation includes an acknowledgement that learning at school will be effective to the extent that the presentation and processing of curriculum content takes account of learners' action knowledge, what they have learnt outside school. The practice of encouraging the use of home languages in class and exploring similarities and differences between them and English and Irish depends on a commitment to exploratory and interpretative modes of talk in which pupils participate as experts. As the examples we have presented in Chapters 2–5 confirm, expert status engages the individual pupil's interest and reinforces her motivation. Learning by transmission is essentially a matter of understanding, remembering and regularly demonstrating that one has remembered. Learning by exploration and interpretation involves participation and collaboration; progression in learning is measured not only by the ability to pass tests but by pupils' individual and collaborative contributions to the life of the classroom. ELLs clearly need focused language support, but that does not mean that they need to be taught English as though it were a foreign language. From the beginning they should be treated as fully integrated members of their class and provided with support of the kind we have illustrated – support that repeatedly scaffolds and models the various forms of oral and written discourse on which their participation depends.

David Little has long argued that foreign language teachers cannot be expected to promote autonomous learning in their classrooms if they have not themselves experienced what it is to be an autonomous language learner (see, e.g., Little 1995, 2007; also Little, Dam and Legenhausen 2017, Chapter 8). The same consideration applies to the use of exploratory and interpretative talk to integrate the teaching of English and Irish as required by the new Primary Language Curriculum. At least some of the courses taught in Irish colleges of education should include both languages in much the same way as in Scoil Bhríde's classrooms. Course content should be presented in Irish as well as English, and students should be required to process that content in both languages, in writing as well as orally. What is more, key concepts and the nature of fundamental processes should be explored with reference to all the other languages available to the members of a given class: foreign languages learnt at school and the home languages of students from immigrant families. If student primary teachers were educated in this way they would know from personal experience not only how to achieve the aims of the new Primary Language Curriculum but also how to make use of ELLs' home languages.

From record-keeping to reflective practice

In Ireland as elsewhere, accountability has been a key issue in education for at least the past two decades. The 1998 Education Act (Irish Statute Book 1998) focuses on evaluation and the need periodically to report the results of evaluation to pupils and their parents. This entails developing appropriate assessment procedures, creating and maintaining individual records of pupils' progress and achievement, and providing parents with clear and accessible assessment reports. Circular 0056/2011, on 'Initial Steps in the Implementation of the National Literacy and Numeracy Strategy', likewise draws attention to the importance of documentation:

> Parents play a critical role in supporting their children's learning. Schools can strengthen the capacity of parents to support their children in this way by sharing meaningful information with parents about the progress that children are achieving in the education system. This information needs to draw on the different sources of evidence that teachers use, such as conversations with

the learner, examination of students' own self-assessment data, documented observations of the learner's engagement with tasks, outcomes of other assessment tasks and tests, and examples of students' work. In turn, parents will often be able to enrich teachers' knowledge of their students' progress through providing further information about the students' learning at home. (Department of Education and Skills 2011: 7)

Circular 0018/2012, on 'Supporting Assessment: Standardised Testing in Primary Schools' (Department of Education and Skills 2012), explains the function of standardized tests of English reading and maths but points out that they are not the only way of gathering information about children's learning.

Primary teachers keep an 'assessment folder' containing a class list and pupils' standardized test results from the previous year (or other evidence of learning achievement in the Infant years, for which there are no standardized tests). The folder also includes a plan for each subject per term, a plan for each week or fortnight (newly qualified teachers are obliged to make weekly plans; a fortnightly plan is all that is officially required of teachers who have completed their probation) and monthly reports. Teachers also keep an individual folder on each pupil in which they collect evidence of that pupil's learning: the results of weekly spelling and maths tests, examples of independent work and projects, a record of progress in reading, the pupil's own reports on books he or she has read, and literacy development work; the pupil folder may also include copies of particularly interesting or praiseworthy examples of written work. In Scoil Bhríde, pupil folders are also used to record memorable contributions to class discussions that focus on language. There is every indication that pre-service primary teacher education endows its graduates with well-developed record-keeping skills. These are an essential foundation for reflective practice, and they stand students in good stead when they undertake action research projects based on their teaching practice. Without such a regime of documentation, of course, this book could not have been written.

Some concluding thoughts on 'plurilingual and intercultural education'

Scoil Bhríde is an example of plurilingual education in action: the way in which all languages present in a given classroom are taught, learnt and used ensures that each language in play is part of at least one pupil's 'everyday lived language', a fully integrated component of her emerging plurilingual repertoire.

Our understanding of this phenomenon would be significantly enhanced by further exploration carried out within the framework of successful practice and using the techniques of action research (McNiff 2004, Burns 1999, 2009) and exploratory practice (Allwright 2003, Hanks 2017). For example, we have noted pupils' use of their home language to communicate with speakers of the same or a related language in the classroom and the schoolyard, but a systematic record of such language use lies beyond the bounds of routine documentation. In any case, the languages in question are mostly unknown to the teachers. One way of finding out more would be to engage Fifth and Sixth Class pupils in a project to gather information on the use of their home languages throughout the school, using a video recorder or tablet to capture examples of language use to match their descriptions of the kind of interactions they and their peers engage in. This would constitute a substantial PhD research project for an enterprising teacher.

We have presented numerous instances of texts pupils have written in their home languages in parallel with texts in English, Irish and French. Given the length of the texts, the evident fluency of the language and the confidence of the handwriting, we have no reason to doubt the validity of this dimension of their literacy. But it lies beyond our competence and the scope of this book to attempt a linguistic analysis of home language texts. It would nevertheless be interesting to know more about them. Do they, for example, include features borrowed or transferred from English or Irish? And how do they compare with texts written by pupils of the same age in the country of origin? There are various ways in which these issues might be investigated – by engaging directly with parents or with those members of the home language community who provide weekend classes to support literacy development and, more ambitiously, by establishing partnerships with schools and universities in selected countries of origin. Again, this would provide an appropriately qualified teacher or postgraduate student with a significant topic of PhD research.

Work of this kind would contribute to a better understanding of the very foundation of plurilingual education, the 'communicative competence to which all knowledge and experience of language contributes and in which languages interrelate and interact' (Council of Europe 2001: 4); it would also help to dispel some of the confusions inherent in the CEFR's definition of the concept, to which we drew attention in Chapter 3 (pp. 81–4 above). Carefully constructed interviews with individual learners might throw much needed light on how languages 'interrelate and interact', not only in classroom discourse but in plurilingual minds.

Equally important, and again within the framework of successful practice, we need to find out more about the intercultural component of 'plurilingual and intercultural education'. In Chapter 3 (pp. 83–4 above) we noted the problematic nature of the link the CEFR assumes between language and culture. We also pointed out that when learning in the primary classroom is rooted in language use, the various languages in play contribute to the development of a learning culture in which classroom discourse mediates between curriculum content and the pupils' developing plurilingual repertoires. Drawn from their action knowledge and thus influenced by the culture of the home, pupils' own contributions cumulatively create a hybrid culture that is unique to their collective educational experience. The Council of Europe promotes 'intercultural education' as a means of preparing learners to cope with the challenges of 'otherness' (see especially Coste and Cavalli 2015). When pupils come from a wide variety of linguistic and cultural backgrounds their successful inclusion presupposes acceptance of diversity and difference. But if diversity and difference are dwelt on by teachers and pupils as markers of 'otherness', harmony can easily be undermined and barriers erected. Precisely because of this potential trap it is necessary to explore in as much depth as possible the cultural roots of pupils' action knowledge, perhaps following the example of the 'funds of knowledge' research reported by González, Moll and Amanti (2005). Such an exploration should include native-born Irish as well as immigrant families: the stories pupils hear from their grandparents, for example, are equally important, whether those grandparents live in Ireland, Nigeria, Poland or the Philippines.

We decided to write this book because we believed that a 'thick description' of Scoil Bhríde's approach to language education would be of interest to anyone who is critically involved with language education at primary level and especially those charged with educating pupils from immigrant families. We hope that our description will encourage other primary schools, in Ireland and elsewhere, to create their own version of plurilingual education, documenting and in due course reporting on their experience. Above all, we hope that other schools will be encouraged to include home languages in the life of the classroom because – as we have shown – to do so converts linguistic diversity into educational capital, enhances individual pupils' self-esteem, and motivates them to become confident and autonomous learners; by fostering respect for diversity, it also helps to lay the foundations of social cohesion.

Appendix
Scoil Bhríde (Cailíní) – Language Policy Statement

An integrated approach to language teaching and learning

By not creating a context for bilingual language exploration in our classroom, we miss out on one of the most powerful tools that children have to develop their literacy and awareness of language. … the cognate connections between the languages provide enormous possibilities for linguistic enrichment, but not if the programme is set to ensure that the two languages never meet. (Jim Cummins)

Languages should be taught in relation to one another rather than in isolation. (David Little)

Each pupil's home language is the default medium of her self-concept, her self-awareness, her consciousness, her discursive thinking, and her agency. It is thus the cognitive tool that she cannot help but apply to formal learning, which includes mastering the language of schooling. (David Little)

An integrated approach to language teaching and learning is used in Scoil Bhríde (Cailíní) to

- enhance cognitive development and thus support all learning;
- develop reflective, analytical, conceptual skills that can be used in all areas of learning;
- support communication and social cohesion within the various linguistic groups that are part of our school community;
- introduce and develop the skills needed for independent and lifelong learning.

Language mission statement

Language teaching and learning in primary education strives to empower all pupils to reach their full potential as individuals and to become fully integrated members of the community of the school and the wider social community, while respecting and valuing the richness of cultures and linguistic diversity.

Introduction

The language policy of Scoil Bhríde (Cailíní) is developed in collaboration with the Partners in Education, namely:

Parents
Teachers
Management

The policy itself is developed and its implementation is achieved through the active involvement of the partners representing the whole school community.

Aim

Based on the idea of an integrated approach to language learning and teaching, the aim of the language policy is the promotion and achievement of

- excellent English language skills at all levels, for both native speakers and English as an Additional Language (EAL) learners alike;
- excellence in the Irish language, using children's unique experience of language in general as a support;
- a positive attitude to all mother tongues within the school;
- a positive attitude to Irish culture and the cultures of all pupils by validating every child's identity through the language learning experience.

Language support

As language underpins all formal learning, developing English language proficiency for all pupils is of crucial importance to the child's success in school. All elements of the curriculum incorporate the learning of language and all teachers are, therefore, teachers of language. Given the diversity of languages encountered in Scoil Bhríde (Cailíní), with 80 per cent of its pupil population composed of newcomers, representing more than fifty different countries – and languages – the concept of plurilingualism as a means of enhancing language awareness, understanding and learning of languages for all learners in this school is of particular relevance (*Common European Framework of*

Reference for Languages; Council of Europe 2001). In this approach, there is an emphasis on 'commonality' of language through interconnectedness and linkage. In learning a language, the pupil is not unlearning another. The child's profile among her peers can be raised when her knowledge of and reference to her own language allows her to actively participate in class. This facility of language awareness enhances the experiential learning of all pupils, and their language learning skills are promoted. Initiatives, including modern language teaching and learning, Léargas projects, *We Are Writers!*, and participation in local radio programmes, are very suitable vehicles for developing this kind of learning. In terms of Gaeilge, there is the opportunity to focus on its use as a real means of communication.

Staff roles

All school staff, including teachers, special needs assistants and ancillary staff, are made aware of the importance of mother tongue (home language, L1) in the child's development. Parents are also actively encouraged to enhance their child's language learning through maintenance and development of their child's mother tongue.

Class teacher

The role and responsibility of the class teacher is to teach the curriculum to all the pupils in the class (native speakers of English, EAL pupils, special needs pupils), being mindful of the strengths and weaknesses brought by children to the task of learning.

Language support teacher

The primary responsibility of the language support teacher is to promote the pupil's development of English language proficiency so that she can gradually gain access to the curriculum, ultimately achieving the same educational opportunities as English-speaking peers so that she can reach her potential as a fully participative learner within the school. The language support teacher delivers a programme of English language tuition which is based on the requirements of the primary curriculum and which prepares and supports the child in

- accessing classroom learning;
- socializing with peers.

Ongoing liaison between the language support teacher and the mainstream teacher is crucial to EAL learner success, which is achieved by

- working in collaboration with the mainstream class teacher to set relevant and achievable learning targets for each pupil;
- preparing the pupil, on an ongoing basis, to access mainstream learning, initially in part and later more fully;
- helping the pupil to develop appropriate strategies and skills to support future formal education in general.
 (*Up and Away*, Dublin: Integrate Ireland Language and Training, 2006: 5)

The joint objective of both class and language support teachers is to

- ensure that the newly arrived pupil can understand and use the basic language of the classroom (e.g. toilet, be quiet, copy from board etc.);
- equip the pupil with knowledge of the rules and procedures of the school so that she does not unwittingly infringe them;
- help the pupil to understand different norms of behaviour that may exist in the new culture/society (in classroom, school, playground etc.);
- help to build the confidence and self-esteem of the pupil who may feel different, excluded and less able than those around her. Valuing the home language of the pupil is a crucial step in this process.

Practical strategies

Every effort is made to bring a child to the point where she can function successfully within the mainstream system. Scoil Bhríde (Caíliní) supports the idea that when children have reached level B1.3 in the four language competences according to the DES *Primary School Assessment Kit* (Dublin: Integrate Ireland Language and Training, 2007) they are ready for inclusion in the mainstream classroom without language support. (Being in a position to 'dip in' when necessary to the language support room is always desirable.)

Group 1

Junior level receives maximum oral language support.

Group 2

Older children receive maximum oral language support, utilizing their L1 literacy and existing language skills to support learning.

Early support strategies

- Parents are encouraged to maintain and develop home language
- Language support for all pupils from the beginning of schooling
- Buddy system to be set up on informal basis, for example, yard
- Language pairing – children from the same country
- Literacy pairing – older children with the same L1 skills are paired with each other and with younger children with same linguistic background

N.B. The child's needs are paramount when putting the language support plan into place. Good communication between mainstream and language teachers is vital for success (*Primary School Assessment Kit*, pp. 24, 47).

Consultation

The partners in education, as outlined in the introduction, will be consulted on matters concerning development and review of the school's language policy.

Training and resources

The school recognizes that there are implications for training and resources in implementing the language policy.

Ratification and review

This policy was ratified by the Board of Management in March 2010. The language policy is to be reviewed by the partners in education in the light of changing needs. It was reviewed in 2012, January 2014 and March 2015.

References

Alexander, R. J. (2006a), *Towards Dialogic Teaching: Rethinking Classroom Talk*, York: Dialogos.

Alexander, R. J. (2006b), *Education as Dialogue: Moral and Pedagogical Choices for a Runaway World*, York: Dialogos.

Alexander, R. (2008), 'Pedagogy for a Runaway World', in R. Alexander, *Essays on Pedagogy*, 121–53, London: Routledge.

Allwright, D. (2003), 'Exploratory Practice: Rethinking Practitioner Research in Language Teaching', *Language Teaching Research*, 7 (2): 113–41.

August, D., and T. Shanahan, eds (2006), *Developing Literacy in Second-language Learners*, Mahwah, NJ: Erlbaum.

Barnes, D. (1976), *From Communication to Curriculum*, Harmondsworth: Penguin.

Barnes, D. (1977), *Fra samvær til læseplan*, trans. H. Bertelsen, Copenhagen: Forum.

Barnes, D. (2008), 'Exploratory Talk for Learning', in N. Mercer and S. Hodgkinson (eds), *Exploring Talk in School*, 1–15, London: Sage.

Beacco, J.-C., and M. Byram (2007), *From Linguistic Diversity to Plurilingual Education: Guide for the Development of Language Education Policies in Europe*, Strasbourg: Council of Europe. Available online: https://rm.coe.int/CoERMPublicCommonSearchServices/DisplayDCTMContent?documentId=09000016802fc1c4 (accessed 1 March 2019).

Beacco, J.-C., M. Byram, M. Cavalli, D. Coste, M. Egli Cuenat, F. Goullier and J. Panthier (2015), *Guide for the Development and Implementation of Curricula for Plurilingual and Intercultural Education*, Strasbourg: Council of Europe. Available online: https://www.coe.int/en/web/language-policy/guide-for-the-development-and-implementation-of-curricula-for-plurilingual-and-intercultural-education (accessed 1 March 2019).

Bracken, S., M. Hagan, B. O'Toole, F. Quinn and A. Ryan (no date), *English as an Additional Language in Undergraduate Teacher Education Programmes in Ireland: A Report on Provision in Two Teacher Education Colleges*, Armagh: Standing Conference on Teacher Education, North and South (SCoTENS). Available online: http://scotens.org/site/wp-content/uploads/english-as-an-additional-language.pdf (accessed 27 June 2018).

Britton, J., T. Burgess, N. Martin, A. McLeod and H. Rosen (1975), *The Development of Writing Abilities (11–18)*, London: Macmillan.

Burns, A. ([1999] 2010), *Collaborative Action Research for English Language Teachers*, Cambridge: Cambridge University Press.

Burns, A. (2009), *Doing Action Research in English Language Teaching: A Guide for Practitioners*, Abingdon: Routledge.

Ćatibušić, B., and D. Little (2014), *Immigrant Pupils Learn English: A CEFR-related Empirical Study of L2 Development*, Cambridge: Cambridge University Press.

Cavalli, M., D. Coste, A. Crişan and P. van de Ven (2009), 'Plurilingual and Intercultural Education as a Project', Strasbourg: Council of Europe. Available online: https://rm.coe.int/CoERMPublicCommonSearchServices/DisplayDCTMContent?documentId=09000016805a219f (accessed 1 March 2019).

Central Statistics Office (2017), *2016 Census Results, Part I*, Dublin: Central Statistics Office. Available online: https://www.cso.ie/en/media/csoie/newsevents/documents/census2016summaryresultspart1/Census2016SummaryPart1.pdf (accessed 1 March 2019).

Coelho, E. (1994), 'Social Integration of Immigrant and Refugee Children', in F. Genesee (ed.), *Educating Second Language Children*, 301–28, Cambridge: Cambridge University Press.

Cook, V. J. (1991), 'The Poverty-of-the-stimulus Argument and Multi-competence', *Second Language Research*, 7 (2): 103–17.

Cook, V. (2002), 'Background to the L2 User', in V. Cook (ed.), *Portraits of the L2 User*, 1–28, Clevedon: Multilingual Matters.

Coste, D., M. Cavalli, A. Crişan and P.-H. van de Ven (2009), 'Plurilingual and Intercultural Education as a Right', Strasbourg: Council of Europe. Available online: https://rm.coe.int/CoERMPublicCommonSearchServices/DisplayDCTMContent?documentId=09000016805a219d (accessed 1 March 2019).

Coste, D. and M. Cavalli (2015), *Education, Mobility, Otherness: The Mediation Functions of Schools*, Strasbourg: Council of Europe. Available online: https://rm.coe.int/education-mobility-otherness-the-mediation-functions-of-schools/16807367ee (accessed 1 March 2019).

Council of Europe (2001), *Common European Framework of Reference for Languages: Learning, Teaching, Assessment*, Cambridge: Cambridge University Press. Available online: https://rm.coe.int/1680459f97 (accessed 4 July 2018).

Council of Europe (2008), 'Living Together as Equals in Dignity', *White Paper on Intercultural Dialogue*, Strasbourg: Council of Europe. Available online: https://www.coe.int/t/dg4/intercultural/source/white%20paper_final_revised_en.pdf (accessed 1 March 2019).

Council of Europe and Department of Education and Skills (Ireland) (2008), *Language Education Policy Profile: Ireland*, Strasbourg and Dublin: Council of Europe and Department of Education and Skills. Available online: https://rm.coe.int/language-education-policy-profile-ireland/16807b3c2f (accessed 4 July 2018).

Creese, A., and A. Blackledge (2010), 'Translanguaging in the Bilingual Classroom: A Pedagogy for Teaching and Learning', *The Modern Language Journal*, 94 (1): 103–15.

Cummins, J. (1979), 'Linguistic Interdependence and the Educational Development of Bilingual Children', *Review of Educational Research* 49 (2): 222–51.

Cummins, J. (1981), 'The Role of Primary Language Development in Promoting Educational Success for Language Minority Students', in California State Department of Education (ed.), *Schooling and Language Minority Students: A Theoretical Framework*, 3–49, Los Angeles, CA: California State University, Evaluation, Dissemination and Assessment Center.

Cummins, J. (1991), 'Conversational and Academic Language Proficiency', *AILA Review*, 8: 75–89.

Cummins, J. (2007), 'Rethinking Monolingual Instructional Strategies in Multilingual Classrooms', *Canadian Journal of Applied Linguistics*, 10 (2): 221–40.

Cummins, J. (2008), 'Teaching for Transfer: Challenging the Two Solitudes Assumption in Bilingual Education', in J. Cummins and N. Hornberger (eds), *Encyclopedia of Language Education*, 2nd edn, Vol. 5, *Bilingual Education*, 65–75, New York: Springer.

Cummins, J. (2017), 'Teaching Minoritized Students: Are Additive Approaches Legitimate?' *Harvard Educational Review* 87 (3): 404–25.

Cummins, J., and M. Early, eds (2011), *Identity Texts: The Collaborative Creation of Power in Multilingual Schools*, Stoke on Trent (UK): Trentham Books.

Cummins, J., S. Hu, P. Markus and M. K. Montero (2015), 'Identity Texts and Academic Achievement: Connecting the Dots in Multilingual School Contexts', *TESOL Quarterly* 49 (3): 555–81.

Curriculum and Examinations Board (Ireland) (1986), *Report of the Board of Studies for Languages*, Dublin: Curriculum and Examinations Board.

Dam, L. (1995), *Learner Autonomy 3: From Theory to Classroom Practice*, Dublin: Authentik.

Department of Education and Science (1996), 'Circular 12/96, Revision of Circular 18/79 on Exemption from the Study of Irish', Dublin: Department of Education and Science. Available online: https://www.education.ie/en/Circulars-and-Forms/Active-Circulars/pc12_96.pdf (accessed 26 June 2018).

Department of Education and Science (2009), 'Circular 0015/2009 – Meeting the Needs of Pupils Learning English as an Additional Language (EAL)', Dublin: Department of Education and Science. Available online: https://www.education.ie/en/Circulars-and-Forms/Active-Circulars/cl0015_2009.pdf (accessed 4 July 2018).

Department of Education and Skills (2011), 'Circular 0056/2011 – Initial Steps in the Implementation of the National Literacy and Numeracy Strategy', Dublin: Department of Education and Skills. Available online: https://www.education.ie/en/Circulars-and-Forms/Active-Circulars/cl0056_2011.pdf (accessed 1 March 2019).

Department of Education and Skills (2012), 'Circular 0018/2012 – Supporting Assessment: Standardised Testing in Primary Schools', Dublin: Department of Education and Skills. Available online: https://www.education.ie/en/Circulars-and-Forms/Active-Circulars/Supporting-Assessment-Standardised-Testing-in-Primary-Schools.pdf (accessed 28 June 2018).

Department of Education and Skills (2014), 'Whole School Evaluation Report – Scoil Bhríde (Cailíní), Blanchardstown, Dublin 15', Dublin: Department of Education and Skills. Available online: https://www.education.ie/en/Publications/Inspection-

Reports-Publications/Whole-School-Evaluation-Reports-List/report1_18047C.pdf (accessed 1 March 2019).

Department of Education and Skills (2015), *Primary Language Curriculum: English Language 1 and Irish Language 2*, Dublin: Department of Education and Skills. Available online: https://www.curriculumonline.ie/getmedia/524b871d-1e20-461f-a28c-bbca5424112d/Primary-Language-Curriculum_1.pdf (accessed 26 June 2018).

Department of Education and Skills (2017a), *Languages Connect: Ireland's Strategy for Foreign Languages in Education, 2017–2016*, Dublin: Department of Education and Skills. Available online: https://www.education.ie/en/Schools-Colleges/Information/Curriculum-and-Syllabus/Foreign-Languages-Strategy/fls_languages_connect_strategy.pdf (accessed 1 March 2019).

Department of Education and Skills (2017b), *Languages Connect: Ireland's Strategy for Foreign Languages in Education, 2017–2026 – Implementation Plan, 2017–2022*, Dublin: Department of Education and Skills. Available online: https://www.education.ie/en/Schools-Colleges/Information/Curriculum-and-Syllabus/Foreign-Languages-Strategy/fls_languages_connect_implementation_plan.pdf (accessed 1 March 2019).

Department of Education and Skills (2018), 'Chief Inspector's Report January 2013 – July 2016, Executive Summary', Dublin: Department of Education and Skills. Available online: https://www.education.ie/en/Publications/Inspection-Reports-Publications/Evaluation-Reports-Guidelines/insp_chief_inspectors_report_2013_2016.pdf (accessed 1 March 2019).

Diocesan Advisers for Religious Education in Primary Schools (2004), *International Children in Primary Schools: Fingal North, Finglas, Maynooth*, Dublin: Diocesan Advisers for Religious Education in Primary Schools.

Evensen, L. S. (2008), '"With a Little Help from My Friends"? Theory of Learning in Applied Linguistics and SLA', *Journal of Applied Linguistics*, 4 (3): 333–53.

Flores, N. (2013), 'The Unexamined Relationship between Neoliberalism and Plurilingualism: A Cautionary Tale', *TESOL Quarterly* 47 (3): 500–20.

Flores, N., and O. García (2014), 'Linguistic Third Spaces in Education: Teachers' Translanguaging across the Bilingual Continuum', in D. Little, C. Leung and P. Van Avermaet (eds), *Managing Diversity in Education: Languages, Policies, Pedagogies*, 243–56, Bristol: Multilingual Matters.

García, O. (2017), 'Problematizing Linguistic Integration of Migrants: The Role of Translanguaging and Language Teachers', in J.-C. Beacco, H.-J. Krumm and D. Little (eds), *The Linguistic Integration of Adult Migrants: Lessons from Research/ L'intégration linguistique des migrants adultes: Les enseignements de la recherche*, 11–26, Berlin: De Gruyter Mouton.

García, O., and Li Wei (2014), *Translanguaging: Language, Bilingualism and Education*, Basingstoke: Palgrave Macmillan.

García, O., and C. E. Sylvan (2011), 'Pedagogies and Practices in Multilingual Classrooms: Singularities and Pluralities', *The Modern Language Journal*, 95 (3): 385–400.

Gardner, H. (1993), 'On Teaching for Understanding: A Conversation with Howard Gardner', *Authentic Learning*, 50 (7): 4–7.

Geertz, C. (1973), *The Interpretation of Cultures*, New York: Basic Books.

Genesee, F., K. Lindholm-Leary, B. Saunders and D. Christian (2006), *Educating English Language Learners: A Synthesis of Research Evidence*, Cambridge: Cambridge University Press.

González, N., L. C. Moll and C. Amanti, eds (2005), *Funds of Knowledge: Theorizing Practices in Households, Communities and Classrooms*, New York and London: Routledge.

Government of Ireland (1999a), *Primary School Curriculum: Introduction/Curaclam na Bunscoile: Réamhrá*, Dublin: Stationery Office. Available online: https://curriculumonline.ie/getmedia/93de2707-f25e-4bee-9035-92b00613492e/Introduction-to-primary-curriculum.pdf (accessed 1 March 2019).

Government of Ireland (1999b), *Primary School Curriculum: English*, Dublin: Stationery Office. Available online: https://www.curriculumonline.ie/getmedia/5b514700-e65c-46a7-a7d0-c8e05e115bf9/PSEC01a_English_Curriculum.pdf (accessed 4 July 2018).

Hanks, J. (2017), *Exploratory Practice in Language Teaching: Puzzling about Principles and Practices*, London: Palgrave Macmillan.

Heugh, K. (2015), 'Epistemologies in Multilingual Education: Translanguaging and Genre – Companions in Conversation with Policy and Practice', *Language and Education*, 29 (3): 280–5.

Holec, H. ([1979] 1981), *Autonomy and Foreign Language Learning*, Oxford: Pergamon.

Integrate Ireland Language and Training (2003a), *English Language Proficiency Benchmarks for Non-English-speaking Pupils at Primary Level*, Dublin: Integrate Ireland Language and Training.

Integrate Ireland Language and Training (2003b), *English Language Proficiency Benchmarks for Non-English-speaking Students at Post-primary Level*, Dublin: Integrate Ireland Language and Training.

Integrate Ireland Language and Training (2006), *Up and Away*, Dublin: Integrate Ireland Language and Training.

Irish Statute Book (1998), *Education Act, 1998*. Available online: http://www.irishstatutebook.ie/eli/1998/act/51/enacted/en/html (accessed 28 June 2018).

Kasper, G., and J. Wagner (2011), 'A Conversation-analytic Approach to Second Language Acquisition', in D. Atkinson (ed.), *Alternative Approaches to Second Language Acquisition*, 117–42, London: Routledge.

Kerfoot, C., and A.-M. Simon-Vandenbergen, eds (2015), *Language in Epistemic Access: Mobilising Multilingualism and Literacy Development for More Equitable Education in South Africa*, Special issue (29 [3]) of the journal *Language in Education*.

Kirwan, D. (2009), 'Language Support for Newcomer Learners in Irish Primary Schools: A Review and a Case Study', PhD thesis, University of Dublin, Trinity College, Dublin.

Kirwan, D. (2015), 'Cultivating a Plurilingual Environment: Opportunities in Pre-school, Primary School and Beyond', *ETBI Newsletter*, Spring 2015, 60–2, Naas (Ireland): Education and Training Boards Ireland. Available online: http://www.etbi.ie/wp-content/uploads/2015/02/ETBI_Spring15_final_low-res.pdf (accessed 12 July 2018).

Larsen-Freeman, D. (2002), 'Language Acquisition and Language Use from a Chaos/ Complexity Theory Perspective', in C. Kramsch (ed.), *Language Acquisition and Language Socialization: Ecological Perspectives*, 33–46, London: Continuum.

Lave, J., and E. Wenger (1991), *Situated Learning: Legitimate Peripheral Participation*, Cambridge: Cambridge University Press.

Lewis, G., B. Jones and C. Baker (2012), 'Translanguaging: Origins and Development from School to Street and Beyond', *Educational Research and Evaluation*, 18 (7): 641–54.

Li Wei (2014), 'Who's Teaching Whom? Co-Learning in Multilingual Classrooms', in S. May (ed.), *The Multilingual Turn*, 167–90, Abingdon: Routledge.

Little, D. (1991), *Learner Autonomy 1: Definitions, Issues and Problems*, Dublin: Authentik.

Little, D. (1995), 'Learning as Dialogue: The Dependence of Learner Autonomy on Teacher Autonomy', *System* 23 (2): 175–81.

Little, D. (2003), 'Languages in the Post-primary Curriculum: A Discussion Paper', Dublin: National Council for Curriculum and Assessment.

Little, D. (2007), 'Language Learner Autonomy: Some Fundamental Considerations Revisited', *Innovation in Language Learning and Teaching*, 1 (1): 14–29.

Little, D. (2010), 'The Linguistic and Educational Integration of Children and Adolescents from Migrant Backgrounds', Strasbourg: Council of Europe. Available online: https://rm.coe.int/the-linguistic-and-educational-integration-of-children-and-adolescents/16805a0d1b (accessed 17 July 2018).

Little, D., L. Dam and L. Legenhausen (2017), *Language Learner Autonomy: Theory, Practice and Research*, Bristol: Multilingual Matters.

Little, D., and B. Lazenby Simpson (2009), 'Teaching Immigrants the Language of the Host Community: Two Object Lessons in the Need for Continuous Policy Development', in J. C. Alderson (ed.), *The Politics of Language Education: Individuals and Institutions*, 104–24, Bristol: Multilingual Matters.

Little, D., B. Lazenby Simpson and B. Finnegan Ćatibušić (2007), *Primary School Assessment Kit*, Dublin: Department of Education and Science.

McNiff, J. (2004), *Action Research: Principles and Practice*, London: Routledge.

Mercer, N. (1995), *The Guided Construction of Knowledge: Talk amongst Teachers and Learners*, Clevedon: Multilingual Matters.

Mercer, N. (2000), *Words and Minds: How We Use Language to Think Together*, London and New York: Routledge.

Mercer, N., and S. Hodgkinson, eds (2008), *Exploring Talk in School*, London: Sage.

Mercer, N., and K. Littleton (2007), *Dialogue and the Development of Children's Thinking: A Sociocultural Approach*, Abingdon: Routledge.

National Council for Special Education (Ireland) (2014), *Delivery for Students with Special Educational Needs*, Dublin: National Council for Special Education. Available online: http://ncse.ie/wp-content/uploads/2014/09/Allocating_resources_1_5_14_ Web_accessible_version_FINAL.pdf (accessed 1 March 2019).

Ó Ceallaigh, T. J., and Á. Ní Dhonnabháin (2015), 'Reawaking the Irish Language through the Irish Education System: Challenges and Priorities', *International Electronic Journal of Elementary Education* 8 (2): 179–98. Available online: https:// files.eric.ed.gov/fulltext/EJ1085869.pdf (accessed 17 July 2018).

Ó Duibhir, P., and J. Cummins (2012), 'Towards an Integrated Language Curriculum in Early Childhood and Primary Education', Dublin: National Council for Curriculum and Assessment.

Olson, D. R. (1979), 'Literacy as Metalinguistic Activity', in D. R. Olson and N. Torrance (eds), *Literacy and Orality*, 251–70, Cambridge: Cambridge University Press.

Olson, D. R. (1994), *The World on Paper: The Conceptual and Cognitive Implications of Writing and Reading*, Cambridge: Cambridge University Press.

Olson, D. R. (1995), 'Writing and the Mind', in J. V. Wertsch, P. Del Río and A. Alvarez (eds), *Sociocultural Studies of Mind*, 95–123, Cambridge: Cambridge University Press.

Olson, D. R. (2016), *The Mind on Paper: Reading, Consciousness and Rationality*, Cambridge: Cambridge University Press.

Pulinx, R., P. Van Avermaet and C. Extramiana (2014), *Linguistic Integration of Adult Migrants: Policy and Practice*. Final Report on the 3rd Council of Europe Survey, Strasbourg: Council of Europe. Available online: https://rm.coe.int/16802fc1ce (accessed 4 July 2018).

Schleppegrell, M. (2013), 'The Role of Metalanguage in Supporting Academic Language Development', *Language Learning*, 63, Supplement 1: 153–70.

Scollon, R. (2004), 'Teaching Language and Culture as Hegemonic Practice', *The Modern Language Journal*, 88 (2): 271–4.

Sfard, A. (1998), 'On Two Metaphors for Learning and the Dangers of Choosing Just One', *Educational Researchers*, 27 (2): 4–13.

Shohamy, E. G. (2006), *Language Policy: Hidden Agendas and New Approaches*, London and New York: Routledge.

Shuell, T. J. (1986), 'Cognitive Conceptions of Learning', *Review of Educational Research*, 56 (4): 411–36.

Sierens, S., and P. Van Avermaet (2014), 'Language Diversity in Education: Evolving from Multilingual Education to Functional Multilingual Education', in D. Little, C. Leung and P. Van Avermaet (eds), *Managing Diversity in Education: Languages, Policies, Pedagogies*, 204–22, Bristol: Multilingual Matters.

Sinclair, J. McH., and M. Coulthard (1975), *Towards an Analysis of Discourse: The English Used by Teachers and Pupils*, Oxford: Oxford University Press.

Singleton, D. (2016), 'A Critical Reaction from Second Language Research', in V. Cook and Li Wei (eds), *The Cambridge Handbook of Linguistic Multi-competence*, 502–20, Cambridge: Cambridge University Press.

Stanat, P., and G. Christensen (2006), *Where Immigrant Students Succeed: A Comparative Review of Performance and Engagement in PISA 2003*, Paris: OECD.

Swain, M. (2006), 'Languaging, Agency and Collaboration in Advanced Second Language Proficiency', in H. Byrnes (ed.), *Advanced Language Learning: The Contribution of Halliday and Vygotsky*, 95–108, London: Continuum.

Tharp, R., and R. Gallimore (1988), *Rousing Minds to Life: Teaching, Learning, and Schooling in Social Context*, Cambridge: Cambridge University Press.

Tyler, R. ([1949] 2013), *Basic Principles of Curriculum and Instruction*, Chicago: University of Chicago Press.

Wells, G. (2009), *The Meaning Makers: Learning to Talk and Talking to Learn*, 2nd edn, Bristol: Multilingual Matters.

Wenger, E. (1998), *Communities of Practice: Learning, Meaning and Identity*, Cambridge: Cambridge University Press.

Williams, C. (2002), *A Language Gained: A Study of Language Immersion at 11–16 Years of Age*, Bangor: University of Wales, School of Education.

Wong Fillmore, L. (1991), 'When Learning a Second Language Means Losing the First', *Early Childhood Research Quarterly*, 6: 323–46.

Wood, D., J. S. Bruner and G. Ross (1976), 'The Role of Tutoring in Problem-solving', *Journal of Child Psychology and Psychiatry*, 17 (2): 89–100.

Index